'*Global Human Trafficking* is a wonderful contribution to the research literature on trafficking. While most writing on the topic has been evidence-thin or anecdotal, this book contains important empirical studies of various dimensions of trafficking. And departing from the usual exclusive focus on sex trafficking, the contributors examine labor and organ trafficking as well. The book shows how trafficking can be much more complex and variegated than the monolithic and sensationalized image so common in the media and in policymaking throughout the world.'

Ronald Weitzer, Professor of Sociology,
George Washington University, USA

'*Global Human Trafficking* is an essential resource for anyone interested in the study of human trafficking and anti-trafficking policies and practices. It challenges common assumptions about the problem by showcasing rich empirical studies from the global North and South and by providing critical insights into key debates about what is to be done about trafficking. An excellent volume on one of the most important socio-criminological topics of our time.'

Maggy Lee, Professor of Criminology, Department of Sociology,
University of Hong Kong, Hong Kong

Global Human Trafficking

Human trafficking has moved from relative obscurity to a major area of research, policy, and teaching over the past ten years. Research has sprung from criminology, public policy, women's and gender studies, sociology, anthropology, and law, but has been somewhat hindered by the failure of scholars to engage beyond their own disciplines and favored methodologies. Recent research has begun to improve efforts to understand the causes of the problem, the experiences of victims, and policy efforts and their consequences in specific cultural and historical contexts.

Global Human Trafficking: Critical issues and contexts foregrounds recent empirical work on human trafficking from an interdisciplinary, critical perspective. The collection includes classroom-friendly features, such as introductory chapters that provide essential background for understanding the trafficking literature, text boxes explaining key concepts, discussion questions for each chapter, and lists of additional resources, including films, websites, and additional readings for each chapter.

The authors include both eminent and emerging scholars from around the world, drawn from law, anthropology, criminology, sociology, cultural studies, and political science. The book will be useful for undergraduate and graduate courses in these areas, as well as for scholars interested in trafficking.

Molly Dragiewicz is Associate Professor in the School of Justice, Faculty of Law at Queensland University of Technology in Brisbane, Australia. Dr. Dragiewicz is author of *Equality with a Vengeance: Men's rights groups, battered women, and antifeminist backlash*. She received the Critical Criminologist of the Year Award from the American Society of Criminology Division on Critical Criminology in 2012 and the New Scholar Award from the American Society of Criminology Division on Women and Crime in 2009.

Global Issues in Crime and Justice

Global Human Trafficking

Critical issues and contexts

Edited by Molly Dragiewicz

Routledge
Taylor & Francis Group

LONDON AND NEW YORK

First published 2015
by Routledge
2 Park Square, Milton Park, Abingdon, Oxon OX14 4RN

and by Routledge
711 Third Avenue, New York, NY 10017

*Routledge is an imprint of the Taylor & Francis Group,
an informa business*

British Library Cataloguing-in-Publication Data
A catalogue record for this book is available from the British
Library

Library of Congress Cataloging-in-Publication Data
Global human trafficking : critical issues and contexts / edited by
   Molly Dragiewicz.
     pages cm. — (Global issues in crime and justice ; 2)
   1. Human trafficking.   I. Dragiewicz, Molly.
   HQ281.G55 2014
   306.3'62—dc23
   2014019859

ISBN: 978-0-415-71109-8 (hbk)
ISBN: 978-0-415-71110-4 (pbk)
ISBN: 978-1-315-88182-9 (ebk)

Typeset in Times New Roman
by Apex CoVantage, LLC

MIX
Paper from
responsible sources
FSC
www.fsc.org   FSC® C013056

Printed and bound in Great Britain by
TJ International Ltd, Padstow, Cornwall

Contents

Contributors

Aziza Ahmed is Associate Professor of Law at Northeastern University School of Law in Boston, Massachusetts. She served as an expert member of the Technical Advisory Group on HIV and the Law convened by the United Nations Development Programme (UNDP) and as an expert for the American Bar Association. She is on the board of the Center for Health and Gender Equity (CHANGE) and the Sexuality Information and Education Council of the United States (SIECUS).

Kum-Kum Bhavnani is Professor of Sociology at the University of California Santa Barbara, with affiliations to Global and Feminist Studies. She has written books and articles (e.g. *Talking Politics* [1991], *Feminism and "Race"* [2001]), and, most recently, has made three documentary films: *The Shape of Water* (2006), *Nothing Like Chocolate* (2012) (both narrated by Susan Sarandon) and *Lutah* (2013).

Melissa Hope Ditmore has written about human trafficking in books and journal articles. Her other publications address gender, migration, development, sex work, and drug use.

Molly Dragiewicz is Associate Professor of Justice in the Faculty of Law at Queensland University of Technology in Brisbane, Australia. Her research interests focus on violence, gender, critical criminology, and the sociology of law.

Elżbieta M. Goździak is Director of Research at the Institute for the Study of International Migration at Georgetown University and Editor of *International Migration*. Currently, she directs a National Institute of Justice funded project to present a profile of adult survivors of human trafficking assisted by the Office of Refugee Resettlement's Anti-Trafficking Services Programs and to evaluate the effectiveness of intervention programs.

Neil Howard is a Marie Curie Fellow at the European University Institute in Florence, Italy. Research for the article in this volume was conducted for the author's doctorate in International Development at the University of Oxford.

Samantha Lyneham is a Research Analyst at the Australian Institute of Criminology, where her research focuses on human trafficking and slavery in Australia and the Asia-Pacific region. Samantha has completed a Bachelor of Social Science in Criminology from the University of New South Wales and a Postgraduate Diploma in Criminology from the University of Melbourne.

Anna Maternick collaborated on The Road North Study as a research intern for the Sex Workers Project. Anna is interested in studying the impact of trauma on youth. She currently works as a research associate in the Department of Family Medicine and Population Health at Virginia Commonwealth University in Richmond, Virginia.

Simona Morganti is an anthropologist. She completed her Ph.D. in Anthropology at the University of Modena, Italy, after extensive fieldwork in Southern Benin (2003–2009). In Cotonou, she also acted as a consultant for NGOs and International Agencies engaged in child protection.

Erin O'Brien is Senior Lecturer in the School of Justice, Queensland University of Technology, Australia. She researches the spectrum of political activism, particularly the interplay between activists and the state in the construction of knowledge and formation of policy, on issues of sex, gender, and justice. Her current research focuses on the political discourse surrounding human trafficking and irregular migration.

Julia O'Connell Davidson is Professor of Sociology at the University of Nottingham. She has researched and written widely on a variety of forms of sex commerce, and also on "trafficking"—especially on the conceptual, definitional, and political problems associated with the term itself. She currently holds a Leverhulme Major Research Fellowship for a project titled "Modern slavery and the margins of freedom: Debtors, detainees, and children."

Joyce Outshoorn is Professor Emeritus of Women's Studies at the University of Leiden, where she is affiliated to the Institute of Political Science. She is editor of *The Politics of Prostitution* (2004) and, with Johanna Kantola, *Changing State Feminism* (2007). She has published extensively on women's movements, women's equality policy, and body politics, notably abortion and prostitution.

Claire M. Renzetti is the Judi Conway Patton Endowed Chair for Studies of Violence against Women, and Professor and Chair of the Sociology Department at the University of Kentucky, U.S.A. She is editor of the international, interdisciplinary journal, *Violence Against Women* (Sage Publications); co-editor of the Interpersonal Violence Book Series (Oxford University Press); and editor of the Gender and Justice Book Series (University of California Press).

Kelly Richards holds a Ph.D. in criminology from the University of Western Sydney. After five years as a senior researcher at the Australian Institute of Criminology, she recently joined the School of Justice at Queensland University of

Technology as a Lecturer. Her research interests include restorative justice, youth justice, sexual violence, and human trafficking. Kelly is an Associate Editor for the *Australian Journal of Social Issues*.

Nancy Scheper-Hughes is Professor of Medical Anthropology at the University of California, Berkeley where she directs the doctoral program in Critical Studies in Medicine, Science, and the Body. Scheper-Hughes' lifework concerns the violence of everyday life examined from a radical existentialist and politically engaged perspective. Her examination of structural and political violence, of what she calls "small wars and invisible genocides" has allowed her to develop a so-called "militant" anthropology, which has been broadly applied to medicine, psychiatry, and to the practice of anthropology.

Emily Schneider is a Ph.D. candidate in the department of Sociology at the University of California Santa Barbara. Prior to attending UCSB, she received a BA in Sociology from Colorado College. Her research examines the effects of alternative tourism with a focus on the Middle East, diaspora identity, and sexuality.

Meena Seshu is a co-founder of Sampada Gramin Mahila Sanstha (SANGRAM), a non-governmental organization in Sangli, India that works with sex workers to stop the spread of HIV/AIDS. She has more than 20 years of experience working with grassroots, rights-based organizations (particularly with people in sex work) on issues related to HIV/AIDS, sexual and reproductive health, violence against women, poverty alleviation, and gender and sexual minority rights. Seshu is part of the UNAIDS Reference Group on Human Rights and HIV, and in 2002 she won a Human Rights Watch award for her work.

Rebecca Surtees is an anthropologist and senior researcher at NEXUS Institute, a human rights policy and research center in Washington, DC. She has conducted research in Southeast Asia, Southeast Europe, the former Soviet Union, and West Africa. Her research interests include less considered forms and experiences of trafficking as well as the challenges and complexity of family and community reintegration. She has also written on research methods and ethics in the trafficking field.

Michael Wilson is a student researcher in the School of Justice, Queensland University of Technology, Australia. His research interests center on the disconnect between the principles of justice and the realities of human behavior, specifically the representation and treatment of refugees and migrants within society.

Acknowledgments

Like every book, this project was a collective effort. This book would not have been possible without help from a number of people. It would not exist at all without encouragement from Thomas Sutton, Senior Editor for Criminology and Criminal Justice at Routledge, who repeatedly suggested at subsequent American Society of Criminology meetings that a book on human trafficking might be a good idea. Heidi Lee, Editorial Assistant, has provided helpful information and persistent reminders about approaching deadlines throughout the process. I feel very lucky to have found such a friendly, professional, and supportive editorial team with Routledge.

Emily van der Meulen, my friend and colleague from Toronto, was to co-edit this book in the original plan, but our divergent scholarly interests took her away from the project. Still, Emily's input was invaluable in the early stages and I am grateful for her contributions and research about possible contributors, thoughts about organizing the book, and research and drafting for the text boxes. Ann Jordan provided early advice and ideas for possible contributors, stressing the need for empirical research in this area. Thank you to Joan and Richard Zorza for hosting me at your lovely house in Washington, DC during the American Society of Criminology meeting where I decided to do the book.

Many thanks to the authors who took time out of their busy schedules to write and revise chapters for the book. I am so pleased that the collection comprises distinguished and emerging scholars as well as advocates and practitioners. Although they may disagree with one another, they are united by a shared interest in serving the interests of adults and children affected by all kinds of inequality and exploitation and dedicated to scholarship to inform work in that direction.

Thanks also to *The Anti-Trafficking Review*, the Australian Institute of Criminology, Sienna Baskin, Crystal DeBoise and the Sex Workers Project (SWP), the NEXUS Institute and Oxford University Press, who all kindly agreed to let us publish material that had previously appeared in other publications.

This project was supported financially by Queensland University of Technology, which first hosted me on a sabbatical visit and then let me stay on permanently in a wonderful faculty. I am especially grateful to John Humphrey and Kerry Carrington who supported the move and the rest of my QUT colleagues and students for making my job a delight.

My family provided emotional support throughout the writing process, with Matt Brenner moving all the way from Canada to Australia, Lucy and Kay enduring quarantine and numerous veterinarian visits, Judy Dragiewicz and Larry Dragiewicz coming to visit, Shirley Carlson providing moral support by phone, and Marc Dragiewicz scheduling commuting phone calls. Thank you for your love and support.

Chapter 1

Introduction

Molly Dragiewicz

Human trafficking has moved from relative obscurity to a major area of publishing, policy, and law in less than 20 years. Prior to the passage in 2000 of the United Nations Protocol to Prevent, Suppress, and Punish Trafficking in Persons, Especially Women and Children, and the United States Trafficking Victims Protection Act, a comprehensive review of the trafficking literature unearthed fewer than 100 research publications devoted to the subject. At that time, a literature search on "trafficking" was much more likely to produce content on drugs and weapons than trafficking in people (Dragiewicz, 2008). By 2005, the number of published sources had tripled (Laczko, 2005). The literature continues to grow. As of May 2014, a Google Scholar search for "human trafficking" yields about 34,800 results. The first peer-reviewed journal on human trafficking, *Anti-Trafficking Review*, was founded in 2011. The *Journal of Human Trafficking* is due to be launched in 2015 (Younis, 2013). Interest in human trafficking is undeniable. However, the proliferation of publications has significantly outpaced the empirical research in this area. As Anne Gallagher puts it, "Human trafficking has attracted a great deal of attention over the past decade, but many have rightly questioned the quality of much research and writing on this issue" (2012, p. 2).

The difficulties of studying trafficking are many and include definitional problems, the clandestine nature of the activity, criminalization of traffickers and those who are trafficked, and the vulnerability of trafficking victims along lines of social inequality (Laczko, 2005; Lee, 2007). The increasingly restrictive professional imperatives of scholarly production have also shaped the literature. Scholars in some places like Australia, Canada, New Zealand, the U.S., and U.K. face increasingly onerous institutional research ethics requirements which can effectively deter or prevent research on children and illegal activity (Becker-Blease & Freyd, 2006). Replication of routinized, pre-determined, and discipline specific research methodologies, including over-reliance on quantitative methods in the social sciences, has also dissuaded empirical work on this complex issue.

The development of knowledge about trafficking has also been hindered by scholars' failure to read and engage beyond our own disciplines. Following a recent meeting of scholars, practitioners, and funders working in the field, Sarah Scraggs, Rebecca Surtees, and Lisa Taylor noted that "opportunities for sharing research, including exploring methodological strengths and limitations, ethical issues, avenues for improvements and engaging in peer review, have been limited" (2011, p. 2). Despite these formidable challenges, there is a growing body of exciting empirical research on trafficking that moves beyond efforts to count trafficking victims, recount their tragic (composite) tales, or rehash intractable policy debates.

Recent research has begun to improve efforts to understand the causes of the problem, the experiences of victims, changes in law and policy, and their consequences within specific cultural and historical contexts. Books like Marie Segrave, Sanja Milivojevic, and Sharon Pickering's *Sex Trafficking: International Context and Response* (Willan, 2009), Susan Kneebone and Julie Debeljak's *Transnational Crime and Human Rights: Responses to Human Trafficking in the Greater Mekong Subregion* (Routledge, 2012), Ato Quayson and Antonela Arhin's collection *Labour Migration, Human Trafficking and Multinational Corporations: The Commodification of Illicit Flows* (Routledge, 2012), Pardis Mahdavi's *Gridlock: Labor, Migration, and Human Trafficking in Dubai* (Stanford University Press, 2011), and Rhacel Parreñas' *Illicit Flirtations: Labor, Migration, and Sex Trafficking in Tokyo* (Stanford University Press, 2011) provide deeply contextualized, empirically based accounts of the history, nature, and impact of anti-trafficking policies in specific locations. These books challenge dominant discourses on trafficking, complicating the issue well beyond the caricatures of traffickers and trafficking victims that feature so prominently in media coverage and policy debates.

Global Human Trafficking aims to contribute to the growing knowledge base on human trafficking by drawing together contemporary empirical research on a variety of forms of labor and exploitation in multiple locations. The collection takes a critical view of trafficking and responses to it, informed by the voices and experiences of those affected and involved. It is essential to note that this is a field marked by deep ideological and theoretical differences. Scholars who might have shared affinities with critical, feminist, and pro-human rights perspectives disagree with one another about how to best understand and address trafficking. *Global Human Trafficking* includes chapters by established and emerging international scholars who work in criminology, anthropology, political science, women's studies, and law. The primary goal of the book is to present empirical work on a variety of forms of trafficking, regardless of the discipline from which it emerges. Accordingly, the contributions address a number of types of labor as well as organ trafficking. The book is organized into three sections: Critical Contexts for Thinking about Trafficking; Key Issues in Trafficking Research; and Trafficking Policy: Intent and Outcomes. **Section I: Critical Contexts for Thinking about Trafficking** offers essential background for understanding the field, with chapters reviewing the policy debates and issues in data collection that provide a foundation for understanding this area of research. **Section II: Key Issues in Trafficking Research** takes up trafficking for sex work, fishing, marriage, domestic work, and organ transplant, highlighting the complex and contradictory experiences of adults and children, all of whom exercise agency while navigating economic survival in locations marked by social stratification across gender, sexuality, income, age, ethnicity, and nationality. **Section III: Trafficking Policy: Intent and Outcomes** addresses the origins of policy and the impact of policy changes on the ground, with a critical focus on criminal justice practices. This section includes research on the ideological origins of U.S. trafficking policy, service providers' perspectives, and critical assessment of "end demand" approaches. **Section IV: Moving Forward** highlights efforts to address the social problems ascribed to trafficking via local action and organizing for social justice. Chapters on sex workers' organizing and resistance to raid and rescue operations, and efforts to address child labor in the chocolate business help to bring the discussion of trafficking policy to the local level. Finally, the conclusion points to future directions for research and research-informed policies. This section aims to focus calls for awareness and outrage down to the level of practice and impact in order to promote the development of research-informed programs and practices that are accountable to the groups of people who are ostensibly the beneficiaries of changes.

Throughout the book, I have inserted text boxes which explain key terms and concepts. The text boxes provide references and links to original sources and further information. In addition, each chapter is followed by questions for discussion, study, and reflection. A list of multimedia resources is provided at the end of each chapter to facilitate further reading, viewing, and investigation. This collection provides snapshots of multiple facets of the phenomenon of human trafficking for multiple forms of labor in different locations around the world. I hope that the book will serve as a starting point for those interested in learning more about the topic. I also hope that the chapters will provide inspiration for students, scholars, and others who can ultimately contribute to this growing body of knowledge in order to better understand, respond to, and ultimately prevent human trafficking and other forms of exploitation.

References

Becker-Blease, K.A., & Freyd, J.J. (2006). Research participants telling the truth about their lives: The ethics of asking and not asking about abuse. *American Psychologist, 61*(3), 218–226.

Dragiewicz, M. (2008). Teaching about trafficking: Opportunities and challenges for critical engagement. *Feminist teacher, 18*(3), 185–201.

Gallagher, A.T. (2012). Editorial. *Anti-Trafficking Review, 1*, 2–9.

Kempadoo, K., Sanghera, J., & Pattanaik, B. (Eds.) (2011). *Trafficking and prostitution reconsidered: New perspectives on migration, sex work, and human rights* (2nd ed.). Boulder: Paradigm Publishers.

Kneebone, S., & Debeljak, J. (Eds.) (2012). *Transnational crime and human rights: Responses to human trafficking in the Greater Mekong Subregion.* New York: Routledge.

Laczko, F. (2005). Data and research on human trafficking. *International Migration, 43*(1–2), 5–16.

Lee, M. (Ed.) (2007). *Human trafficking.* London, U.K.: Willan.

Mahdavi, P. (2011). *Gridlock: Labor, migration, and human trafficking in Dubai.* Palo Alto, CA: Stanford University Press.

Parreñas, R. (2011). *Illicit flirtations: Labor, migration, and sex trafficking in Tokyo*. Palo Alto: Stanford University Press.

Quayson, A., & Arhin, A. (Eds.) (2012). *Labour migration, human trafficking and multinational corporations: The commodification of illicit flows*. London: Routledge.

Scraggs, S., Surtees, R., & Taylor, L. R. (2011). *The state of counter-trafficking research: Researcher, programmer, and donor perspectives* (No. GMS-09). Bangkok, Thailand: Strategic Information Response Network (SIREN).

Segrave, M., Milivojevic, S., & Pickering, S. (2009). *Sex trafficking: International context and response*. London, U.K.: Willan.

Younis, L. (2013). Professor creates world's 1st human trafficking journal. (2013). *Daily Nebraskan*. Retrieved April 30, 2014, from http://www.dailynebraskan.com/news/unl-professor-creates-world-s-st-human-trafficking-journal/article_e03d58b4-5e32-11e3-8a16-001a4bcf6878.html

Section I

Critical contexts for thinking about trafficking

Molly Dragiewicz

This introductory section provides background information that is essential to understanding the rest of the chapters in the collection and, indeed, the rest of the trafficking literature. The discussion about human trafficking has been taken up by a number of interest groups which have argued and lobbied to institutionalize different understandings of trafficking, based on a variety of values and beliefs. Because the issue has been so deeply politicized, it is essential to place any study or discussion of human trafficking within this context.

In Chapter 2, "The Trafficking Policy Debates," Joyce Outshoorn, Professor of Women's Studies at Leiden University in the Netherlands, provides an updated overview of the debates over anti-trafficking policy. Central to the disagreement is a difference of opinion over the relationship of prostitution to human trafficking. As Outshoorn shows, parties on all sides of this debate share an interest in promoting human rights and women's safety, but differ sharply on the best way to proceed in order to reach that goal. Outshoorn focuses on the European context which has been the location for debates about how to frame trafficking in the United Nations. Outshoorn reviews the historical development of interest in trafficking, tracing the shifting focus of UN conventions. She then lays out the core beliefs of the sex workers' rights and sexual domination approaches to trafficking, explaining how they understand prostitution, sexuality, and their relationship to trafficking. Outshoorn describes the opposing transnational alliances against trafficking that have brought individuals and organizations with different foci together in efforts to influence human rights policy. She concludes with a call for greater attention to the realities of international migration in work against exploitation.

In Chapter 3, "Data Matters: Issues and Challenges for Research on Trafficking," Elżbieta M. Goździak, Director of Research at the Institute for the Study of International Migration at Georgetown University in the United States, provides a synthesis of empirical research. Goździak draws from an extensive review of the empirical literature funded by the National Institutes of Justice as well as her own research on trafficking to the United States. She describes a research landscape heavy on commentary and light on empirical studies, with a higher concentration of empirical studies published as reports than journal articles. The chapter describes the approaches taken to trafficking research, including promising methodological approaches and shortcomings. In addition, she describes a dearth of theory in the literature. Finally, she outlines gaps in the literature.

These two contextualizing chapters provide a foundation for readers new to the trafficking issue and an update about the current state of the literature for those returning to the topic. The issues raised in Section I can be linked to all of the other chapters in the book as well as other texts on trafficking. The section will help anyone seeking to understand or comment on the trafficking debate to understand the conversation they are entering. This background offers a concise point of entry for critical interpretations of the trafficking literature.

Learning objectives for Section I

1. Understand the debates about how to approach human trafficking policy.
2. Explain why the relationship between prostitution and trafficking is controversial.
3. Name the "sides" in the trafficking debate.
4. Identify challenges for researching trafficking.
5. Describe the current state of empirical research on trafficking.

Chapter 2

The trafficking policy debates*

Joyce Outshoorn

Introduction

Historically, attention to trafficking of women has been focused on prostitution. The first international debates on the topic started in the 1880s, culminating in the 1949 United Nations (UN) International Convention for the Suppression of the Traffic in Persons. Trafficking and prostitution then largely disappeared from the international policy agenda until the 1980s, when many Western countries, the UN and the European Union (EU) began to react to evidence of the expansion of a globalizing market for sexual services. Migration grew immensely at this time, spurred on by increasing gaps between the rich and poor, better transportation, and improved communication networks. This wave of immigration contributed to a shift in the composition of sex work labor markets in the West, with renewed interest in sexual demands from customers and concerns about migrants from poorer countries being trafficked in order to provide the services.

Box 2.1 The United Nations

The United Nations (UN) is an international organization that was founded in 1945 by 51 member-states following the atrocities of World War II. As of 2014, the UN had a membership of 193 sovereign nations. It sets out to address a variety of international concerns with the support of its members and affiliated organizations, together forming the UN System. Its primary goals are: "To keep peace throughout the world; To develop friendly relations among nations; To help nations work together to improve the lives of poor people, to conquer hunger, disease and illiteracy, and to encourage respect for each other's rights and freedoms; To be a centre for harmonizing the actions of nations to achieve these goals." The UN System is constituted by cooperative agreements with 13 specialized agencies such as the World Bank, the International Monetary Fund, the World Health Organization, and the International Labour Organization. These organizations are responsible for collaborating with the UN on a number of social and economic fronts, although they remain autonomous. According to the UN website, "The Organization works on a broad range of fundamental issues, from sustainable development, environment and refugees protection, disaster relief, counter terrorism, disarmament and non-proliferation, to promoting democracy, human rights, gender equality and the advancement of women, governance, economic and social development and international health, clearing landmines, expanding food production, and more, in order to achieve its goals and coordinate efforts for a safer world for this and future generations."

For further information:

UN at a glance, http://www.un.org/en/aboutun

These developments contributed to the emergence of a widespread and often ferocious debate about the nature of prostitution and its relationship to trafficking, defined here as recruiting and transporting women across national borders for work or services by means of violence or threat or abuse of authority or other forms of coercion. Prostitution usually refers to the exchange of sex or sexual services for money or other material benefits. As feminist theorists have pointed out, it usually occurs within unequal gendered power relations (O'Connell Davidson, 1998, p. 9). Prostitution has long been an issue of concern for women's political activism. During the "first wave," advocates for women's rights opposed prostitution as part of campaigns to improve the treatment of women. During the "second wave," multiple political positions emerged as some feminists conceptualized prostitution as inherently violent to women. Other feminists preferred the term "sex work," and characterized prostitution primarily as a form of labor. Crucial to the debate is the relationship between trafficking and prostitution: does prostitution lead to trafficking, or is trafficking a more general form of labor exploitation? In this chapter I will focus on women's movement organizations' involvement in the international debates over the last three decades, and examine the widely divergent discourses they developed in Western democratic states and the UN and EU arenas, where they are attempting to make their discourses hegemonic to influence policies on trafficking and prostitution.

The re-emergence of the issues

Trafficking arose as a social problem at the end of the nineteenth century in Europe and North America when industrialization, urbanization, and unequal distribution of wealth led to increased migration,with accompanying worries about the free movement of women. Trafficking was then defined as transporting women across borders for sexual exploitation. At the time, trafficking and prostitution became major issues for feminists who demanded the abolition of state regulation of brothels and an end to trafficking.

Box 2.2 The Contagious Diseases Acts

The British Parliament passed the first *Contagious Diseases Acts* in 1864 to prevent the spread of sexually transmitted infections in the armed forces. The *Acts* were amended in 1866 and 1869. It was believed that, while prostitution was a "necessary evil" for men to accommodate their "biological urges," prostitutes were passing infections to soldiers, who needed to be kept disease-free. Targeting prostitutes as the "vectors of disease" was seen as a way to re-establish military efficacy and national security. Among other provisions, the *Acts* authorized police officers to arrest women whom they deemed prostitutes, and bring them before a magistrate who would either confirm or deny the arresting officer's suspicions. Following confirmation, the magistrate would order the prostitute to register and undergo a medical examination. If found to carry a venereal disease, she would be forcibly confined to a "Lock Hospital" for up to nine months, and if she refused, she would be imprisoned. The *Acts* did not mandate military men to get tested for sexual infections, nor did they enforce confinement of men who were found to be infected. By the late 1860s, opposition to the *Acts* was beginning to build. The social reformer Josephine Butler was one of the more vocal critics, arguing that the clients of prostitutes, not prostitutes themselves, should be held responsible for the spread of venereal diseases, as well as for exploiting and violating vulnerable women. The *Acts* were suspended in 1883 and repealed in 1886.

For further information:

Spiegelhalter, D. (2004). The Contagious Diseases Acts: A controlled experiment in criminal justice. *Significance*, June, 88–89.

After widespread public upheaval about "white slavery" – the recruitment of (white) women into prostitution in the 1880s – trafficking of women was outlawed in international law in 1904. It was coded as bringing women across borders for purposes of prostitution, and subsequently enacted into many national legal systems. The 1949 UN Convention called on all states not only to suppress trafficking, but also prostitution, regardless whether they occur with the consent of the woman involved. The Convention superseded earlier international agreements and set the standard for the next decades despite the fact that many states did not ratify it, partly because of its abolitionist intent. As trafficking then faded from the public eye and prostitution ceased to be a prominent political issue, there was little pressure on implementation (Outshoorn, 2005, p. 142).

Box 2.3 Convention for the Suppression of the Traffic in Persons and of the Exploitation of the Prostitution of Others (1949 Trafficking Convention)

The *Convention for the Suppression of the Traffic in Persons and of the Exploitation of the Prostitution of Others*, otherwise referred to as the *1949 Trafficking Convention*, was published by the United Nations General Assembly on December 2, 1949 and entered into force on July 25, 1951. The preamble states: "[P]rostitution and the accompanying evil of the traffic in persons for the purpose of prostitution are incompatible with the dignity and worth of the human person and endanger the welfare of the individual, the family and the community." It mandates party states to punish any person who: procures, entices, or leads away, for purposes of prostitution, another person, even with the consent of that person; exploits the prostitution of another person, even with the consent of that person; keeps or manages, or knowingly finances or takes part in the financing of a brothel; and knowingly lets or rents a building or other place or any part thereof for the purpose of the prostitution of others. These offenses are subject to prosecution and punishment, including extradition. The *1949 Trafficking Convention* also requests party states to take steps to prevent prostitution and to rehabilitate its victims, and to be vigilant of immigration and emigration channels that might give rise to traffic in persons for the purpose of prostitution.

For further information:

Text of the 1949 Trafficking Convention: http://www1.umn.edu/humanrts/instree/trafficinperson.htm
1949 Trafficking Convention participants: http://treaties.un.org/Pages/ViewDetails.aspx?src=TREATY&mtdsg_no=VII-11-a&chapter=7&lang=en

---

However, with the increase in international tourism, growing prosperity and liberalization of the sexual mores in the West since the mid-1970s, an increasing global sex industry confronted states with new challenges. Sex tourism developed along with cheap travel and affluence among Western males. Reports of trafficking started to emerge at the beginning of the 1980s. At first trafficked women in Western Europe came from South East Asia; in the 1980s the "supply" started to come from Latin America, the Caribbean, and West Africa. After the fall of the Berlin Wall and the demise of communism in Eastern and Central Europe, the bulk of the women trafficked into Western Europe came from these regions. In Australia, trafficked women come mainly from South East Asia; while in the U.S. the major recruitment is from Latin America and Asia. Policy agenda status for trafficking was also facilitated by the emergence of AIDS in the early 1980s, giving fuel to worries about the health hazards of sex. Prostitutes were seen as sources of contamination and authorities were keen to increase control of their activities.

The dynamics of trafficking are best explained by migration theory, which utilizes an economic perspective to analyze the flow of human migration in terms of demand-pull factors. Factors such as high levels of economic development and prosperity, access, and employment prospects make affluent regions, like the Organisation for Economic Co-operation and Development (OECD) states, attractive for migrants. Demand for sex led to a proliferation of new forms of sexual services such as escort services, telephone sex and peep shows, as well as the expansion of more traditional types of prostitution such as streetwalking and rent-a-rooms in cheap hotels. This led to citizens' complaints, putting pressure on local authorities to act. Once the existence of trafficking had been established by research (often provided by feminist NGOs), national governments were also compelled to take the issue seriously.

Supply-push factors also drive migration. In the countries of origin, bad economic conditions, political instability, and social breakdown motivate relocation (Truong, 2003). Structural adjustment policies in developing countries and the introduction of markets in Eastern Europe have redrawn gender segregation lines in the labor market, destroying women's local job opportunities even as financial responsibility for families has fallen more squarely onto women. Women bear the brunt of poverty and seek ways to migrate to the more prosperous countries where they have become a major source of "typical female" labor in sectors such as domestic services, care work, and sexual services. Migration then becomes an important alternative option for women to make a living, making the migration market a highly gendered affair. A variety of transport networks profit off of the demand for migration, transferring migrants from one region to another. These channels can be utilized by those seeking to profit from labor exploitation, including women who are being trafficked for the sex industry.

Feminists in the second wave of women's movements arising in the late 1960s disagreed sharply about the definition of prostitution and its link to trafficking. Although it was not a central issue in mainstream feminist organizing, issue-specific women's movement groups developed in many countries at the time, demanding reform of national prostitution regimes. At the same time, women in prostitution organized to voice their demands, giving rise to sex workers' rights movements in many countries (Doezema,1998; Jenness, 1993; Kempadoo & Doezema, 1998; Mathieu, 2003; Pheterson, 1989).

These diverse groups were able to have considerable impact on prostitution policy by promoting or blocking new legislation in many countries. Most post-industrial democracies have revised their prostitution laws in the last two decades (Outshoorn, 2004, 2011). Many countries did so early in the 1970s as part of the international mood to modernize and liberalize criminal law. For instance, Australia, Canada, Sweden, and Finland all repealed their vagrancy laws which had been used to indict prostitutes. Britain abolished criminalization in the early 1970s. Spain removed articles which stipulated that prostitutes be sent to detention camps from the old Franquist Penal Code in the 1990s, limiting the offense to forced prostitution. In that same decade, France reformed its Penal Code by providing clearer definitions of pimping and soliciting which were less punitive to prostitutes. The Netherlands and some states in Australia (Victoria, New South Wales, and the Australian Capital Territory) repealed the ban on brothels and regulated prostitution as sex work in the course of the 1990s. New Zealand legalized prostitution in 2003. Austria and Germany recognized sex work as work and granted workers social security and equitable taxation. Sweden and the city of Helsinki in Finland took the unique move of criminalizing only the client in prostitution. Norway followed in 2009. In the United States, however, no changes occurred in prostitution policy. All U.S. states except Nevada continue to prohibit prostitution and make both prostitutes and others living off the income earned from prostitution liable to prosecution (Weitzer, 2012, p. 87).

After 2000, in response to the new UN Protocol on Trafficking (Palermo Protocol 2000) and shifting EU regulations, many states also adjusted their criminal law in the area of trafficking. Most states broadened the definition of the offense to include the trafficking of boys and men, refined the concepts of deceit and coercion used to recruit and hold women in sexual exploitation, and raised the penalties for traffickers. Several states also started to provide aid to victims of trafficking, providing temporary residency permits and limited social assistance to those women willing to testify against their traffickers up to and during the trial.

The feminist debates on prostitution and trafficking

There are deep divisions within feminism about what prostitution is and its relation to trafficking of women. Different feminist groups have diametrically opposed positions on such basic issues as the definition and nature of prostitution and its relationship to trafficking.

During the "first wave" of feminism in the latter half of the nineteenth century, most women activists agreed to the abolitionist goal of ending state regulation of brothels and deploying state power to stop all practice of prostitution. The prostitute had to leave prostitution and be "saved." Major abolitionist associations, often with strong connections to the Roman Catholic Church, as well as women's organizations, particularly from Southern Europe, still subscribe to these basic tenets today. Second wave feminism spawned two new major discourses, one of which originated in radical feminist thought and is compatible with traditional abolitionism; the other is the new discourse framing prostitution as sex work, which developed from liberal and socialist feminist thought.

The radical feminist or "sexual domination" discourse views prostitution as the epitome of women's oppression (e.g. Barry, 1979, 1995; Hughes & Roche, 1999; Jeffries, 1997; Raymond, 1998). This perspective sees prostitution as sexual slavery and the most extreme expression of sexual violence against women, making it essential to abolish it and to penalize all those profiting from sexual exploitation, except the prostitute herself. She is portrayed as a victim who requires help to escape slavery and set up a new life. To those holding this position, prostitution is forced by definition, making the concept of "forced prostitution" a pleonasm. Adherents of this position therefore reject the notion of "voluntary prostitution," maintaining that no woman would prostitute herself out of choice or truly free will. This position focuses on the patriarchal oppression of women by men rather than other causes of prostitution and trafficking. It does not focus on the economic analysis of the sex industry or the market for sexual services, instead prioritizing the symbolic meanings of prostitution and the consequences for women that occur within it (Outshoorn, 2005, p. 145).

The other major discourse to emerge was the pro-rights or sex workers' rights approach, which sees prostitution as an option for income generation or a strategy for survival which is to be respected (Bell, 1994; Chapkis, 1997; Pheterson, 1989, 1996). Advocates for sex workers' rights aim for decriminalization of prostitution and its inclusion in labor legislation to normalize the sex trade and guarantee sex workers' labor rights. This perspective argues that women have the right to work as a sex worker and to sexual self-determination. According to this position, sex workers should be able to work in decent labor conditions and to migrate to do sex work elsewhere. Advocates for sex workers' rights seek to destigmatize sex workers and sex work rather than eliminating it. In this view, prostitution itself is not the problem, rather exploitation and abuses such as forced prostitution, trafficking, and bad working conditions are problematic. Adherents to this position focus on fighting forced prostitution and improving working conditions – strategies firmly rejected by radical feminists who adopt the abolitionist position and see all prostitution as forced. An important weakness of the sex workers' rights frame is that in practice it often is hard to draw the line between forced prostitution and voluntary sex work (Outshoorn, 2005, p. 146). For example, some adult women entered prostitution as minors but characterize it as their choice as adults or their other options for income are so constrained as not to present a meaningful alternative.

Underlying the difference between the two positions are conflicting views of male and female sexuality. In the sexual domination discourse, male sexuality is the problem, being seen as intrinsically connected to violence and domination. In the sex work discourse, male sexuality is a given. Both views share an essentialist conception of male sexuality and the male sexual drive, which implicitly is held to be unchangeable and ever present. Here lies a parallel with traditional abolitionism, which also regards the male sexual drive as a given and as a natural and potentially dangerous trait which needs to be controlled. As to female sexuality, in the sexual domination discourse it is denied – women are seen as passive victims of male lust, while the sex work discourse allows for sexually active women. Here again the parallel between the sexual domination discourse and traditional abolitionism should be noted, as both deny active female sexuality. These parallels have enabled the strong alliance between traditional abolitionist organizations and feminists adhering to the sexual domination frame in the Western world (Outshoorn, 2005, p. 146).

The divide between these two feminist perspectives on prostitution also structures the ways in which trafficking and women's migration for sex work are viewed. As trafficking was originally defined in criminal law as the transfer of women across borders for the purposes of prostitution, it was intrinsically linked to prostitution. The focus was very much on how women were recruited, often framed as being lured or duped, into "sexual exploitation." In the sexual domination view, migrating to do sex work is always seen as non-consensual; women who do so are by definition victims of trafficking. Trafficking is also regarded as caused by demand for prostitution, making the best way to fight trafficking the abolition of prostitution. In this view, legalizing the sex trade leads to new demands for prostitutes and thus to more trafficked women. As Doezema has noted, some adherents to this view actually suggest restricting young women's travel as a good way to stop trafficking (Doezema, 2002, p. 25).

For those adhering to the sex workers' rights position, women can be victims of trafficking, but not all sex workers crossing borders are victims of forced prostitution. Many women migrate to work in the sex industry in order to make a living. Here, the unequal distribution of wealth on a global scale is seen as the most important causal factor for sex commerce and migration. In this view, prostitution is only trafficking when the woman is forced into prostitution against her will. According to this perspective, much of what is called trafficking is actually the smuggling of human beings, which enables undocumented people to migrate to other countries to make a living in better circumstances. Among those smuggled are women who intend to work in the sex industry. While smuggling of aliens is a crime against the state to which the person is smuggled, trafficking of women against their will is viewed as a form of violence against women and infringement of their basic human rights (Wijers, 2001, p. 214).

Many proponents of the sex workers' rights position have argued that trafficking for the sex industry is no different than coercing people into other forms of forced labor or slavery, and can best be fought against as such. In this way, trafficking is disconnected from prostitution and linked instead to labor exploitation. This approach degenders the issue, as the link to prostitution reminds us that it is usually women who are trafficked for the purposes of sexual gratification of men. Critics of this approach argue that linking trafficking and prostitution creates a space to discuss the origin of male demands for commercial sex and the construction of masculine sexualities. Proponents of sex workers' rights acknowledge this degendering, but justify it by pointing out that the focus on policing the movement of women and girls will reproduce gender-specific repression by restricting their mobility. This perspective also notes that boys and men are also being trafficked for sexual purposes. Advocates for sex workers' rights expect that, given strong (inter)national law on labor and slavery, this framing makes for more effective strategies against trafficking practices. With the expansion of the trafficking definition in the Palermo Protocol and subsequent EU policies, this strategy is becoming mainstream.

The sex workers' rights position has been strengthened in recent years by a new post-colonial critique that sees abolitionism as a Western, white middle-class women's movement seeking to "protect" women from non-Western countries, a position taken by Doezema (2001, 2010). Agustín has called the concern about trafficking "obsessive" and indicative of Western feminists' attempt to "help" and "save" migrant women (Agustín, 2007). She argues that many women working in the sex industry in the rich industrialized countries are little different to those women migrants working in domestic labor or the entertainment business as waitresses, barmaids, or dancers. Only if one sees sexual contact as utterly different from other kinds of bodily contact can one isolate sex work from other types of services providing care for the body such as hairdressing, nursing, or massage.

According to Agustín (2002), many young women from developing countries are in fact tourists, working their way around the world, and sometimes the work involves sex work. Occasionally this brings them into abusive situations or even sexual slavery. Agustín's strength is that she provides fruitful insights about the construction of demand for commercial sexual services. She links it to Western ideas about sexual liberation and the search for a personal sexual identity. In their later work Agustín (2007) and Doezema (2010) have argued that we should do away with the term "trafficking" altogether, with its suspect genealogy in the "white slavery" scare in the nineteenth century and its traditional link to abolitionism.

A weak spot in their analyses is downplaying the importance of intermediary actors involved in prostitution and prostitution-related migration: those who recruit sex workers, arrange transportation, documents, and jobs in various parts of the sex industry. Many scholars (e.g. Truong, 2003), feminist-inspired NGOs like La Strada in Europe, and authorities such as Europol, have provided evidence of the existence of international criminal networks, running a range from small-scale family-run operations to large-scale crime syndicates involved in international sex commerce. These provide the infrastructure for the increasingly global sex market, in which prostitution-related migration can result in forced labor and exploitation.

The international political arena

The opposing policy positions within the trafficking debate are reflected in two opposing transnational alliances against trafficking. The U.S.-led Coalition Against Trafficking in Women (CATW), in which the well-known U.S. feminists Kathleen Barry and Janice Raymond play an active role, advocates a sexual domination and abolitionist approach. CATW advocates increased penalties for pimps, traffickers, and clients, and the decriminalization of prostitutes. The Global Alliance against Traffic in Women (GAATW), founded in 1994 and based in Thailand, subscribes to the distinction between forced and voluntary prostitution, allowing for sex work. GAATW calls for decriminalization of prostitution and focusing anti-trafficking efforts on forced prostitution and other forms of abuse and exploitation. GAATW's position was backed by the International Committee for Prostitutes' Rights (ICPR), the first transnational manifestation of prostitutes' rights movements, which is also in favor of decriminalization to improve sex workers' position, but is critical of the distinction between forced and voluntary prostitution. ICPR argues that this still relies on state regulation and does little in the way of securing rights for sex workers (Doezema, 2002, p. 25).

Debates on trafficking in the UN recommenced with the adoption of the 1979 Convention on the Elimination of All Forms of Discrimination Against Women (CEDAW). It calls on states "to suppress all forms of traffic in women and the exploitation of prostitution." As no definition was provided for "exploitation," it could be interpreted to allow for abolitionist or non-abolitionist positions. Since then, every new UN treaty or convention on the issues has invited a new round of debate. The UN Vienna Declaration on the Elimination of Violence Against Women (1993) marked the first shift away from abolitionism; it condemns *forced* prostitution and trafficking, but not prostitution *per se*. In 1995, the *Platform for Action* adopted at the Beijing UN Women's World Conference called for fighting *forced* prostitution and trafficking. By the end of the 1990s, trafficking had been incorporated into discourses on the battle against transnational crime: the Palermo Protocol is a supplement to the UN Convention Against Transnational Organized Crime.

The Palermo Protocol on Trafficking defined the issue as the recruitment and transfer of persons by means of the threat or use of force or coercion, fraud, deception or abuse of power for the purpose of exploitation (Protocol, 2000, p. 2). In the final Protocol, exploitation includes the prostitution of others, sexual exploitation, forced labor or services, slavery, servitude, or the removal of organs. The Protocol requires state parties to penalize trafficking and to protect victims of trafficking and grant them temporary or permanent residence in the countries of destination.

Predictably, debates during drafting of this Protocol centered on the definition of trafficking and its relationship to prostitution. Hotly contested was whether the document should state that trafficking could occur "irrespective of the consent of the person." Abolitionists argued that including this phrase in the Protocol would ensure that traffickers could not claim consent as a defense against trafficking complaints. The other side argued that the rest of the definition specifying coercion, force, abduction, fraud, etc. made it clear that consent was not a viable defense to trafficking and would blur the distinction between trafficking and people smuggling (Gallagher, 2001).

In this debate, CATW allied with other abolitionists within the International Human Rights Network, which opposed any kind of legalization of prostitution. The network insisted that the phrase "use in prostitution" should be included among the end purposes named for trafficking, potentially shifting the focus of law enforcement from trafficking to prostitution (Gallagher, 2001). On the other side, GAATW formed an alliance with the International Human Rights Group in the Human Rights Caucus to oppose criminalization of consensual sex work. The Caucus backed the proposals of the UN Convention Committee to expand the definition of trafficking to include forced labor, debt bondage, and forced marriage. As a participant in this debate, Doezema (2005) has described how the

Network of Sex Work Projects (NSWP) allied with the Caucus in support of this position. However, in the process of lobbying, the sex workers themselves became invisible. Doezema observes that even in the non-abolitionist liberal feminist discourse, sex workers are still visible primarily as victims of sexual violence rather than advocates for labor and migration rights.

The Palermo Protocol has proved open to several interpretations. CATW maintains that, according to the Protocol, any migration that involves sex work now falls under the definition of trafficking. Accordingly, all migrating sex workers should be treated as victims of trafficking (Raymond, 2002). The Caucus, on the other hand, holds that the Protocol *intentionally* does not define "the exploitation of prostitution of others or other forms of sexual exploitation," as a compromise between conflicting policy positions among states. The Caucus thus interprets the Protocol as a departure from the 1949 Convention as it permits focus on the coercive elements of labor exploitation and does not require an abolitionist approach to prostitution (Sullivan, 2003, pp. 82–83).

The Palermo Protocol has therefore not ended the debates on trafficking or its relation to migration and prostitution. While it has provided a new definition confirming existing rights, it contains a number of weaknesses in its instruments, leaving too much to the ratifying states and lacking mandatory protection for victims (Gallagher, 2001, p. 1004). Notably, despite its self-definition as a world leader in anti-trafficking efforts (see O'Brien and Wilson in this volume), the U.S. has not ratified the Palermo Protocol and continues to prioritize the abolition of prostitution via foreign and development policy as well as domestic law enforcement efforts (Doezema, 2010, pp. 141–142; Weitzer, 2007, p. 462).

Within the EU, prostitution and trafficking have been on the policy agenda since 1986. During a successful feminist lobby in the European Parliament (EP) on violence against women, a new framing of prostitution in an official report recognized the distinction between forced and voluntary prostitution. However, trafficking continued to be tied to prostitution until the early 1990s, when feminist members of the Greens/European Free Alliance party in the EP coalesced with feminist researchers and activists from sex workers' rights organizations to promote an approach to trafficking that advocates sex workers' rights and decriminalization of prostitution (Outshoorn, 2004, p. 12). This alliance resulted in an EP resolution, calling on member-states to protect victims of trafficking, to set up witness protection programs and provide temporary residency permits for those willing to testify against their traffickers. In this context, there was no mention of taking measures against prostitution.

The de-linking of trafficking and prostitution was also in evidence in subsequent reports and measures of the EP and later the European Commission (EC). The Commission also adopted the distinction between voluntary and forced prostitution and recognized that many trafficked women are in fact migrants. They did not call for eliminating all prostitution as a way to address trafficking. Despite opposition from conservative members, the EP in general has maintained this line. However, the fall of the Berlin Wall and the ensuing increase in migration also moved the EC to take action. It realized that the planned enlargement of the EU in 2004 meant that the EU would no longer just be at the "receiving end" of trafficking, but would be responsible for women from the Central and Eastern European States. In this context, the new Swedish Eurocommissioner, Anita Gradin, acted as policy entrepreneur. She was an abolitionist on prostitution and opposed to the de-linking of the issue from trafficking, but she did set up the first EU conference on trafficking in Vienna in 1996 and initiated the STOP and DAPHNE programs for funding projects on violence against women (Outshoorn, 2005, p. 151).

Gradin found a political ally in the European Women's Lobby. This large platform organization was formed in 1990 at the instigation of the European Commission, which preferred to deal with a single organization of lobby groups. The European Women's Lobby now includes more than 3,000 women's organizations from all member-states, including traditional and religious groups. Prior to the Fourth World Conference on Women in Beijing in 1995, it had no position on prostitution, but when confronted with the adoption of the distinction between forced and voluntary prostitution in the Beijing Platform for Action, it backed an abolitionist position.

In this alliance, traditional French abolitionists united with Swedish left wing feminists against the increasing support for sex workers' rights and the de-linking of trafficking and prostitution. This resulted in a strong resolution from the European Women's Lobby condemning both trafficking and prostitution in 1998. Soon after that, the European Women's Lobby joined forces with CATW, culminating in a second resolution calling on members to lobby their national states and push for client criminalization in 2001 (Outshoorn, 2005, p. 152). Although this approach has considerable support in the Committee of Women's Rights of the European Parliament, many other Members of European Parliament continue to advocate for a distinction between forced prostitution and sex work and the separation of prostitution and trafficking.

Despite substantial support for the abolitionist position within the EP, the separation of trafficking and prostitution is in alignment with the various Treaties of the EU which make trafficking a transnational issue under EU jurisdiction and maintain prostitution as a matter of national jurisdiction. Accordingly, the European Commission and the Council of Ministers have continued to focus on trafficking as distinct from prostitution, such as in the 1997 Joint Action of the Council on Trafficking (Joint Action, 1997). This Action obliged member-states to penalize trafficking of persons, to pass measures to prosecute profiteers of trafficking and to confiscate their profits, and to support and protect victims of trafficking. In 2002 the Council adopted the Framework on Combating Trafficking in Human Beings, replacing earlier measures (Council, 2001). The Framework called on member-states to outlaw trafficking, to protect victims of trafficking, and to develop a common policy against illegal migration. Again there is no mention of prostitution *per se*; the Framework therefore allows for voluntary prostitution. Since then, the EU has developed several action plans to combat trafficking. In the European Parliament, abolitionists have tried repeatedly to include prostitution in EU regulations against trafficking and to stop funding to NGOs that take a pragmatic sex workers' rights position. However, the abolitionists have failed to obtain a majority.

In 2011, a new EU directive on trafficking was adopted which replaces the Framework. The European Commission had been working on a revision to remedy the Framework's shortcomings, which included few effective prosecutions, insufficient aid to victims and inadequate monitoring of the situation. However, the Lisbon Treaty (forming the EU's new constitutional base) of 2009 did away with Framework programs, so that a new binding directive was developed. A new Directive on Preventing and Combating Trafficking in Human Beings was passed in 2011 by the European Parliament (Directive, 2011). The Directive more or less retains the Framework's definition of the offense, but adds begging and the removal of organs to the list of offenses for trafficking. The Directive also directs more attention to supporting victims and protecting them in criminal proceedings, as well as discouraging and reducing demand for trafficked labor.

Conclusion

Since the re-emergence of trafficking on the policy agenda, women's movement groups have developed two primary frames which have informed debates at the national and international level. Following the older abolitionist position, which set out to end all selling of sexual services, eliminate state regulation of prostitution, and extricate women from prostitution, second wave feminism spawned two new positions on prostitution that feed into human trafficking policies. The sexual domination frame, developed by radical feminists, regards all prostitution as inherently violent and the epitome of patriarchal oppression of women. According to this position, trafficking is primarily caused by prostitution, therefore ending prostitution is a necessary precondition for preventing trafficking. The similarity between the sexual domination position and old-style abolitionism has made for a strong international alliance to fight the competing frame of sex work. The second position developed from second wave feminism accepts sex work as an income-generating strategy for women to avoid poverty. This position opposes only forced prostitution and sees "trafficking" as often about women migrating to work in the sex industry. Proponents of this position allied with the novel phenomenon of sex workers' rights organizations, which claim equal rights for prostitutes and women's right to sexual self-determination.

In many Western nations, there has been a gradual move to legalize prostitution since the 1970s. A number of states have implemented policies that decriminalize the prostitute, allow certain types of prostitution, and regulate prostitution as sex work. At the UN and EU level, however, ongoing conflict between these two positions on prostitution has deeply marked international debates on measures to combat trafficking. At the EU level the sex workers' rights position currently dominates, due in part to states' jurisdiction over prostitution and EU jurisdiction over trafficking. However, at the UN level, compromises over the approach to prostitution and trafficking have resulted in ambiguous policies, allowing for diverse interpretations by member-states.

Despite these deep divisions, all policy approaches to trafficking advocate stiffer criminal penalties for traffickers. However, efforts to monitor and combat trafficking have had the unintended consequence of making life harder for migrating women, especially those in the sex trade. Women's movement organizations will have to come to terms with the realities of international migration and rethink their definition of women's interests when addressing the old question of prostitution and its historical link to trafficking.

Note

* This chapter contains revised material from the article originally published by Oxford University Press as Outshoorn, J. (2005). The political debates on prostitution and trafficking of women. *Social Politics: International Studies in Gender, State and Society, 12*(1), 141–155.

References

Agustín, L. M. (2002). Challenging "place": Leaving home for sex. *Development, 45*(1), 110–116.
— (2007). *Sex at the margins: Migration, labour markets and the rescue industry*. London/ New York: Zed Books.
Barry, K. (1979). *Female sexual slavery*. Englewood Cliffs, NJ: Prentice-Hall.
— (1995). *The prostitution of sexuality*. New York: New York University Press.
Bell, S. (1994). *Reading, writing and rewriting the prostitute body*. Bloomington: Indiana University Press.
Chapkis, W. (1997). *Performing erotic labor*. New York: Routledge.
Council (2001). *Council Framework Decision on combating trafficking in human beings— proposal by European Commission*. 2001 COM (2000)854/2-2001/0024.
Directive (2011). Directive 2011/36/EU of the European Parliament and of the Council of 5 April 2011 on preventing and combating trafficking in human beings and protecting its victims, and replacing the Council Framework Decision 2002/629/JHA (OJ L 101 of 15.4.2011). Retrieved on April 17, 2014 from http://eur-lex.europa.eu/legal-content/EN/ TXT/?uri=CELEX:32011L0036
Doezema, J. (1998). Forced to choose: Beyond the voluntary v. forced prostitution dichotomy, in Kempadoo, K. and Doezema, J. (Eds.), *Global sex workers: Rights, resistance, and redefinition*. London: Routledge, pp. 34–51.
— (2001). Ouch! Western feminists' "wounded attachment" to the Third World prostitute. *Feminist Review, 67*(Spring), 16–38.
— (2002). Who gets to choose? Coercion, consent, and the UN trafficking protocol. *Gender and Development, 10*(1), 20–27.
— (2005). Now you see her, now you don't: Sex workers at the UN trafficking protocol negotiation. *Social & Legal Studies, 14*(1), 61–89.
— (2010). *Sex slaves and discourse masters: The construction of trafficking*. London/New York: Zed Books.
Gallagher, A. (2001). Human rights and the new UN protocols on trafficking and migrant smuggling. *Human Rights Quarterly, 23*(4), 975–1004.
Hughes, D. M. & Roche C. (Eds.) (1999). *Making the harm visible: Global sexual exploitation of women and girls. Speaking out and providing services*. Kingston, RI: CATW.

Jeffries, S. (1997). *The idea of prostitution*. Melbourne: Spinifex Press.

Jenness, V. (1993). *Making it work: The prostitutes' rights movement in perspective*. Hawthorne, NY: Aldine de Gruyter.

Joint Action (1997). *Joint Action of 24 February 1997, concerning action to combat human beings and sexual exploitation of women*. 97/154/JHA.

Kempadoo, K. & Doezema J. (Eds.) (1998). *Global sex workers: Rights, resistance, and redefinition*. New York/London: Routledge.

Mathieu, L. (2003). The emergence and uncertain outcomes of prostitutes' social movements. *European Journal of Women's Studies*, *10*(1), 29–50.

O'Connell Davidson, J. (1998). *Prostitution, power and freedom*. Cambridge: Polity Press.

Outshoorn, J. (Ed.) (2004). *The politics of prostitution: Women's movements, democratic states and the globalisation of sex commerce*. Cambridge: Cambridge University Press.

— (2005). The political debates on prostitution and trafficking, *Social Politics*, *12*(1/ Spring), 141–156.

— (2011). The politics of prostitution revisited: Trends in policy and research, in Jónasdóttir, A. G., Bryson, V. and Jones, K. B. (Eds.), *Sexuality, gender and power: Intersectional and transnational perspectives*. New York/London: Routledge, pp. 127–142.

Pheterson, G. (Ed.) (1989). *A vindication of the rights of whores*. Seattle: Seal Press.

— (1996). *The prostitution prism*. Amsterdam: Amsterdam University Press.

Protocol (2000). *Protocol to prevent, suppress and punish trafficking in persons, especially women and children, supplementing the United Nations Convention Against Transnational Organized Crime*. (December) Retrieved on April 17, 2014 from https://treaties.un.org/pages/viewdetails.aspx?src=ind&mtdsg_no=xviii-12-a&chapter=18&lang=en

Raymond, J. G. (1998). Prostitution as violence against women. *Women's Studies International Forum*, *21*(1), 1–9.

— (2002). The new UN Trafficking Protocol. *Women's Studies International Forum*, *25*(5), 491–502.

Sullivan, B. (2003). Trafficking in women: Feminism and new international law. *International Feminist Journal of Politics*, *5*(1), 67–91.

Truong, T. (2003). Gender, exploitative migration, and the sex industry. *Gender, Technology and Development*, *7*(1), 31–52.

Weitzer, R. (2007). The social construction of sex trafficking: Ideology and institutionalization of a moral crusade. *Politics and Society*, *35*(3), 447–475.

— (2012). *Legalizing prostitution: From illicit vice to lawful business*. New York: New York University Press.

Wijers, M. (2001). European Union policies on trafficking in women, in Rossilli, M. (Ed.), *Gender policies in the European Union*. New York: Peter Lang, pp. 209–220.

Discussion questions

1. What position on prostitution is incorporated in the contemporary UN human trafficking protocols?
2. How is the human trafficking problem characterized by advocates for sex workers' rights?
3. What do abolitionists want to abolish?
4. What is the legal approach to prostitution advocated by proponents of the sexual domination position?
5. How do the International Human Rights Network and the Human Rights Caucus differ?

Additional resources

Coalition Against Trafficking in Women
http://www.catwinternational.org

Global Alliance Against Traffic in Women
http://www.gaatw.org

United Nations Convention against Transnational Organized Crime
http://www.unodc.org/unodc/en/treaties/CTOC

Protocol to Prevent, Suppress and Punish Trafficking in Persons, Especially Women and
    Children, supplementing the United Nations Convention against Transnational Orga-
    nized Crime (Palermo Protocol)
http://www.ohchr.org/EN/ProfessionalInterest/Pages/ProtocolTraffickingInPersons.aspx

World Charter for Prostitutes' Rights
http://www.walnet.org/csis/groups/icpr_charter.html

Chapter 3

Data matters

Issues and challenges for research on trafficking

Elżbieta M. Goździak

Introduction

Human trafficking continues to capture the imagination of the global public. Sensational stories about women kept as sexual slaves and children sold into domestic servitude appear on front pages of newspapers, in academic journals, and in popular books (e.g. Batstone, 2007; Kara, 2009; Malarek, 2004; Skinner, 2008). The term is used to discuss a wide range of phenomena without much consideration of whether they meet the legal definition of trafficking in persons or deal with a wider set of abuses and exploitation. However, despite the increased interest in human trafficking, little research has been done on this issue. There are a lot of *writings* about human trafficking, mainly for sexual exploitation, but there is significantly less *literature* based on empirical research (Goździak & Bump, 2008).

Critical observations about the state of data and research-based knowledge of human trafficking are not mere academic reflections but are recognized by key international organizations (Huijsmans, 2011). For example, the United Nations Inter-Agency Project (UNIAP), established in 2000 to facilitate coordination of anti-trafficking responses in the Mekong subregion of mainland Southeast Asia, considered to be a hot-spot of global trafficking (Piper, 2005; ILO, 2002), wrote on its website: "even after nearly ten years of attention to human trafficking, estimates of the number of human trafficking victims are very limited and lack empirical merit . . . the counter-trafficking community has yet to come up with reliable methodologies for getting those numbers" (UNIAP, 2008).

At the same time, "the amount of money to combat human trafficking has increased exponentially over the years—from $31.8 million in 2001 to $185.5 million in 2010" (Coburn, 2011, p.11). These resources have been earmarked almost exclusively for provision of services to trafficked persons and technical assistance to service providers assisting them. Media campaigns to raise public awareness and concern for the trafficked victims have also been financed. However, these activities have taken place without a clear idea of the extent of the problem or a uniform methodology for determining the scope of the issue (Bump et al., 2005; Coburn, 2011). Assistance to victims has been provided without the benefit of empirical research aimed at identifying their service needs or evaluating the outcomes and impacts of rehabilitation programs to integrate survivors of human trafficking into the wider society and prevent repeat victimization. The dominant anti-trafficking discourse is not evidence-based but remains grounded in the construction of a particular mythology of trafficking (Sanghera, 2005).

In this chapter I discuss the state of empirical literature on trafficking in persons and explore some of the challenges involved in conducting empirical research, particularly studies involving survivors of human trafficking. I concentrate on cross-border trafficking of adults and children for labor and sexual exploitation. I illustrate my points with examples from the analysis of global research on human trafficking undertaken in preparation for the special issue of *International Migration* (Laczko & Goździak, 2005) and a review, supported by a grant from the National Institute of Justice (NIJ), of research-based English-language publications on human trafficking carried out in 2008 (Goździak & Bump, 2008) and updated in 2011, as well as my own research with children, mainly girls, trafficked to the United States for labor and sexual exploitation (see Goździak & MacDonnell, 2007; Goździak, 2008, 2011). Both reviews of the literature indicated that the field had not moved beyond estimating the scale of the problem; mapping routes and relationships between countries of origin, transit, and destinations; and reviewing legal frameworks and policy responses. The situation is not much different in 2014; there is still no reliable data on the scope of the trafficking phenomenon or the characteristics of the victims and perpetrators.

Growing number of publications, little empirical data

The 2008 survey of English-language publications on human trafficking mentioned above yielded some 2,388 references, including 1,249 reports, 736 journal articles, and 403 books. Fewer than 20 percent of the journal articles were based on empirical research. However, almost half of the non-empirical articles were published in peer-reviewed journals. This challenges traditional notions of the type of research published in peer-reviewed periodicals. Peer review is the process of subjecting a work to the critical eye of experts in the same field and has the important function of promoting high standards and preventing poorly researched or unwarranted claims. For this reason, studies that are not subject to peer review are often considered to lack scientific rigor and to be of lesser quality. Scholars and editors deem peer review necessary because it allows for mistakes and oversights to be caught and provides an opportunity to improve the analysis or presentation of research results. While some have critiqued the peer review system as "biased, incomplete, and unaccountable," it remains one of the standard benchmarks of academic rigor and quality (Horton, 2000).

It seems that peer-reviewed journals have published non-empirical research on trafficking in persons because of the dynamic created by the sudden and intense political interest in human trafficking following the passage of the UN Palermo Protocol and the U.S. Trafficking Victims Protection Act (TVPA) of 2000.

Additionally, the difficulty of conducting empirical research on human trafficking, including impeded access to victims, law enforcement, and prosecutors, as well as the length of time it takes to conduct empirical research, have also contributed to the predominance of non-empirical studies. Journal editors realized that their readership desired more information about human trafficking, but few empirical studies were conducted, thus non-empirical papers, mostly in the form of literature and data reviews or descriptions and analyses of anti-trafficking policies, have been published.

In contrast to journal articles, the vast majority (or 68 percent) of reports identified in the survey were based on empirical research. These reports were produced by numerous organizations: governments, the United Nations, intra-governmental organizations, international organizations, and U.S. and international non-governmental organizations. The fact that more than two-thirds of the surveyed reports were authored by international NGOs or intra-governmental organizations is an important factor in the analysis of where and how most trafficking research is currently being conducted. Much of the research conducted by these organizations took place in the developing world. It seems that research conducted by non-academic and non-governmental entities in the developing world may face fewer barriers than research projects carried out by scholars whose studies are subject to approval by Institutional Review Boards or Ethics Committees, whether they study human trafficking in the developed or developing countries.

Empirical research on trafficking in persons is most prevalent in the social sciences. At the time of my 2008 literature review, the majority of empirical research focused on sex trafficking. Only three journal articles dealt with trafficking for labor exploitation (Goździak & Bump, 2008; De Lange, 2007; Shigekane, 2007) and one with domestic servitude (Constable, 1996). Sixty percent of the analyzed reports also dealt with trafficking for sexual exploitation. The situation has improved recently and more empirical studies on labor trafficking are beginning to emerge (e.g. Brennan, 2014; Coghlan & Wylie, 2011; Mahdavi, 2011; Vlieger, 2012). However, the majority of recent publications still deal with legal frameworks or the anti-trafficking discourse/s (e.g. Huijsmans, 2011; Shoaps, 2013; Stoyanova, 2013).

Theoretical frameworks

"*In no area* of the social sciences has ideology contaminated knowledge more pervasively than in writings on the sex industry," asserts Ronald Weitzer, a sociologist at the George Washington University. This claim certainly extends to trafficking for sexual exploitation, an area "where cannons of scientific inquiry are suspended and research deliberately skewed to serve a particular political [and moral] agenda" (Weitzer, 2005, p. 934; see also Weitzer, 2007; Rubin, 1984, 1993; Goode, 1997). Much of the early U.S. research on human trafficking for sexual exploitation has been conducted by activists involved in anti-prostitution campaigns (e.g. Hughes, 2004, 2005; Raymond, 1998, 2004). These activists adopt an extreme (i.e. absolutist, doctrinaire, and unscientific) version of radical feminist theory, which does not distinguish between trafficking for forced prostitution and voluntary migration (legal or irregular) for sex work and claims that all sex workers are victims of trafficking. As Weitzer points out, few of the radical feminist claims about sex trafficking are amenable to verification or falsification (Weitzer, 2005, p. 936).

Moral crusades propagated by activists and to a certain extent by service providers whose funding depends on maintaining the gravity of the trafficking problem "typically rely on horror stories and 'atrocity tales' about victims in which the most shocking exemplars of victimization are described and typified" (Weitzer, 2007, p. 448). In reality, limited numbers of victims have been identified and even fewer have been studied to be able to make such gross generalizations. The radical feminist theory (or sexual domination theory as described by Outshoorn in this volume) conflates trafficking for sexual exploitation with prostitution and suggests, among other things, that there is a causal link between legal prostitution and sex trafficking. Research does not support these claims. Both conceptually and empirically, it is inappropriate to fuse prostitution and sex trafficking (Weitzer, 2007). There is no evidence that the majority of prostitutes have been trafficked and the causal link between legal prostitution and sex trafficking has not been empirically established.

Research on trafficking for labor exploitation is disconnected from theory as well. There are virtually no attempts to analyze issues of cross-border trafficking for labor exploitation within existing international migration theories. There is also no attempt to develop a new theoretical framework in which to comprehensively analyze the phenomenon. "Poverty and the aspiration for a better way of life are by far the major 'push factors' and are also among the principal reasons why parents send their children away to work" (Williams & Masika, 2002, p. 5). My own research suggests that virtually all victims of child trafficking came to the United States intent on finding employment. Child labor is common and widely accepted in the countries of origin of many of the trafficked minors I studied (Goździak & Bump, 2008). The International Labour Organization (ILO) estimates that 250 million children between the ages of 5 and 14 living in developing countries qualify as child laborers. At least 120 million children work full-time. Sixty-one percent of child laborers are in Asia, 32 percent in Africa, and 7 percent in Latin America. Their work varies, from helping with family farms to performing physically demanding tasks in manufacturing, construction, and extractive industries (Henne & Moseley, 2005).

Methodological approaches

Development of innovative methodologies to study human trafficking is in its infancy. Qualitative methodologies dominated journal articles identified in the course of the 2008 literature review. Interviews were the predominant methodology. As an anthropologist, I certainly value in-depth, open-ended, and systematic ethnographic interviews, but am fully aware that interviews conducted by

Box 3.1 International Labour Organization

The International Labour Organization (ILO) was founded in 1919 as part of the Treaty of Versailles that ended World War I. It was founded based on the belief that social justice is a prerequisite to peace, and that ensuring decent labor conditions across international borders was an essential part of this. The ILO opposed the exploitation of workers in industrializing countries at that time and recognized the need to promote similar working conditions in all countries, due to increasing globalization, in order to maintain peace and develop prosperity worldwide. It has played an important role in developments such as maximum work weeks and hours and the minimum wage. ILO is devoted to promoting social justice and human and labor rights. The organizing principle of the ILO is that "labour peace is essential to prosperity." ILO's current objectives are to "promote rights at work, encourage decent employment opportunities, enhance social protection and strengthen dialogue on work-related issues." The ILO *Special Action Programme to Combat Forced Labour (SAP-FL)* is responsible for leading its anti-forced labor and anti-human trafficking initiatives.

For further information:

International Labour Organization http://www.ilo.org/global/about-the-ilo/lang--en/index.htm

ILO history
http://www.ilo.org/global/about-the-ilo/history/lang--en/index.htm

untrained researchers often amount to no more than an anecdote. Victims' and stakeholders' narratives are important but need to be augmented by participant observation. People do not necessarily do what they say. Participant observation is needed, but difficult. The main obstacle to conducting empirical qualitative research on human trafficking is related to gaining access to trafficked persons. For obvious reasons, to study them while they are still in the hands of traffickers is impossible and dangerous.

But is it easier to engage trafficked persons in research once they have been rescued? In order to conduct research on trafficking to the United States, particularly research that highlights the perspectives of the trafficked persons themselves, researchers have to work closely with service providers. Trafficked persons are considered an extremely vulnerable population and service providers are charged with protecting them from further exploitation as well as from the possible adverse effects of recounting their trafficking experiences in the course of a research project. Many social service providers do not see research as a way to empower trafficked persons by providing an opportunity to bring about justice and to affect policy making and program design from the ground up. Researchers often lament how difficult it is to convince practitioners—service providers, attorneys, and law enforcement—about the value of research and gain their permission to recruit trafficked persons, both adults and children, to participate in empirical studies (Brennan, 2005). Researchers who are successful in developing close working relationships with and gaining the trust of service providers and their charges often meet with criticism from fellow-researchers who point out that precisely because of the close connection between the researchers and the practitioners the study would be less "objective" and the involvement of the practitioners in the study would be self-serving.

Quantitative methodologies are noticeably scarce (e.g. Curtol et al., 2004; Hennink & Simkhada, 2004). The scarcity of quantitative studies results from either unavailability of datasets on trafficking in persons or difficulties in gaining access to existing databases. It is not uncommon for authors of research articles on trafficking in persons to address the difficulty of accessing quality data on this issue. Some authors suggest that quantitative research is impossible without access to the existing—very few—databases. For example, the database developed by the International Organization for Migration (IOM), described in the Government Accountability Office report (GAO, 2006), is yet to be made available to outside researchers. The U.S. Federal Government is also not sharing much statistical information on trafficked victims in federal care. In a recent conversation, a representative of the Bureau of Justice Assistance (BJA) said he could not allow my colleague and I to access the Human Trafficking Reporting System (HTRS) because "the data integrity is not of a satisfactory standard to permit valuable conclusions to be drawn from it." Lack of datasets on the number and characteristics of trafficked victims, the number of traffickers, and even the number of prosecutions has forced researchers to rely on qualitative methodologies.

Sweeping generalizations based on small samples

Reliance on unrepresentative samples is widespread. Most studies continue to rely on interviews with "key stakeholders" who do have a stake in promoting certain views of human trafficking and its victims. Studies that do include interviews with victims are limited to very small samples (e.g. Caliber Associates, 2003; Human Rights Center and Free the Slaves, 2004; Human Rights Center, 2005). The well-known dangers of generalizing from small convenience samples and from anecdotal stories are routinely ignored in publications on human trafficking. There is a need to emphasize the limitations of small samples for generalizations and extrapolations, while at the same time stressing the value of ethnographic investigations for formulating hypotheses for further studies, including preparation of survey questionnaires.

The majority (85 percent) of social science journal articles identified in the 2008 literature review were based on undiscernible samples. Most authors did not identify the sample size upon which they were basing their observations, and many did not specify the gender and age of the victims they were discussing. Only two papers were based on random samples and three on population samples. The remaining articles were based on convenience samples. The majority of law and criminal justice papers focused on legislation and policies and for obvious reasons the authors did not need to sample victims. However, many authors stated that their analyses were based on interviews with policy makers and representatives of law enforcement but failed to indicate both the number of interviewed individuals and the way they selected study participants (Goździak & Bump, 2008).

Focus on "women and children"

The vast majority of publications identified in the survey—approximately 80 percent—focused on "women and children." Child victims were often subsumed under the women and children heading without allowing for analysis of their special needs. Thirty percent of publications on trafficked children did not differentiate between male and female children (Goździak & Bump, 2008). It is interesting that women and children are lumped together in anti-trafficking legislation and the dominant trafficking paradigm when in all other instances, including labor laws, great care is being taken to separate child labor from adult labor. Many writers use the word "children" but focus on young women. Research on trafficked boys is virtually non-existent, as is research on men trafficked both for sexual and labor exploitation (see Allais, 2013; Macy & Johns, 2011).

The focus on women (and girls) is also related to the fact that the trafficking discourse centers on trafficking for sexual exploitation, resulting in the neglect of trafficking for other forms of labor (Anker & van Liempt, 2012; Mahdavi, 2011). Women and girls are considered to be particularly vulnerable to trafficking because in many parts of the world they have low social status, limited access to education, lack of rights to property, and possess few opportunities to participate in the political process (Shelly, 2010).

The gendered (as well as raced, classed, and sexualized) discourse on human trafficking stems from the current disconnect "between the broad legal definition that embraces any worker who experienced force, fraud, or coercion, and the narrow latitude of activist and policy discussions that focuses on sex work" (Mahdavi, 2011, p. 13). The centrality of women in the trafficking discourse "maintains the gendered divide around which earlier definitions of trafficking settled and thus reinforces the general, dominant image of trafficking as pertinent only to women's and girls' lives." The concept of gendered inequality continues to guide research, "with situations of poor women and girls becoming the main concern of those involved with anti-trafficking work" (Kempadoo et al., 2005, p. ix).

And finally, the gendered dimension of human trafficking relates to broader issues of women and migration. Despite the continued feminization of migration— half of the world's migrants are women (Zlotnik, 2003)—there remains a "bias that women and girls need constant male or state protection from harm, and therefore must not be allowed to exercise their right to movement or right to earn a living in a manner they choose" (Kempadoo et al., 2005, p. 29). "Some countries (e.g. Bangladesh, Myanmar, Nepal) have even prohibited women from migration because of the fear that they will end up in trouble" (Anker & van Liempt, 2012, p. 8). This bias often conflates migration with trafficking and contributes to the notion that women are the main victims of trafficking. Critics have argued that anti-trafficking measures have been used not necessarily to protect women from exploitation, but to police, punish, and racialize female migrants (Chapkis, 2003; Kapur, 2002; Sharma, 2005).

The discourse on trafficked children parallels in many ways the discourse on trafficked women and assumes that "migrants can be neatly divided into moral categories such as adult (strong, active, agent) and child (weak, passive, victim), and smuggled (complicit in a crime against the state) and trafficked (victim of a crime against the person)" (O'Connell Davidson, 2005, pp. 74–75). Hashim (2003) shows the inadequacies of these binaries. Her research in Tempane Natinga, Ghana shows that children who remain in their place of birth, working for their own families, can be exploited, but migrant children who move for work may have positive experiences that provide them the opportunity to develop skills and earn an income that they can spend on necessities. However, Western child and anti-trafficking advocates often see minors as "child laborers" and "victims of trafficking," rather than working children (Hashim, 2003; see also O'Connell Davidson, 2005).

Neglected issues and topics

Research fulfills a number of roles, one of which is to offer an independent and critical assessment of current policy and practice. The list of issues that need to be explored in future research projects is long, but the most important arena which needs urgent exploration is the way the knowledge upon which the public debate about trafficking for sexual and labor exploitation is based is generated. Where does this knowledge come from and how is it used? The U.S. government prides itself in leading the anti-trafficking movement and providing policy and programmatic guidance to other governments. The data and the knowledge the U.S. uses must therefore be valid, reliable, and based on empirical research.

In order to acquire the broadest possible picture of the trafficking phenomenon, several different data collection methods, including quantitative and qualitative methods, need to be tested. Estimation methods that have been gaining currency in studies of hidden populations include rapid assessment, capture-recapture methodology, and Respondent-Driven Sampling (RDS). These methods have been successfully used to study the homeless (Williams & Cheal, 2002), street children (Gurgel et al., 2004), and women in street prostitution (Brunovskis & Tyldum, 2004). Researchers in Norway, for example, were quite successful in employing telephone surveys of sex workers operating through individual advertisements (Tyldum & Brunovskis, 2005). It seems that collaboration with scholars who have had a long history of conducting research on prostitution could be very fruitful in testing the applicability of data collection methods developed and utilized within the sex work research arena to studies of trafficking in persons. Similar collaboration ought to occur with researchers studying illegal migration. I am yet to see anyone discussing the applicability, or lack of such, of methods utilized by Jeffrey Passel (2005, 2006) or George Borjas (1991, 2001) to estimate the number of undocumented immigrants in the U.S. to arrive at similar estimates of the number of persons trafficked into the United States.

Trafficking in persons is often portrayed as the world's fastest growing criminal enterprise, with profits that rival the illegal drugs and arms trade. Reports repeatedly quote the number of seven billion dollars in profit to indicate the magnitude of the phenomenon (Denisova, 2001; Roby, 2005; Scarpa, 2006; Spangenberg, 2002). Reports also talk about networks of international organized crime which are attracted to the trade in human beings because of low risk and because the criminal penalties for human trafficking are light in most countries (Pochagina, 2007; Tiefenbrun, 2002; Zhang et al., 2007). Different *Trafficking in Persons Reports* produced by the U.S. Department of State reiterate this assertion, describing how traffickers enjoy virtually no risk of prosecution by using sophisticated modes of transportation and communication and avoid punishment by operating in places where there is little rule of law, lack of anti-trafficking laws, poor enforcement of such laws, and widespread corruption (United States Department of State, *Trafficking in Persons Report*, 2003–2007). Media and international organizations also talk about the fact that the crime of trafficking in persons offers international organized crime syndicates a low-risk opportunity to make billions in profits by taking advantage of unlimited supply and unending demand for trafficked persons (Burke et al., 2005; Claramunt, 2002; ILO, 2002).

Given the lack of research findings and statistical data, it is difficult to accurately assess the scope of organized crime's involvement in human trafficking (Bruckert & Parent, 2002, p. 13). The distinction between trafficking and smuggling is not always easy to make. According to John Salt (2000, p. 43), the notion that human trafficking and organized crime are closely related is widespread despite lack of evidence to support this assertion. This alleged connection is based on the fact that people of different nationalities are part of the same group of trafficked victims; that trips over long distance require a well-oiled organization; that substantial amounts of money are involved; that itineraries change quickly; that legal services are available very quickly; and that there is a strong reaction to counter-offensives by law enforcement agencies (Bruckert & Parent, 2002). These arguments developed by Europol (Salt, 2000) are also shared by others (e.g. Juhasz, 2000; Taibly, 2001). Some researchers also point to a close connection between organized crime and trafficking for sexual exploitation, indicating that the magnitude and geographic scope of the sex industry are phenomenal and organized crime is involved at various levels (Caldwell et al., 1999; Shannon, 1999).

Although many reports indicate involvement of large criminal networks in human trafficking, family involvement in trafficking should not be underestimated. These smaller operations based on kinship or friendship ties may, of course, be part of larger criminal networks. In my own recently concluded study of 146 children trafficked to the United States, we did not find any direct evidence of connections to organized crime. Moreover, the trafficked children did not speak of criminal networks, but rather focused on the close relationships between themselves and those who helped them cross the U.S. border. Some were quite upset when law enforcement or service providers referred to their family members as traffickers, and even the children who felt wronged by their loved ones had difficulty conceptualizing their actions as criminal.

There is a need for both quantitative and qualitative research that would provide both macro-and micro-level understanding of the trafficking phenomenon. Methodologically sound compilation of official statistics on the number of trafficked victims would enable quantitative analysis and inform appropriation of funds for counter-trafficking efforts and services to victims. Sadly, as of August 2006 the Office of Refugee Resettlement (ORR) in the U.S. Department of Health and Services (DHHS) ceased to provide data on trafficked persons in their care. Prior to August 2006, researchers were able to get access to limited non-identifiable data on victims, including their ethnicity/nationality, date of birth and age at the time of rescue, gender, marital status, and number of children. U.S. data related to trafficking prosecutions is also currently unavailable.

Rigorous ethnographic and sociological studies based on in-depth interviews with trafficking survivors would provide baseline data on trafficked victims and their characteristics. Too often victims of trafficking remain one-dimensional figures whose stories are condensed and simplified, which does not bode well for the development of culturally appropriate services. In order to develop appropriate assistance and treatment programs for trafficking survivors, increased attention needs to be paid to the expertise and practical knowledge of non-governmental organizations (NGOs) and their experience in working with different groups of trafficking survivors, including women, men, and children. In the already mentioned study of children trafficked to the United States, my colleagues and I found that most programs followed a "cookie-cutter" approach. In theory, the children could choose from a menu of services; however, in reality they were encouraged to enroll in all available programs, including mental health services, whether they felt they needed counseling or not.

Given the fact that services to trafficked persons are in their infancy, monitoring and evaluation studies should be an integral part of every assistance program, public and private. Well-designed monitoring and evaluation studies, particularly external evaluations, can identify effective policies and "best practice" approaches as well as assess the success of different programs. Particularly important are longitudinal studies of the effects of rehabilitation programs on the ability of survivors to integrate into the new society or re-integrate into their native one. The U.S. has spent a considerable amount of resources supporting

Box 3.2 Non-governmental organizations (NGOs)

Non-governmental organizations (NGOs) are not-for-profit groups that operate independently of government membership or affiliation, although they are often funded through government grants. They comprise people who come together around a particular social cause or issue. It is common for NGOs to have less bureaucratic structures than governments, allowing them more flexibility in providing programs and services; however, a common challenge for NGOs is a lack of core funding, which can make service provision and sustainability an issue. NGOs exist on local, regional, national, and transnational levels, with some collaboration amongst the different levels and the varying organizations. It is common for NGOs to participate in policy analysis and policy making processes in a variety of ways. They can also act to encourage civil and political participation and dissent. NGOs have been on the rise since the 1980s, mostly spearheading activities related to social and economic development. The United Nations, for instance, works with approximately 33,000 NGOs around the world. NGOs have the capacity to build or contribute to multileveled strategies, and to conduct large-scale research, depending on the size and scope of the organization.

For further information:

United Nations, resources on NGOs: http://www.unrol.org/article.aspx?article_id=23
United Nations NGO Branch: http://csonet.org/index.php?menu=14
Yadama, G. N. (1997). Tales from the field: Observations on the impact of nongovernmental organizations. *International Social Work*, 40(2), 145–162.

"Rescue and Restore" initiatives around the world but no follow-up study has been conducted on any of the victims returned to their home countries. Have survivors of trafficking for sexual exploitation been accepted by their families and local communities? Are survivors of trafficking for labor exploitation at risk of revictimization? How are the children who had been trafficked with the approval of their families doing?

There is also a need for effective cooperation and coordination of research within and between countries. In addition, there is a need to establish a forum where research results can be exchanged between different scholars as well as shared with policy makers and service providers; such a forum can take the form of a specialized publication or an international task force. This forum should be free of moral and political influences and devoted solely to scholarly pursuits. The need to fill in the gaps in our knowledge and share research results is urgent. As Liz

Kelly observed, "Lack of research-based knowledge may inadvertently deepen, rather than loosen the factors that make trafficking both so profitable and difficult to address" (Kelly, 2002, p. 60).

References

Allais, C. (2013). The profile less considered: The trafficking of men in South Africa. *South African Review of Sociology*, *44*(1), 40–54.

Anker, C., & van Liempt, I. (Eds.) (2012). *Human rights and migration: Trafficking for forced labour*. Hampshire, England: Palgrave.

Batstone, D. (2007). *Not for sale. The return of the global slave trade and how we can fight it*. New York: Harper Collins. (Revised updated edition, 2009. New York: HarperCollins e-books.)

Bennett, J. W. (1996). Applied and action anthropology. Ideological and conceptual aspects. *Current Anthropology*, *36*(1), S23–S53.

Borjas, G. J. (1991). *Friends or strangers: The impact of immigrants on the U.S. economy*. New York: Basic Books.

— (2001). *Heaven's door: Immigration policy and the American economy*. Princeton: Princeton University Press.

Brennan, D. (2005). Methodological challenges in research with trafficked persons: Tales from the field. *International Migration*, *43*(1/2), 35–54.

— (2014). *Life interrupted. Trafficking into forced labor in the United States*. Durham, NC: Duke University Press.

Bruckert, C., & Parent, C. (2002). *Trafficking in human beings and organized crime: A literature review*. Ottawa: Research and Evaluation Branch, Royal Canadian Mounted Police.

Brunovskis, A., & Tyldum, G. (2004). *Crossing borders: An empirical study of trans-national prostitution and trafficking in human beings* (No. Fafo report 426) (p. 134). Oslo, Norway: Fafo. Retrieved on August 17, 2014 from http://www.fafo.no/pub/rapp/426/426.pdf

Bump, M. N., Duncan, J., Goździak, E. M., & MacDonnell M. (2005). 2nd conference on identifying and serving child victims of trafficking. *International Migration*, *43*(1/2), 343–363.

Burke, A., Ducci, S., & Maddaluno, G. (2005). *Trafficking in minors for commercial sexual exploitation: Costa Rica*. Torino: UNICRI.

Caldwell, B., Pieris, I., Barkat-e-Khuda, Caldwell, J., & Caldwell, P. (1999). Sexual regimes and sexual networking: The risk of an HIV/AIDS epidemic in Bangladesh. *Social Science and Medicine*, *48*(8), 1103–1116.

Caliber Associates (2003). *Needs assessment for service providers and trafficking victims*. Fairfax, VA: Caliber Associates.

Chapkis, W. (2003). Trafficking, migration and the law: Protecting innocents, punishing immigrants. *Gender and Society*, *17*(6), 923–937.

Claramunt, M. C. (2002). *Commercial sexual exploitation of minors: Costa Rica*. Geneva: ILO.

Coburn, T. (2011). Blind faith: How Congress is failing trafficking victims. Unpublished Report. Washington, DC: Office of Tom Coburn, U.S. Senate.

Coghlan, D., & Wylie, G. (2011). Defining trafficking/denying justice? Forced labour in Ireland and the consequences of trafficking discourse. *Journal of Ethnic and Migration Studies, 37*(9), 1513–1526.

Constable, N. (1996). Jealousy, chastity and abuse. Chinese maids and foreign helpers in Hong Kong. *Modern China, 22*(4), 448–479.

Curtol, F., Decarli, S., Di Nicola, A., & Savona, E. U. (2004). Victims of human trafficking in Italy: A judicial perspective. *International Review of Victimology, 11*(1): 163–174.

Denisova, T. A. (2001). Trafficking in women and children for purposes of sexual exploitation: The criminological aspect. *Trends in Organized Crime, 6*(3/4), 30.

Goode, E. (1997). *Deviant behavior*. Upper Saddle River, NJ: Prentice Hall.

Government Accountability Office (GAO) (2006). *Human trafficking: Better data, strategy and reporting needed to enhance U.S. antitrafficking efforts abroad*. Washington, DC: GAO.

Goździak, E. M. (2008). On challenges, dilemmas, and opportunities in studying trafficked children. *The Anthropology Quarterly, 81*(4), 903–923.

— (2011). *Challenges, dilemmas, and opportunities in studying trafficked children in the United States*. CourseReader eBooks. Belmont: Wadsworth Cengage Learning.

Goździak, E. M., & Bump, M. N. (2008). *Victims no longer: Research on child survivors of trafficking for sexual and labor exploitation in the United States*. NIJ Grant No. 2005-IJ-CX-0051. Final Report. Washington, DC: National Institute of Justice.

Goździak, E. M., & MacDonnell, M. (2007). Closing the gaps: The need to improve identification and services to child victims of trafficking. *Human Organization, 66*(2), 171–184.

Gurgel, R.Q., da Fonseca, J. D.C., Neyra-Castañeda, D., Gill, G. V., & Cuevas, L. E. (2004). Capture and recapture to estimate the number of street children in a city in Brazil. *Archives of Disease in Childhood, 89*(3), 222–224.

Hashim, I. (2003). Discourse(s) of childhood. Conference paper cited in O'Connell Davidson, J. (2005). *Children in the global sex trade*. Cambridge: Polity.

Henne, K., & Moseley, D. (2005). Combating the worst forms of child labor in Bolivia. *Human Rights: Journal of the Section of Individual Rights and Responsibilities, 32*(1), 12–15.

Hennink, M., & Simkhada, P. (2004). *Sex trafficking in Nepal: Context and process*. Southampton, University of Southampton, Discussion Papers in Opportunities and Choices, No. 11.

Horton, R. (2000). Genetically modified food: consternation, confusion, and crack-up: The controversy over genetically modified food exposes larger issues about public trust in science and the role of science in policymaking. *The Medical Journal of Australia, 172*(4), 148–149.

Hughes, D.M. (2004). *Myths and realities concerning child trafficking*. Brussels: Fafo Institute for Applied International Studies.

— (2005). *The demand for victims of sex trafficking*. Report prepared for the U.S. Department of State.

Huijsmans, R. (2011). The theatre of human trafficking. A global discourse on Lao stages. *International Journal of Social Quality, 1*(2), 66–84.

Human Rights Center (2005). Freedom denied: Forced labor in California. Retrieved on August 17, 2014 from http://www.oas.org/atip/country%20specific/Forced%20Labor%20in%20California.pdf

Human Rights Center and Free the Slaves (2004). Hidden slaves: Forced labor in the United States. Retrieved on August 17, 2014 from https://www.freetheslaves.net/Document.Doc?id=17

International Labour Organization (2002). *Unbearable to the human heart: Child trafficking and actions to eliminate it.* Geneva: ILO.

Juhasz, J. (2000). Migrant trafficking and human smuggling in Hungary, in Laczko, F. & Thompson, D. (Eds.), *Migrant trafficking and human smuggling in Europe: A review of evidence with case studies from Hungary, Poland, and Ukraine.* Geneva: IOM, pp. 167–232.

Kapur, R. (2002). The tragedy of victimization rhetoric: Resurrecting the "native" subject in international/post-colonial feminist legal politics. *Harvard Human Rights Journal, 15,* 1–37.

Kara, S. (2009). *Sex trafficking: Inside the business of modern slavery.* New York: Columbia University Press.

Kelly, E. (2002). *Journeys of jeopardy: A review of research on trafficking in women and children in Europe.* International Organization for Migration. (Migration Series No. 11.)

Kempadoo, K., Sanghera, J., & Pattanaik, B. (2005). *Trafficking and prostitution reconsidered: New perspectives on migration, sex work and human rights.* Boulder, CO: Paradigm Publishers.

Laczko, F., & Goździak, E. M. (2005). Data and research on human trafficking: A global survey. Special Issue of *International Migration, 43*(1/2), 5–16.

De Lange, A. (2007). Child labour migration and trafficking in rural Burkina Faso. *International Migration, 45*(2), 147–167.

Macy, R. J., & Johns, N. (2011). Aftercare services for international sex trafficking survivors: Informing U.S. service and program development in an emerging practice area. *Trauma Violence Abuse, 12*(2), 87–98.

Mahdavi, P. (2011). *Gridlock. Labor, migration, and human trafficking in Dubai.* Stanford: Stanford University Press.

Malarek, V. (2004). *The Natashas. Inside the new global sex trade.* New York: Arcade Publishing.

O'Connell Davidson, J. (2005). *Children in the global sex trade.* Cambridge: Polity.

Passell, J. S. (2005). *Estimates of the size and characteristics of the undocumented population.* Pew Hispanic Center. Retrieved on August 15, 2014 from http://pewhispanic.org/files/reports/44.pdf

— (2006). *The size and characteristics of the unauthorized migrant population in the U.S.: Estimates based on the March 2005 Current Population Survey.* Pew Hispanic Center. Retrieved on August 15, 2014 from http://pewhispanic.org/files/reports/61.pdf

Piper, N. (2005). A problem by a different name? A review of research in trafficking in South East Asia and Oceania. *International Migration, 43*(1/2), 203–233.

Pochagina, O. (2007). Trafficking in women and children in present-day China. *Far Eastern Affairs, 35*(1), 82.

Raymond, J. G. (1998). Prostitution as violence against women: NGO stonewalling in Beijing and elsewhere. *Women's Studies International Forum, 21*(1), 1–9.

— (2004). Prostitution on demand. Legalizing the buyers as sexual consumers. *Violence against Women, 10*(10), 1156–1186.

Roby, J. (2005). Women and children in the global sex trade: Toward more effective policy. *International Social Work, 48*(2), 136–147.

Rubin, G. (1984). Thinking sex: Notes for a radical theory of the politics of sexuality, in Vance, C. (Ed.), *Pleasure and danger.* Boston: Routledge, pp. 267–319.

— (1993). Misguided, dangerous and wrong: An analysis of anti-pornography politics, in Assiter, A., & Carol, A. (Eds.), *Bad girls and dirty pictures: The challenge to reclaim feminism*. London & Boulder Colorado: Pluto Press, pp. 267–319.

Salt, J. (2000). Trafficking and human smuggling: a European perspective. *International Migration, 38*(3), 31–56.

Sanghera, J. (2005). Unpacking the trafficking discourse, in Kempadoo, K., Sanghera, J., & Pattanaik, B. (Eds.), *Trafficking and prostitution reconsidered: New perspectives on migration, sex work, and human rights*. Boulder: Paradigm Publishers, pp. 3–24.

Scarpa, S. 2006. *Trafficking in human beings. Modern slavery*. Oxford: Oxford University Press.

Shannon, S. (1999). Prostitution and the Mafia: The involvement of organized crime in the global economy, in Williams, P. (Ed.), *Illegal migration and commercial sex. The new slave trade*. London: Frank Cass Publishers, pp.119–144.

Sharma, N. (2005). Anti-trafficking rhetoric and the making of a global apartheid. *NWSA Journal, 17*(3), 88–111.

Shelly, L. (2010). *Human trafficking. A global perspective*. Cambridge: Cambridge University Press.

Shigekane, R. (2007). Rehabilitation and community integration of trafficking survivors in the United States. *Human Rights Quarterly, 29*(1), 112–136.

Shoaps, L. L. (2013). Room for improvement. Palermo Protocol and the Trafficking Victims Protection Act. *Lewis & Clark Law Review, 17*(2), 931–972.

Skinner, E. B. (2008). *A crime so monstrous: Face-to-face with modern-day slavery* (reprint edition). New York: Free Press.

Spangenberg, M. (2002). *International trafficking of children to New York City for sexual purposes*. Brooklyn, NY: ECPAT-U.S.A.

Stoyanova, V. (2013). The crisis of a definition: Human trafficking in Bulgarian law. *Amsterdam Law Forum, 5*(1), 64–79.

Taibly, R. (2001). *Organized crime and people smuggling/trafficking in Australia*. Canberra, Australian Institute of Criminology.

Tiefenbrun, S. W. (2002). Sex sells but drugs don't talk: trafficking of women sex workers and an economic solution. *Thomas Jefferson Law Review, 24*(2), 161–189.

Tyldum, G., & Brunovskis, A. (2005). Describing the unobserved: Methodological challenges in empirical studies on human trafficking. *International Migration, 43*(1/2), 17–34.

UNIAP (2008). Trafficking estimates initiative. Retrieved on August 17, 2014 from http://www.no-trafficking.org/siren_estimates.html

Vlieger, A. (2012). Domestic workers in Saudi Arabia and the Emirates: Trafficking victims? *International Migration, 50*(6), 180–194.

Weitzer, R. (2005). Flawed theory and method in studies of prostitution. *Violence against Women, 11*(7), 934–949.

— (2007). The social construction of sex trafficking: Ideology and institutionalization of a moral crusade. *Politics and Society, 35*(3), 447–475.

Williams, M., & Cheal, B. (2002). Can we measure homelessness? A critical evaluation of the method of "capture-recapture." *International Journal Social Research Methodology, 5*(4), 313–331.

Williams, S., & Masika, R. (2002). Editorial, in Masika, R. (Ed.), *Gender, trafficking and slavery*. Oxfam Focus on Gender, pp. 2–9.

Zhang, S. X., Chin, K-L., & Miller, J. (2007). Women's participation in Chinese transnational human smuggling: A gendered market perspective. *Criminology*, *54*(3),
699–733.
Zlotnik, H. (2003, March 1). The global dimensions of female migration. Retrieved on
October 30, 2014 from http://www.migrationpolicy.org/article/global-dimensions-
female-migration

Discussion questions

1.   What are some of the challenges in studying human trafficking?
2.   Why are most publications on human trafficking not empirically based?
3.   How does the available research relate to the dominant discourses on trafficking?
4.   What has most of the trafficking funding been spent on?
5.   What is the most important area for future research on trafficking?

Additional resources

ILO Asia Pacific Forced Labour Network
http://apflnet.ilo.org

IOM Global Human Trafficking Database
https://www.iom.int/jahia/webdav/shared/shared/mainsite/activities/ct/iom_ctm_database.
   pdf

Section II

Key issues in trafficking research

Molly Dragiewicz

Section II comprises the majority of this collection. It draws together new empirical work on trafficking issues from Mexico, the United States, Ukraine, Benin, South Africa, China, Israel, and Australia. This section covers various types of labor trafficking within and across borders. It includes trafficking for prostitution, commercial fishing, and domestic service. The section also includes chapters on other types of trafficking, including marriage trafficking and the traffic in organs. Each of the chapters utilizes innovative methodological approaches to collecting and analyzing data on trafficking and the impact of trafficking policies. The chapters in this section provide information about the dynamics of trafficking even as they raise questions about the utility of existing interventions.

In Chapter 4, "Sex, Violence, and the Border: Trafficking for Sex Work from Mexico to the U.S.," Anna Maternick and Melissa Ditmore draw from 37 affidavits prepared in application for T visas and interviews with six of the affiants in order to understand the experiences of people whose experience met the legal definition of trafficking as defined by the U.S. Trafficking Victims Protection Act. Maternick participated in the study as a research intern for the Sex Workers Project. She is currently working as a research associate in the Department of Family Medicine and Population Health at Virginia Commonwealth University in the United States. Ditmore is an independent scholar and consultant who has studied human trafficking as well as gender, migration, development, sex work, and drug use. The sample in their chapter comprises 36 women, including two transgender women, and one man. The T visa applicants in their study describe lives of hardship leading to a variety of forms of exploitative labor and experiences of abuse which are shaped by gender transgressions. This chapter contributes valuable information to our understanding of how gender shapes risks and experiences of trafficking. These insights go well beyond the simple association of trafficking victimization with women and girls, providing details about how normative gendered social expectations contribute to abuse and trafficking. The chapter also calls into question the raid and rescue tactics promoted by some anti-trafficking organizations, since they are focused on repatriation and family reunification outcomes that are inappropriate when so many of the trafficking victims left home to escape abuse or were trafficked by family members.

In Chapter 5, "At Sea: The Trafficking of Seafarers and Fishers from Ukraine," Rebecca Surtees describes the situation faced by 46 men who had been trafficked to Russia, Turkey, and South Korea. Surtees is an anthropologist and senior researcher at NEXUS Institute, a human rights policy and research center in Washington, DC in the United States. Her study is based on case files from victims assisted by the International Organization for Migration and its non-governmental organization partners and interviews with a subsample of the men and other key stakeholders. This chapter describes deceptive recruiting procedures, inhumane working conditions, and captivity on boats while offshore or in port. Significantly, the stories of these men point out that education is not all that is needed to prevent trafficking. Most of the men in the sample had tertiary education and professional qualifications, but a lack of employment opportunities forced them to take jobs under any circumstances they could. This chapter illustrates the importance of data collection on identified victims of trafficking to help fill the gaps in our understanding of trafficking for multiple forms of labor.

In Chapter 6, "Human Trafficking in 'Fresh' Organs for Illicit Transplants: A Protected Crime," Nancy Scheper-Hughes describes the international dynamics of kidney trafficking. Scheper-Hughes is Professor of Medical Anthropology at the University of California, Berkeley in the United States. Scheper-Hughes describes the way she came to learn about kidney selling as a result of investigations into transplant tourism. As she became aware of illegal selling of kidneys, she co-founded Organs Watch, an advocacy organization which studies and tracks global organ trafficking. Scheper-Hughes' chapter presents some of the first empirical research on organ trafficking, which has the status of an urban legend but is increasingly recognized as an international social problem. Her chapter highlights ethical questions about how to best respond to the organ transplant trade. While she cautions that her approach may not provide a methodological model for others to follow, her work demonstrates how unorthodox methods can contribute to awareness and research of this type of trafficking.

Chapter 7, "(Not!) Child trafficking in Benin," draws on fieldwork with teenage labor migrants to explore the relationship between service provider narratives about child trafficking and young people's own understandings of their situation. Neil Howard got his Ph.D. in International Development, and is currently Marie Curie Fellow at the European University Institute in Florence, Italy. Simona Morganti is an anthropologist who has conducted extensive fieldwork in Southern Benin and acted as a consultant for NGOs engaged in child protection. Their chapter makes clear the importance of listening to the voices of those affected by anti-trafficking policy, including children. The chapter challenges dominant discourses about naïve children being duped into exploitative situations. It also highlights the difficulty of aligning human rights goals for child protection with socio-economic contexts in which young people must work for survival at the moment.

Chapter 8, "Bride Traffic: Trafficking for Marriage to Australia," was written by Kelly Richards, a Lecturer in the School of Justice at Queensland University of Technology in Australia, and Samantha Lyneham, a Research Analyst at the

Australian Institute of Criminology. Their chapter investigates the role of partner migration in trafficking to Australia. Their study is based on a mixed methods study conducted by the Australian Institute of Criminology. Their study was based on case files and interviews with eight women identified as victims or survivors of human trafficking to Australia as well as interviews with 17 key stakeholders from government, NGO, law enforcement, and victim support agencies. The study was informed by examined case law from the United Nations Office on Drugs and Crime international human trafficking case law database and the University of Queensland's database of trafficking cases. Their small sample documented cases of exploitation that involved exploitation of Australia's partner immigration schemes. Their findings challenge the sex/labor trafficking distinction as well as a number of other assumptions replicated in popular anti-trafficking discourses. These include: the idea that human trafficking perpetrators are primarily motivated by economic profit; the assumption that human trafficking victim/survivors are primarily vulnerable to being trafficked due to socio-economic "desperation"; and the idea that human trafficking is a type of organized crime.

Together, the chapters in this section challenge many aspects of the dominant discourses on human trafficking. At the same time, they confirm the relevance of other factors that recur in these discussions. These chapters provide some inspiring examples of the potential for empirical research on trafficking in spite of its illegality and clandestine nature. They share an emphasis on the importance of speaking to those affected in their specific cultural and economic locations. Finally, the chapters point to the need to consider the voices of those affected by anti-trafficking policy in crafting policies and assistance practices.

Learning objectives for Section II

1. List multiple contexts (types of work and locations) for human trafficking.
2. Recall reasons that the "trafficking" label may be a misnomer.
3. Name specific examples of force, fraud, and coercion.
4. Consider how trafficking overlaps with other forms of abuse and exploitation.
5. Describe the ways that social inequality and structural discrimination contribute to trafficking.

Chapter 4

Sex, violence, and the border

Trafficking for sex work from Mexico to the U.S.

Anna Maternick and Melissa Hope Ditmore

Introduction

This chapter examines stories of people who were trafficked from Mexico to the United States primarily for commercial sex. The stories detailing experiences of trafficking were collected from affidavits written to support T non-immigrant status visa (T visa) applications and supplemented by interviews with six of the affiants. T visas were created via the Trafficking Victims Protection Act (TVPA) for people who have been trafficked according to U.S. law (United States Citizenship and Immigration Services, 2010).

The accounts were analyzed in order to identify traits and common experiences, as well as to raise awareness of challenges faced by people who are trafficked to the United States. Many trafficked persons experienced childhood poverty and violence before being trafficked. Trafficked persons advised communicating with young people about sexual health, healthy relationships, and the fact that predatory people exist.

What is "sex trafficking"?

The legal definition of sex trafficking in the United States can be found in the United States Trafficking Victims Protection Act (TVPA, 2000). This definition differs from other accepted definitions of trafficking, such as the one used by the United Nations (2000), because the U.S. trafficking definition is split into two parts; one relating to "forced labor" and another relating to "commercial sex." Commercial sex is treated separately because if U.S. law defined "trafficking" simply as forced labor, it would exclude prostitution on the grounds that prostitution is not recognized as a form of labor in the U.S.

Trafficking for commercial sex, according to the U.S. Trafficking Victims Protection Act (TVPA), Section 103(8), is when "a commercial sex act is induced by force, fraud, or coercion, or in which the person induced to perform such act has not attained 18 years of age" (2000). The TVPA defines a "commercial sex act" as "any sex act on account of which anything of value is given to or received by any person" (TVPA, Section 103[3], 2000).

This chapter utilizes the legal definition of trafficking for commercial sex from the TVPA as the individuals included in our study sought services and legal status under these terms.

Box 4.1   The T visa

T visas were created by the United States Congress in 2000 as part of the Victims of Trafficking and Violence Protection Act of 2000 (TVPA). T visas are non-immigrant visas intended to facilitate efforts to investigate or prosecute trafficking cases by allowing victims of "severe forms of trafficking" to remain in the country pending a trafficking investigation. They are specifically designed for trafficking victims who are "willing to assist law enforcement in the investigation or prosecution of acts of trafficking." Under the TVPA, severe forms of trafficking includes two types of case: Sex trafficking where there is force, fraud, or coercion, or the person is a minor (under 18 years old); and labor trafficking involving "force, fraud, or coercion for the purpose of involuntary servitude, peonage, debt bondage, or slavery." In order to be eligible, trafficking victims must "Comply with any reasonable request from a law enforcement agency for assistance in the investigation or prosecution of human trafficking" and be able to prove they are at risk of "extreme hardship involving severe and unusual harm if you were removed from the United States." T visas convey temporary rights to work in the U.S. Although 5,000 T visas are available each year, the most requested in any year was 750 (in 2003) and the largest number approved was 447 (in 2010) (See http://www.uscis.gov/USCIS/Resources/Reports/Forms-Data/i-914-T-I-918-data-2011-april.pdf.) T visa holders are eligible to apply for permanent residency once they have been in the U.S. for three years.

For further information:

http://www.uscis.gov/uscis-tags/unassigned/t-nonimmigrant-visas-victims-
   trafficking

Methodology

The information presented in this chapter is derived from *The Road North*, a qualitative study undertaken by the Sex Workers Project in New York City (Ditmore, Maternick, & Zapert, 2012). The report is based on the experiences of 37 people who meet the legal definition of trafficking as set out by the TVPA and were moved from Mexico to the United States for forced labor, including forced commercial sex. The study included 36 women, including two transgender women, and one man. Of these, 34 were from southern and central Mexico and three were from countries south of Mexico.

Data reflecting the experiences of this group was collected from 37 signed affidavits and six interviews. Twenty-five affidavits were provided by the Sex Workers Project and 12 were provided by the Anti-Trafficking Program at Safe Horizon, both New York City based organizations. The affidavits were written to support applications for a T visa for clients of these organizations. Affidavits were selected by the legal staff at these two organizations and were only included if they were written about an experience of trafficking from Mexico or a neighboring country through Mexico. The Mexico-to-U.S. trafficking situation was the focus of this study, undertaken at the behest of organizations in Mexico working with migrant women, many of whom want to travel to the United States.

Throughout the chapter we have drawn on quotes from affidavits and interviews. The quotations are meant to offer the reader insight into the survivors' experiences in their own words. In order to protect the participants' confidentiality and anonymity, identifying information, such as names, has been changed. For more information about the methods used in this study, please see *The Road North* report accessible online (Ditmore et al., 2012).

How people arrived in trafficking situations

This chapter explores the personal stories of people whose experience met the legal definition of trafficking as defined by the TVPA. It is important to remember that the study participants' lives, like those of the authors, are shaped in many ways by governmental policies, cultural beliefs and attitudes, and other social forces. For example, factors that seemed to contribute to trafficking vulnerability were experiences of poverty, exploitation of gender roles, violence (especially gender-based violence), and knowing the trafficker prior to being trafficked.

Financial hardship and poverty during childhood

Seventy-five percent of our sample reported experiencing financial hardship during childhood, which often made it necessary for them to work in order to support their families. Often, working as children would impede going to school as 81 percent of people in the sample (out of 33 who wrote about their educational attainment) did not attend school past the 10th grade.

> My family was very poor, even compared to other families in the village. My parents worked as farmers on other people's lands. They traveled to other states to find work, and they took us with them. I worked alongside my parents starting when I was eight years old. I tried to also go to school, but had to stop after 6th grade because I missed so much school in order to work. The work I generally did was harvesting vegetables.
>
> Camilla

Migrating to find work was a common theme throughout the stories shared by trafficking survivors. Some of the people in the study were under 18 years of age when they undertook migration from a small rural community to a large city in order to find work. Migration at such an early age, often alone, seemed to increase vulnerability to manipulation by a trafficker.

Exploitation of gender roles

While most people associate sex trafficking with young girls, in this study a boy and two transgender women also described being forced to sell sex; all three came from impoverished backgrounds, yet they faced different expectations related to gender. All three left home at exceptionally young ages even for this sample, as young as eight years old. All were forced to sell sex, often in addition to performing other labor, for example, agricultural labor.

The transgender women included left their home communities because they were harassed for not being like the men in their communities, and the young man was exceptionally young when he left an impoverished home and was forced to sell sex to men, violating norms of gender. Because these three individuals did not conform to socially enforced expectations of gender, they were seen as unmanly and therefore as appropriate targets for abuse, particularly sexual abuse.

These three individuals were simultaneously dependent upon the individuals who arranged their sexual encounters to protect them from further violation. Their stories should prompt a wider exploration of trafficking to include men and transgender persons. Because they do not conform to stereotypes of the typical victim, who is perceived to be a young girl, they endured even greater difficulty accessing services than others. The transgender women in particular experienced discrimination when trying to seek help from law enforcement or other social service organizations.

Young women in the study also described being coerced into trafficking situations by people who manipulate gender norms. For example: traffickers tended to exploit socially sanctioned power dynamics between men and women based in patriarchal gender roles; Torres (2009) describes *padrotes* (traffickers) specifically seeking poor young women who have experienced violence at home and who may therefore be eager to leave home, and likely to travel with a suitor.

For young women in rural Mexico, it is uncommon to leave their parents' home until they marry or have to move to find work in a bigger city, usually domestic work. There is also a social stigma against young women spending the night with a man without being married. Once they have left home with a suitor, they are expected to marry and remain with him in almost any circumstance. Many of the women in the study described having a sexual encounter with a man, often a forced encounter, and then feeling pressured to enter into a marriage with the man or live as a married couple. The social pressure to shield their own—and their family's—reputation from the social stigma of sleeping with a man while not being married was so great that often these women and girls would decide to remain with the man who later trafficked them even when they had been raped or saw signs that the man could be dangerous.

These women mentioned not feeling able to seek help from their families either due to social stigma or because they were leaving abusive family situations and did not want to contact them.

> I had already lived with [trafficker] so I could not return to my family's house . . . I was afraid of what my parents would say about my situation—about living with a boy without being married. It was shaming and my family would have been dishonored if I returned to them as a single woman. I had to make my relationship with [trafficker] work no matter what because I had nowhere to go. I believed and loved him and truly believed we would get married when I finally slept with him. I trusted him to take care of me—I was naïve and could not believe he would do anything to harm me. Thus, I was trapped when he eventually became mean and vicious.
>
> Lelia

Violence during childhood

Violence was also common among the experiences of study participants. Fifty-four percent of study participants reported at least one violent experience prior to trafficking. The actual number who experienced violence during childhood could be much higher as not all affidavits described childhood events. These violent experiences were often extreme and included witnessing domestic violence, being a victim of physical or sexual abuse, being a victim of intimate partner violence, witnessing a murder, and being harassed and beaten in school.

> My father drank a lot, and when he drank he was violent. He did not believe that I was his child, and he would beat me and my mother until we bled . . . My first memories are of being beaten.
>
> Tatiana

The transgender women in this study described the highest levels of violence in the sample, often facing harassment and violence from their family as well as their communities. For many affiants, violence in their homes influenced their desire to leave and go with the trafficker. For example, during one interview with a survivor it was revealed that she decided to leave her family home with the man who trafficked her because she believed he could help her escape from the sexual abuse she was facing at home.

One of the effects of suffering violence is to normalize violence: Family violence was accepted by many, with partner violence particularly accepted by their families and communities. The experience of family violence can disrupt norms and expectations associated with love. Childhood experiences are important to take into account because experiences of trauma and violence in childhood may be linked to future experiences of violence and trauma (Desai et al., 2002; Widom et al., 2008; Klest, 2012).

Trafficker was not a stranger

Sixty-seven percent of the people in the study met the trafficker through a family member, friend, or neighbor. In four cases, the trafficker was a family member prior to trafficking. In addition, some people appear to have been directly set up for trafficking by their family members. In other situations, personal connections were exploited to gain the trust of the trafficked person and/or their family.

> I met [trafficker] when he was 17 years old and I was 14 years old. There was a carnival in my hometown . . . and my friend, who is [trafficker's] aunt, introduced us there . . . I was familiar with her because she was a friend of my mother's. [Trafficker] and I did not talk to each other the first time we met but we did on the second day of the carnival.
>
> Inez

The trafficker was able to use his aunt's connection with Inez to manipulate her into leaving with him. Inez soon learned that many of the trafficker's family members, including the aunt who introduced her to him, were involved in trafficking other young women into the United States for commercial sex. It is unclear from the affidavit whether the others who were victimized by this family were also minors.

In our sample, we identified two common sets of circumstances in which study participants left home: firstly, young poor women living with their families in rural areas, most of whom had experienced violence and abuse at home and who may therefore have been very happy to leave home. A second pattern was the recruitment of young poor women working as domestics in towns and cities, who were approached in public on their days off, who may also have had great incentives to take any opportunity for a better life.

In some cases, the trafficker was a neighbor. For example, Luke had experienced extreme violence at home and was often left alone for months at a time. His isolation from his family or other support seemed to increase his vulnerability to trafficking.

> When I was 13 years old, I met an older man, [trafficker]. He was about 52 years old and lived next door to me. He would buy me female clothes and asked me to meet his friends. I was very young and did not understand what he was doing. One day one of his friends forced me to have sex with him. [Trafficker] then forced me to be with other men. Sometimes he would even lock me in the room with them. After some time I realized that he was selling me to these men for payment that he kept [. . .] [trafficker] had me under his control for about 9 months. I would work in the fields to provide for myself. [Trafficker] would use me and sell me for sex every weekend, sometimes more often, and would not give me anything in exchange.
>
> Luke

The commonality of experiences of poverty and violence (especially gender-based violence) across the sample may indicate that experiencing trauma in childhood may increase a person's vulnerability to trafficking. The manipulation of gender norms is also a strong factor during the trafficking process; for example, the knowledge that young women and young men who violate gender norms, even against their will, face difficulties returning home and being accepted in their communities. The very existence of transgender people challenges gender norms and, as we have described, this is linked to their experiences of extreme levels of violence even within this sample.

What types of trafficking situations were people in?

Participants in the study described a variety of types of forced labor. The following includes the frequency of affiants who mentioned having to perform a particular type of labor: Prostitution (32), Domestic Work (16), Restaurant/Bar (3), Factory/Construction (2), Dancing (2), and Stealing (1). Notice that the majority of affiants in this sample who were trafficked to the United States and throughout Mexico were forced to do sex work, especially prostitution. However, these findings about the variety of work done by the affiants indicate that abuses occur in a wide variety of sectors and that to focus exclusively on any single sector, such as commercial sex, is misguided. Many affiants were forced to perform domestic work within the trafficker's home, work in bars or restaurants, and perform other types of labor. Some cases involved affiants being forced to perform multiple types of labor. For example, some women described being forced to do domestic work, including cooking, cleaning, and laundry, for many people associated with the trafficker in addition to being forced into sex work.

> He told me that I would cook and clean for the men in the house. I told him that he would have to pay me if he wanted me to work, so he originally agreed to pay me $100 per week. He never paid me $100; he rarely paid me enough money to cover the groceries that I had to buy to feed the men living in the apartment.
>
> Yvette

In some cases, forced domestic work involved the traffickers' families.

> I was forced to do work in the different houses belonging to his family. I was told to do all the laundry and clean the houses.
>
> Menna

Some survivors were forced to work in restaurants and bars. For example, Teresa was forced to work in food service and later to dance with men at a bar.

I had already paid off my debt to [trafficker] while working at a restaurant. But [trafficker] made me start working as a bartender at another restaurant. I made $500–$600 a week. But I had to give [trafficker] all of my money. I only kept $20.00 for myself to buy food.

[Trafficker] then forced me to take a job at [a bar] where I was paid money to dance and drink with men. After two days, I couldn't stand it anymore, I did not like that kind of job, and told [trafficker] I wanted to quit. He got angry, beat me, threatened me, and told me I had to work there.

Teresa

Forced sex work in Mexico

Almost half of the survivors were forced into prostitution in Mexico before coming to the U.S. Emma, whose story reflects the experiences of many, was forced into prostitution by her husband, whom she had married when she was 14. By the time she was first forced into prostitution she was the mother of two children by the man who trafficked her.

The week before my daughter's first birthday in July 2003 when I was still 17, [trafficker] forced me to get on a bus going to [a Mexican city] with other women so that he could rent my body to make money.

Emma

Forced sex work in the United States

After being forced to work in prostitution for six years in Mexico, Marcella, who was around 31 at the time, was trafficked to the United States. Although she was not legally married to the trafficker, they lived together as a couple and had two children before she was trafficked. In this quote, Marcella describes being forced to travel to many states for sex work.

I started work the next day, only my second day in New York City. [Trafficked woman] told me how to work. She had the names and addresses for our clients. People gave her the telephone numbers of where to go. They made me travel to work. They would put me on a Greyhound and tell me where to work. I have worked all over: in Nebraska, Maryland, Georgia, Virginia, New Jersey in Trenton and Atlantic City, once in Connecticut and twice in Philadelphia. In New York, I never worked in a house. In Maryland and other states, I occasionally worked in houses.

Marcella

In addition to working as a cocktail waitress, Veronica, who was 23 at the time, was forced by a trafficker to perform erotic dances at a bar in the U.S. In this quote, Veronica highlights how "debt" was used by the trafficker as leverage against her. This use of debt as a manipulative tool was something that was frequently described in the affidavits.

> [Trafficker] was very angry that I did not have sex with the customers because he wanted me to make more money for him. I danced in this restaurant to earn more income so he would not force me into prostitution. Men paid $2 for each dance and I had to dance a lot because that was the only way I could make extra money. I had to pay [trafficker] $2,000 for bringing me to U.S. and I danced about 15–20 times a night to help pay off my debt. . . . There were two different shifts so sometimes I worked from 2 p.m.–2 a.m. and the other time, I worked from 5 p.m.–4 a.m. I worked six days a week.
>
> Veronica

At the age of 18, Tabitha was locked in a trafficker's home in New York City. Tabitha was not permitted to leave the house; instead the trafficker would bring men to the house to have sex with Tabitha. This made it even more difficult for her to escape the situation. Tabitha, who is transgender, was forced into sex work and continually raped by the trafficker.

> I was locked in that house for a total of six months. The rapes I faced eventually became very systematic and settled into a routine . . . I was forced to have sex with about 4 or 5 men a day, for about 12 or 14 hours per day . . . I know they were paying [trafficker] because I asked them how much they had paid, and the men told me they paid $45. I spent about 25 to 30 minutes having sex with each of these men.
>
> Tabitha

After escaping from the man who trafficked her, Tabitha worked hard to build a life for herself in the United States. However, she continually faced violence and discrimination due to prejudice about her gender identity. Seven years after the incident described above, Tabitha was incarcerated and facing deportation due to her undocumented immigration status.

Mariana was 25 when she met a man and fell in love. She had recently left her abusive husband and was having a hard time supporting her two children. After dating this man for seven months, he convinced her to go with him to the United States and work at a restaurant so that they could make money to support her kids. One week after arriving in the U.S. her boyfriend and his sister forced Mariana into commercial sex work.

> I soon found out that [trafficker's sister] was not in charge of a restaurant— she was in charge of a brothel. I was shocked. When I found out what kind of work they wanted me to do, I started crying. I refused and said no way. I could not believe what they were telling me . . . I was terrified and did not know what to do or think. I was shocked and scared that [trafficker], who I trusted and loved, was now telling me I had to work in prostitution.

. . . [trafficker] and [trafficker's sister] threatened that they would not send my kids money if I did not work. They said that if I tried to escape, the people outside in the neighborhood would kill me. I was too afraid to leave because of their threats and also because I did not know anyone else in New York who could help me. Even if I could have gotten away, I would not have known what to do or where to go.

Mariana

Mariana was forced to work in prostitution for four years. During this time she was arrested multiple times for prostitution and continually abused and threatened by the trafficker. She was able to escape with the help of a sex worker whom she met while working.

Barriers to escape

"For fear you believe and you have to stay . . . for fear of all the things that could happen."

Menna

Mariana's story, quoted above, is a good illustration of barriers that survivors faced in trying to leave the trafficking situation. Traffickers often used manipulation, threats, and violence to ensure that the survivors would live in fear and find it difficult to leave. In addition, survivors often found themselves unable to communicate with many people outside of the trafficker's circle due to language barriers and isolation. Survivors also described being threatened by traffickers who claimed they would call the police to arrest the survivors. They feared police because they had been told that they would be seen as criminals, and their experiences having been arrested for prostitution bore this out. They also feared being deported as a result of arrest.

[Trafficker] threatened me constantly from the very beginning. He told me that if I ever escaped he would find me and kill me. He told me that if I called the police they would take me to jail and deport us. [Trafficker] would tell me to not speak to anyone and to not take anything from anyone, because some people say they will help you get "papers" but they lie and they call the police instead. He said that this happened to a lot of girls before and I believed him because I had just arrived in the U.S. and I didn't know anything.

Adela

Affiants typically spoke little if any English and felt unable to communicate with others outside their limited range of contacts, and unable to describe their situations to police even if they wanted to.

Once in New York I never thought about going to the police either. I do not speak English—there is no way for me to communicate and say what I'd like to say.

I also didn't realize the police could help me—I thought it would be like it was in Mexico. My only interactions with the police were the times I got arrested for working. These experiences were so scary and confusing. I couldn't communicate with anyone. I never imagined going myself, to the police for help.

Natalia

Affiants felt dependent upon the people who brought them to New York and who committed violence against them. They did not see law enforcement as potentially helpful in any way. For these reasons, they often sought to leave their situations without turning to law enforcement.

Leaving the trafficking situation and life after escape

Affiants met colleagues and clients at their workplaces who were sometimes helpful to them in leaving a trafficking situation.

During the time I was forced to work in New York, I had met a Colombian woman named [friend] . . . [friend] worked as a prostitute but she kept her earnings and did not have to turn them over to anyone. I told her about my situation. She was very good, very nice to me. She let me stay with her after I left [trafficker]. She let me stay at her apartment for one month without making me pay rent. This allowed me to have some time and think about things.

Natalia

Help was offered in the form of places to stay, transportation, and letting people leave work early, before they were to be picked up by the person who trafficked them.

In some cases, the trafficked person initially perceived their relationship with the men who trafficked them as a marriage and sometimes had children with these men. These children were often in the custody of the trafficker's family in Mexico during and after the trafficking situation. Throughout the trafficking situation, many affiants described the trafficker and their family using threats related to their children as a way to remain in control. This manipulation was a barrier to escape for many of these mothers as they were concerned about what would happen to their children and if they would be able to see them again after leaving the trafficking situation.

Thus, after leaving these situations the mothers focused on reuniting with their children. In some cases, this was part of the planning involved prior to leaving coercive situations.

I planned with my mother to rescue my daughters from [trafficker] and his family. I told her to move to a new address. She did this. Through the money I saved, I was able to pay for my children to be transported to my mother's.

> Once my children were in my mother's care, I left [trafficker's uncles] . . . I changed all my contact information so that they [trafficker's family] have no way to reach me.
>
> Laura

In addition to concerns about their children's safety, after leaving a trafficking situation everyone described a precarious existence in the United States with few employment opportunities, especially without a work permit.

> I wanted desperately to start fresh but unfortunately, I could not find work . . . Because I had no money to support myself and no way to get a good job as I had no work papers, I was forced to continue to work in prostitution to provide for myself. I had to stay in the U.S. since [trafficker] kept calling me. I knew that if I went back to Mexico he would find me immediately and I would have no choice but to go back with him. That was something I was not willing to risk.
>
> Diana

Natalia, who described being helped by a brothel colleague who allowed her to share an apartment, and Diana both worked in the sex industry after leaving their coercive situations. This highlights the differences between trafficking and sex work. In their original situations, they were forced to engage in actions they might have otherwise avoided. Yet, after leaving the coercive situation with a trafficker, they each turned to sex work in order to support themselves and their families. Returning to sex work allowed them both to gain autonomy and financial stability that was not possible in less well-paid work available to undocumented immigrants. Their autonomy and financial stability helped them each build a new life and helped prevent them from returning to a trafficking situation.

Ideas for moving forward: Advice from survivors

Our interviews included questions about what participants would recommend to prevent other young people from facing the same ordeals they endured. These interviews were with six women who had experienced forced prostitution in marriage and "theft of the bride" situations (in which a man kidnaps a woman in order to marry her). Each of the women described being sheltered, in line with ideals of young women in their natal communities. Four out of the six recommended that parents speak with their children about sexual and romantic matters and about marriage and their futures, as well as drugs. They frequently referred to being unable to speak with their families about these issues. It is no coincidence that these issues have great bearing on female roles and traditional identities, the very roles and identities that were manipulated during their ordeals.

> My parents didn't talk with us about those things, about drugs, about sex, about any of those things. I think that it is very important to speak with

[children] about everything, to let them know there are bad people outside, to give them signs to let them learn how to recognize behaviors about somebody that is approaching you with some other intentions.

Helena

Conclusion

The experiences discussed throughout this chapter hint at the complexity of human trafficking situations: what human trafficking looks like, who trafficking survivors are, and what is at stake for people involved in a trafficking situation. While each trafficking experience was unique and personal, there were patterns that emerged which reflected social problems relating to poverty and gender-based violence in particular. There was also evidence that people who were living in trafficking situations in the United States and those continuing to work in commercial sex afterwards were especially vulnerable to arrest and deportation due to current immigration policies which criminalize undocumented persons living in the United States and commercial sex workers.

Thus in thinking about how to end human trafficking these societal level issues of poverty, gender-based violence, and lack of support for undocumented persons must be addressed. Additionally, emphasis must be placed on supporting people who are living in or have left trafficking situations by making it easier for people who find themselves in trafficking situations to get access to services when they choose to, which will not just help them leave the situation but support them in building a life after leaving, including help with: legal status and citizenship, finding employment, achieving educational pursuits, reuniting with family members (including children), offering therapy and access to other emotional/social support.

Acknowledgments

The data for this chapter is taken from *The Road North: The Role of Gender, Poverty and Violence in Trafficking from Mexico to the U.S.* (2012) by Melissa Ditmore, Anna Maternick, and Katherine Zapert. The authors and editor would like to thank Sienna Baskin, Crystal DeBoise, and the Sex Workers Project (SWP) for permission to use the data for this chapter. We would also like to recognize the Oak Foundation which funded the original study and the Urban Justice Center which houses SWP. You can access the full text from *The Road North* report at http://sexworkersproject.org/publications/reports/the-road-north

References

Desai, S., Arias, I., Thompson, M.P., & Basile, K.C. (2002). Childhood victimization and subsequent adult revictimization assessed in a nationally representative sample of women and men. *Violence and Victims*, *17*(6), 639–653.

Ditmore, M., Maternick, A., & Zapert, K. (2012). *The Road North: The role of gender, poverty and violence in trafficking from Mexico to the United States*. Retrieved on September 8, 2013 from http://sexworkersproject.org/publications/reports/the-road-north

Klest, B. (May 2012). Childhood trauma, poverty, and adult victimization. *Psychological Trauma: Theory, Research, Practice, and Policy, 4*(3), 245–251.

Torres, O. M. (2009). *Trata de personas: Padrotes, iniciación y modus Operandi*. México, D.F.: Instituto Nacional de las Mujeres. Retrieved on September 8, 2013 from http://www.inmujeres.gob.mx/index.php/programas/prevencion-de-la-trata-de-personas/fuentesdeinformacion

United States Citizenship and Immigration Services (2010). Questions and Answers: Victims of Human Trafficking, T Nonimmigrant Status. Retrieved on September 4, 2014 from http://www.uscis.gov/humanitarian/victims-human-trafficking-other-crimes/victims-human-trafficking-t-nonimmigrant-status/questions-and-answers-victims-human-trafficking-t-nonimmigrant-status

United Nations Optional Protocol to Prevent, Suppress and Punish Trafficking in Persons, Especially Women and Children (2000). Retrieved on September 8, 2013 from http://www.uncjin.org/Documents/Conventions/dcatoc/final_documents_2/convention_%20traff_eng.pdf

United States Trafficking Victims Protection Act (2000). Retrieved on September 8, 2013 from http://www.state.gov/documents/organization/10492.pdf

Widom, C.S., Czaja, S.J., & Dutton, M.A. (2008). Childhood victimization and lifetime revictimization. *Child Abuse & Neglect, 32*(8), 785–796.

Discussion questions

1. What are some of the limitations of conducting research based on this type of sample? What are the benefits?
2. What, if anything, did you find surprising about the trafficking narratives recounted here?
3. According to the authors, how might gender norms and expectations shape trafficking?
4. How does this chapter fit with claims that survivors of trafficking require rescue from prostitution and reunification with their families?
5. What recommendations did trafficking survivors have for addressing the problem?

Additional resources

Instituto para las Mujeres en la Migracion
http://imumi.org/index.php?option=com_content&view=article&id=17&Itemid=118

Sex Workers Project http://sexworkersproject.org and
http://sexworkersproject.org/publications/reports/the-road-north

Chapter 5

At sea: The trafficking of seafarers and fishers from Ukraine*

Rebecca Surtees

Introduction

While anti-trafficking research, policy, and program responses have placed particular emphasis on women and girls trafficked for sexual exploitation, there is
increased recognition of and attention to trafficking for forced labor, not least
in the seafaring and commercial fishing industries. This is a sector where trafficking can and does take place, arguably to a significant degree. This chapter
explores the issue of trafficking at sea through the experiences of 46 Ukrainian
seafarers and fishers trafficked to the waters of Russia, Turkey, and South Korea.
Understanding their experiences can contribute to improved anti-trafficking policies and programs for this form of exploitation. At the same time, the chapter
also highlights aspects of the Ukrainian experience and context that are specific
and unique. This signals different sites of vulnerabilities and experiences and,
thus, different intervention needs and opportunities. Efforts to address trafficking need to pay careful attention and seek to respond to this complexity and
diversity.

Research methodology and data collection

Research methodology

This chapter is based on the experiences of 46 Ukrainian men trafficked within
the seafaring and fishing sectors between 2005 and 2010. The men were assisted
by the International Organization for Migration (IOM) and its non-governmental
organization (NGO) partners between 2005 and 2010. Case files for each man
were reviewed and analyzed—both the quantitative data in the Trafficked
Migrants' Assistance Database (formerly known as the Counter Trafficking Module), IOM's global database on victims of human trafficking, and the qualitative
interviews from individual case files. Preliminary analysis of the IOM database
and case files assisted in the development of key lines of inquiry for fieldwork
interviews.

Box 5.1 The IOM Trafficked Migrants' Assistance Database (previously known as the Counter Trafficking Module)

The Trafficked Migrants' Assistance Database (TMAD) is used by the International Organization for Migration (IOM) to collect information and track IOM's assistance to victims of human trafficking. Among its purposes are enhancing research on human trafficking and strengthening IOM's activities on the ground. The database relies on primary case data, and is the largest of its kind in the world. By the end of May 2006, the Counter Trafficking Module (CTM) database included 9,376 cases of human trafficking. By the end of 2012, the TMAD had grown to include information about "20,000 registered IOM beneficiaries in approximately 85 source countries and 100 destination countries" (http://www.iom.int/files/live/sites/iom/files/pbn/docs/Migration-Management-annual-review-2012.pdf). Approximately half of the recorded cases were accompanied by in-depth accounts of the victims, perpetrators, and individualized scenarios of movement and exploitation, while maintaining anonymity and confidentiality. The TMAD database is part of the IOM's larger counter-trafficking strategy, which centers on the management of migration. The database is currently the most extensive database on trafficking in the world.

For further information:

The IOM Trafficked Migrant Database
http://www.slideshare.net/OECD-GOV/6-s35-nathalie-morandini-tmad

International Organization for Migration's Counter Trafficking Module
http://www.iom.int/cms/countertrafficking

Migrant assistance: Assisted voluntary return & reintegration counter-
    trafficking & assistance to vulnerable migrants Annual Review 2012
http://www.iom.int/files/live/sites/iom/files/pbn/docs/Migration-
    Management-annual-review-2012.pdf

Two rounds of interviews were conducted with trafficked seafarers and fishers in Ukraine—in May 2010 and May 2011. Four trafficked Ukrainian seafarers/fishers were interviewed, with a focus on their trafficking experience (recruitment, transportation, and exploitation), how they left trafficking, the assistance (if any) they needed and received, their current life situation, and their future plans and needs. We also discussed past (non-trafficking) seafaring experiences as a means of identifying key differences between trafficking and non-trafficking situations. Interviews were approximately an hour in length, conducted in the office of the NGO that had assisted the men. Interviews were conducted with the support of a Ukrainian interpreter. We also interviewed one former seafarer who had not been trafficked but who had, over several years of working at sea, been exposed to high-risk situations, difficult conditions, and deception by crewing companies. A second round of interviews was conducted by phone in May 2011 with five trafficked seafarers/fishers. Four were repeat interviews; one was a new seafarer who agreed to be interviewed. Interviews were conducted in Ukrainian.

The experiences of trafficked seafarers and fishers are supplemented by interviews with 30 key stakeholders who work on anti-trafficking in Ukraine as well as organizations and institutions that work with seafarers and fishers. This included anti-trafficking professionals from organizations that worked with trafficked seafarers and fishers (e.g. service providers, law enforcement officers, prosecutors, government agencies, international organizations) and seafaring professionals/experts (e.g. representatives from port inspectorates and authorities, seafarer unions, seafaring associations, trade unions, labor organizations). A second round of key informant interviews was conducted in 2011 aimed at following up on specific issues identified in the course of fieldwork and data analysis, clarifying any outstanding questions raised in the initial fieldwork and gaining a longitudinal perspective on the cases of trafficked seafarers/fishers (including the status of legal proceedings and reintegration).

Defining terms, outlining the context

Trafficking in persons

Human trafficking in this study refers to the generally accepted definition established in international legal documents, namely the *United Nations Protocol to Prevent, Suppress and Punish Trafficking in Persons* (also known as the UN TIP Protocol or the Palermo Protocol), which defines trafficking in article 3a as:

> recruitment, transportation, transfer, harboring or receipt of persons, by means of the threat or use of force or other forms of coercion, of abduction, of fraud, of deception, of the abuse of power or of a position of vulnerability or of the giving or receiving of payments or benefits to achieve the consent of a person having control over another person, for the purpose of exploitation. Exploitation shall include, at a minimum, the exploitation of the prostitution of others or other forms of sexual exploitation, forced labor or services, slavery or practices similar to slavery, servitude or the removal of organs.
>
> (United Nations, 2000)

Trafficking at sea

Trafficking at sea is that which takes place involving seafarers and fishers in the context of at-sea activities (including fishing, transportation and fish processing, while on vessels, rafts, fishing platforms, or otherwise offshore). It does not include shore-based operations (e.g. fish/seafood processing and packaging, port-based work, shore-based fish harvesting).

Seafarer

The *Maritime Labour Convention* (MLC) (2006) Article II(f) defines a seafarer as: "any person who is employed or engaged in any capacity on board a ship to which this Convention applies." The MLC applies to all ships, whether publicly or privately owned, ordinarily engaged in commercial activities, other than ships engaged in fishing (ILO, 2006).

Fisher

The *Work in Fishing Convention* (2007) Article 1(e) defines a fisher as: a person employed or engaged in any capacity or carrying out an occupation on board any fishing vessel, including persons working on board who are paid on the basis of a share of the catch but excluding pilots, naval personnel, other persons in the permanent service of a government, shore-based persons carrying out work aboard a fishing vessel and fisheries observers (ILO, 2007).

Who is trafficked? Trafficked seafarers and fishers from Ukraine

The 46 trafficked seafarers and fishers were adult men. All were Ukrainian citizens. They ranged in age from 18 to 71 years when trafficked—between 26 and 35 years of age (15 or 32.6 percent); 36 and 45 years of age (13 or 28.3 percent) and 18–25 years (10 or 21.7 percent). Of note were the handful of men between 56 and 65 years and, in one instance, 71 years of age. In this latter instance the man worked on a seafood processing platform, off the South Korean shore.

Age can be a factor in vulnerability to exploitative conditions and circumstances. Both younger seafarers (because of their inexperience) and older seafarers (because of their age and, thus, lack of appeal on the job market) may be particularly vulnerable to trafficking as they are more likely to accept (or perhaps even be targeted for) exploitative circumstances.

Twenty-seven (or 58.7 percent) of the men were married or in common-law relationships, while twelve (26.1 percent) had never been married, six (13 percent) were divorced and one (2.2 percent) was widowed. The need to support one's family was a key contributor in some decisions to accept work. However, pressure to support one's family is not unique to seafarers; it has been noted amongst males and females trafficked for both labor and sexual exploitation (as well as in decision-making amongst migrants generally).

Ukrainian men trafficked at sea were not typically "rank and file" sailors; they had professional seafaring qualifications and accreditation. One seafarer described what this typically involved:

> In Ukraine it is usually right after the eighth or ninth year of school that youngsters go to study at the technical college for three and a half years. There they acquire the knowledge and profession of a sailor, so "rank and file". In order to become a navigator one needs to accomplish university studies for five to six additional years.

Of the 46 men, 40 (or 87 percent) had tertiary level education through accredited maritime schools and academies and served as captain, captain's assistant, navigator, cook, and electrician, among other jobs. An additional five of the seafarers had completed high school and one had middle school education with basic level seafaring certification.

Some trafficked seafarers had not been to sea before, which may have contributed to their vulnerability. Reputable companies prefer qualified and experienced crew, leading less experienced seafarers to accept any available offer or be targeted by unscrupulous crewing agencies. One seafarer described how pressure to gain experience could lead to accepting even risky work offers:

> Even if there was someone to [teach about risk] to students in the maritime colleges or universities, they will not take it seriously. They would probably think: "It is not going to happen to me. I need a stamp, I need a contract and I agree to anything to acquire professional experience." In Sakhalin [Russia] they promised me a salary of US$900. Frankly I didn't look at how much they were promising to pay me. I needed to gain professional experience. That is why I agreed to go.

Nonetheless, the majority of trafficked seafarers and fishers had worked at sea prior to being trafficked, many on a number of occasions and for many years. Experience was not in and of itself a sufficiently protective factor, particularly when, as in these cases, recruitment and job offers were consistent with past (non-trafficking) experiences.

An overarching risk factor for Ukrainian seafarers was the economic situation in the country and their limited opportunities; the majority (65.2 percent) reported being poor when recruited. However, seafaring is a comparatively well-paid profession in Ukraine, making it difficult to say if they were objectively "poor" or worse off relative to their past situation. Eight men (17.4 percent) described an average economic situation and seven (15.2 percent) reported being well off. It is important to disentangle economic "need" from "want." One seafarer described family pressure to earn money that would afford the material goods and situation that they aspired to, an important distinction from economic need at the level of basic necessities.

Further, a strong personal desire to work as a seafarer—in their field of training and expertise—was often a significant motivating factor.

Looking for work: Patterns of recruitment

Initial recruitment and crewing agencies

In Ukraine, seafarers are recruited through legally registered and licensed crewing agencies, specialized in placing seafarers on ships. In Odessa alone there are over 100 crewing agencies.

How trafficked seafarers came into contact with crewing agencies differed. In many cases (29 of the 46 men, or 63 percent), recruitment was through personal contacts (commonly friends and seafaring colleagues) who referred them to different crewing companies and, in some cases, with whom they approached the company. Seventeen of the 46 men (or 37 percent), including all men trafficked to Turkey, found their position through newspaper advertisements of crewing companies, while looking for work.

Recruitment was generally consistent with how seafarers had been recruited for past jobs. One experienced seafarer described approaching the crewing agency and asking all of the "right questions," including that the crewing agency provide documentation of its legality and legal contracts with conditions of work and pay. Having been (successfully) to sea many times, he was aware of the official and correct recruitment process:

> We came to the office, they told us about the fishing boat, they said it is a difficult working environment but it is all legal and legitimate and okay . . . I asked if the boat was legal and if fishing was legal and he said, "Yes, the boat had a license to fish crabs" . . . I asked them to give me a copy of the [crewing company] license, which he did.

In one case, recruitment was less formal. The 71-year-old man learned about seafood processing work from a neighbor while visiting his family in Russia. He wanted to earn money for his grandson's wedding. The recruiter promised good working conditions in an automated seafood processing factory at a salary of US$ 1,000 per month. He was instead forced to process seafood on a platform at sea, off the coast of South Korea.

Contracts and agreements

Ukrainian seafarers/fishers trafficked to Russia signed what they understood were legally binding agreements with reliable crewing companies and employers. Each seafarer interviewed still had all of the documents related to their trafficking—i.e. contracts, receipts for recruitment/placement fees, plane tickets, and travel documents—as well as their seafarer documents and accreditation. Contracts were signed prior to departure; however, on arrival these were not honored and were renegotiated for a lesser amount.

The seven seafarers trafficked to Turkey signed their work contract directly with the ship owner upon arrival in Turkey. The contract was not in the Ukrainian language and they did not know the details of the contracts.

Recruitment fees

Thirty-seven of the 46 men in this study (80.4 percent) paid the recruiter some fee or advance payment, usually one to two months' salary. This is consistent with how crewing agencies function in Ukraine, as one experienced seafarer explained, but at odds with international labor standards:

> Many crewing companies in Ukraine ask for a fee for their services of finding work for seafarers . . . It ranges from between US$700 and US$1,000, the sum that we had to pay for employment.

Paying a recruitment fee sometimes meant incurring debt. One seafarer who had been chronically unemployed for five years borrowed US$1,000 from the bank to pay the fee; he used his contract as evidence of his ability to repay the debt.

Agency complicity in trafficking: Regulation of crewing agencies

The extent to which crewing agencies were aware of and complicit in the intended exploitation of Ukrainian seafarers/fishers remains unclear. At least one seafarer trafficked to Russia suggested that the recruitment agency may have been not only aware of, but also invested in, the trafficking operation:

> What we learned from the Russians who spent five years on the boat is that the person who was handling this whole thing in Ukraine was paid money for Ukraine sailors [who he was told] would not come back . . . The Ukrainian recruiter got about US$5,000 for every seaman that he sent that way and he was told that the Ukrainian seamen would never be coming back.

Even when not complicit, the existing regulatory framework for crewing agencies in Ukraine does not provide sufficient safeguards to protect seafarers against fraudulent recruitment. Crewing agencies do not have any responsibility or liability for the well-being (or violation) of seafarers whose placement aboard a vessel they arrange, contrary to international standards.

Facing limited options and alternatives

A number of the trafficked seafarers/fishers faced constrained professional and economic options that influenced decisions around recruitment. Some had been unemployed for some time; others were looking for work experience to start their careers. Information about risk and safe recruitment will have little impact in a context of constrained employment options, as one seafarer and trade unionist explained:

> In my view, one of the ways [to prevent trafficking of seafarers] is to educate seafarers, to give them as much information as possible. But then they are faced with the choice. Because if you have no practice, you have a certificate but currently you are not employed, then you have to find a job. So you go and you know that maybe you can get a good job on a good vessel in one year but now you have to earn some money to feed your family. Well you say: "Okay, I'll go." That's the problem. Basically they do not want to know anything about bad vessels because, being a seafarer, I know that I have to close my eyes and go rather than sit and wait.

That is, many seafarers interviewed for this study had (or felt they had) no alternatives—because of family and economic pressure, the need to gain work experience, and so on.

Going to sea: Transportation and embarkation

Destination countries and flag states

Trafficked seafarers embarked on their vessels in Russia, Turkey, and South Korea. As important, however, is the flag state of the vessel, particularly when operating in international waters. Seafarers trafficked to Turkey embarked on a vessel with a Panamanian flag; those trafficked to Russia were under a Russian flag. This means that these seafarers and fishers were under the legal jurisdiction of these flag states, which have duties under national and international law to protect trafficking victims on vessels flying their flag.

Seafarers/fishers trafficked to Russia carried legal documents and traveled by train and airplane *en route* to Sakhalin Island, in the far east of Russia. Seafarers trafficked to Turkey made their own way to Turkey, flying to Istanbul, where they were met by a company agent with whom they signed a contract. The man trafficked to South Korea traveled with the recruiter (and three other men), who facilitated entry to South Korea.

In Turkey, upon arriving in Istanbul, seafarers immediately embarked on their vessel. The man trafficked to South Korea was turned over, with the other men he'd traveled with, to a Korean man responsible for their embarkation. By contrast, in Russia the men waited for a period of weeks or months before embarkation, with their passports held by the agent. When they did embark, they were transported by boat out to sea because the ships were often unlicensed and crabbing illegally and they feared detection as well as escape by seafarers in port. One seafarer described a journey of several hours to find an illegal fishing vessel that was "hidden" to avoid detection by the authorities.

Life and work at sea: Experiences of exploitation and abuse

Working and living conditions

Ukrainian seafarers and fishers in Russia were engaged in illegal crabbing. Those in Turkey were tasked with transporting cargo from port to port along the Mediterranean coastline. The man trafficked to South Korea was exploited at sea for seafood processing.

Trafficked seafarers and fishers became aware of their precarious situation almost immediately after boarding their vessel, as one man trafficked to Russia explained:

> We were taken on a boat to go to sea and embarked on a ship that did not have any sign and name on it . . . When the boat went, we were told by those who were on board that they were working 24 hours a day, almost without sleep, no money paid, and also that it was impossible to leave since the ship never entered port.

They quickly discovered that the agreed contractual terms would not be honored after they boarded the ship:

> At sea they told us the conditions of the contract, which differed completely from the one we signed back in Ukraine . . . [And] since the contract conditions were violated, we were not about to work there. I was told that if we wanted there was a boat that could take us from the ship and take us home for US$2,000. Certainly no seafarer had more than US$100 or US$200 with him. That is why we had to stay for the minimum period of time that they offered us.

Men trafficked to Turkey also learned at embarkation that the existing crew had not been paid and conditions were extremely harsh. In South Korea, after arrival on the fish-processing platform, the supervisor informed the new crew that they had been sold to and would work for him.

Without exception and regardless of vessel or destination, trafficked Ukrainian seafarers worked seven days a week, for 18 to 22 hours each day. Living and working conditions were universally harsh and inhumane. The men recounted extremely distressing experiences:

> We stood above deck and drew out twine to catch crabs. This continued 24 hours a day, except for days when crabs were overloaded. In addition, everybody executed his professional duties. As a mechanic, I looked after the machines. We were allowed to sleep only a few hours and not every day. There were times when I did not sleep for four days. We rested on short breaks of 15 to 20 minutes.

Even basic necessities, like food and water, were universally scarce, as one seafarer explained:

> They were bringing us [food that was junk] and it was only half of what was needed. There was no water at all. We used to put some seafarers down on an ice flow; we'd put a hose and pump water to drink.

Injuries and illness

Occupational health and safety were serious issues under such brutal working conditions. Harsh and unsafe working conditions regularly led to serious injuries, illness, and even death:

> When we were on the Russian crabbing boat, we slept only two hours a day and all the time we were working. Sometimes people got really hurt when they were standing next to the crab traps. Sailors were standing and literally almost sleeping. The traps were falling and sometimes people lost their hands or legs.

Seafarers/fishers suffered a range of health problems, including kidney and bladder infections, liver problems, heart problems, ear infections, pneumonia, gastric diseases, dental issues, and so on. There was no access to medical care aboard the vessels and no opportunity to obtain medical care when in port. As one trafficked seafarer/fisher explained:

> I worked in ice-cold water, my legs were wet. That's why I had purulent otitis [middle ear infection with purulent discharge]. I asked the captain for medical help but he said that I should hold on, as there were no doctors and no medicine on the ship . . . I started encountering heart problems. I had difficulties breathing. I felt dizzy. However, I was denied any medical help . . . When the ship entered . . . port, I asked the ship owner to provide me with medical help. He said that there was no money and that I must wait.

Contact with land and other vessels

Seafarers/fishers trafficked to Russia had their freedom of movement restricted and were generally not able to leave the ship when in port. Some vessels never entered ports at all. In large part, this was a means of controlling the men. But it may also have been, at least in part, a result of fishing increasingly taking place out at sea, due to fish stock depletion closer to shore. Seafarers/fishers described their experiences of (often limited) contact with land and other vessels:

> When we were in slavery on that old clunker they would not let us enter the port because some seafarers who worked before us tried to escape . . . For the entire duration of my nine months there I managed to leave the ship only

once. It was when I went ashore to collect the telephone SIM cards. I literally walked about five meters to the car to collect the cards. Apart from that, it was not possible to leave the ship during those nine months. They would usually have dogs around so that it would not be possible to go ashore at all.

Those trafficked to Turkey entered ports but their documents were withheld and they had no money. Moreover, the ship owner threatened them with arrest by Turkish authorities should they attempt to leave the vessel (i.e. without documents, visa, etc.).

Violence and physical abuse

While physical abuse was not common amongst men trafficked to Turkey, men trafficked to Russia described frequent and violent abuse, directed against themselves and their colleagues, as a means of control and to prevent rebelliousness over working conditions, as one man explained:

> There was a sort of supervisor. He was overseeing people, making sure everybody was working. He was sometimes beating people. One Russian was bruised so badly, he was spitting blood. Not only Ukrainians [were abused] but Russians also.

On the seafood processing platform off the coast of South Korea, men were beaten by security guards if they refused to work (or did not work satisfactorily).

Lost at sea? Opportunities for identification and escape

A key challenge in combatting trafficking at sea is the identification of trafficked persons because so much trafficking takes place "out of sight," with traffickers consciously and strategically limiting contact between trafficked persons and others, particularly individuals and organizations that might be able to help them. While there are some potential entry points for identification (e.g. port authorities; law enforcement agencies; seafaring associations and unions; and on-board monitoring mechanisms), there are also overarching obstacles to identification.

Isolation at sea and on board

Trafficked seafarers and fishers are literally isolated on their vessels, out at sea. Even when authorities come into contact with vessels at sea, this does not automatically translate into identification. Generally senior officers are interviewed when coast guards conduct routine inspections at sea; contact with law enforcement is limited for lower ranking crew members who are more likely to be trafficked and exploited. Moreover, trafficked seafarers and fishers may not feel able to speak out in such settings, even if interviewed individually and separate from their exploiters. One seafarer trafficked to Russia was detained by the Russian border guards at one stage during his trafficking but was unable to ask for help because the authorities were concerned only with the illegal catch. Trafficked seafarers and fishers may also fear being left in the hands of their traffickers after disclosing their abuse and trafficking or being arrested for their involvement in any illegal activities on board—e.g. illegal crabbing in the case of the Russian seafarers.

Even when vessels are in ports, seafarers and fishers do not generally come into contact with port authorities, particularly if they are prevented from leaving their vessel. And opportunities for vessel inspection are governed by legal/administrative procedures as well as practical constraints like the sheer volume of vessels and crew in the port. Moreover, contacting authorities while in the port is unlikely for seafarers who do not trust the police.

Language barriers

There is often a language barrier between seafarers/fishers and persons who can identify them as trafficked (or at least in need of assistance), making it difficult for authorities to screen for vulnerability and risk. It is equally difficult for seafarers or fishers to ask for assistance or to comprehend assistance offers. As one International Transport Workers Federation (ITF) inspector explained, many Ukrainians faced communication barriers while abroad:

> The other thing for Ukrainian seafarers, for non-English speaking seafarers, they have a big problem once they face problems somewhere abroad, to not be able to explain what problems they are facing, to approach the authorities. They cannot approach the authorities because they do not speak English properly . . . They cannot just call and explain because they do not have an ability to communicate.

Limited capacity and knowledge amongst identifying actors

While many organizations have focused on forced labor in the fishing industry for some time, the extent to which this practice amounts to human trafficking has only been recently highlighted. Individuals likely to interact with victims of trafficking for fishing—i.e. labor unions, fisheries enforcement officials, scientific observers, etc.—are not always aware that forced labor conditions might amount to human trafficking. While they may note very poor living and working conditions, they do not necessarily see this in the context of human trafficking nor is it always within their mandate to investigate human trafficking cases (de Coning, 2011, p. 57; Surtees, 2012, 2013).

Corruption

Corruption (or fear of corruption) was a significant factor in decisions about who to approach for assistance when victims left their trafficking situation. One seafarer opted not to approach authorities who he understood were somehow involved in the illegal crabbing and, thus, unlikely to help him. Another described how men who had tried to escape the Russian ship when in port had been brought back to the ship by law enforcement authorities.

Being assisted (and unassisted)

Assistance abroad

Assistance options for trafficked seafarers and fishers while abroad were extremely limited; none was offered formal anti-trafficking assistance overseas. What assistance was received was *ad hoc* and largely insufficient. Those trafficked to Russia, who were unable to fund their return home, were assisted by the Ukrainian Ministry of Foreign Affairs. The ITF assisted in and funded the return of seafarers trafficked to Turkey and also interceded on their behalf to pursue lost wages through a civil action in Turkish courts. None of the trafficked men sought out and received tangible anti-trafficking assistance abroad, such as medical assistance, accommodation, or counseling. Other assistance was largely the result of personal relationships and individual goodwill. One was given money by Russian seafaring colleagues to buy his ticket home, having left the ship without payment and with no other funds in his possession.

Assistance at home

In Ukraine, trafficked seafarers and fishers received assistance largely through the IOM in Kiev and NGOs working in their area of origin—in Odessa for those trafficked to Russia and in Sevastopol for those trafficked to Turkey. They learned about assistance most commonly through former colleagues who had also been trafficked. Some saw advertisements for assistance organizations; others were referred by the prosecutor's office after they made a statement about their case. At the same time, not all of the men sought out or accepted assistance.

The type of assistance needed depended on a variety of factors such as the nature of trafficking, the period of exploitation, and their individual and family circumstances, among others. Some of the more common assistance needs centered around work, legal issues, and their physical and mental well-being.

Professional opportunities including (re)training and continued education

Many trafficked seafarers felt pressure (sometimes from family, sometimes from themselves) to immediately find work and compensate for not having come home with money. Some men left seafaring, a difficult decision as it involved leaving their profession and "starting at the bottom" in a new profession, as one seafarer explained:

> I have accomplished my seafaring studies in a technical college and then at the university with the rank of navigator. I worked as a navigator and as a senior assistant and now I realize that I came away with almost nothing. I am 37 years of age and I need to start from scratch.

The majority nonetheless continued to work as seafarers, some returning to work shortly after trafficking. One seafarer stressed the value he placed on his profession:

> There is no way I can change my profession. I was a sailor and I will be a sailor.

Trafficked seafarers spoke about their love for life at sea, the adventure and the prestige of their profession, their pride in their professional skills and accomplishment. Leaving seafaring was, therefore, also about their professional (and personal) identity. There were also economic considerations; some were unable to find work on land. For others, staying in seafaring was about supporting one's family at a certain economic level as seafaring was typically better paid than other forms of work. Some who continued as seafarers required assistance in covering the costs of ongoing training and certification. Regularly updating (and paying for) one's certificates and qualifications was often prohibitively expensive.

Legal assistance

Many seafarers felt they had inadequate access to competent legal representation. Trafficking cases are inherently complex and require specialized attorneys who are familiar with the relevant law as well as with the nuances of dealing with a potentially traumatized victim. Trafficking at sea demands an additional familiarity with international and local maritime law and the law of the sea.

Moreover, while many trafficked seafarers were willing to serve as witnesses in criminal or civil proceedings, they were unable to do so due to logistical barriers such as long distances between their homes and the sites of their lawsuits as well as leaving family members behind and loss of income while away. Many were also afraid of their exploiters and the possibility of reprisals for testifying in the case.

Healthcare and medical assistance

Harsh living and working conditions as well as experiences of physical abuse meant that many seafarers returned with serious injuries and medical conditions. Some required intensive rehabilitation and medical treatment, both in the immediate aftermath of their exploitation as well as in the longer term. A number of men developed chronic health problems as a consequence of trafficking—e.g. bronchitis, prostatitis, and the like—which required ongoing treatment or made them vulnerable to other conditions.

While all seafarers received medical care through NGOs and IOM upon their return, their longer-term medical needs posed ongoing problems. The cost of medical treatment can have serious repercussions on the seafarers' and their families' financial situation. One seafarer was recovering from a bout of pneumonia suffered in part because of his compromised immune system. After staying at the hospital for two weeks he had discharged himself to continue treatment at home because he could not afford a continued hospital stay. Ongoing health problems also impeded his ability to work.

Psychological assistance

Many men who returned faced psychological problems, including sleeping disorders, depression, and anxiety and so on. This was often an urgent issue, as one service provider explained:

> We need to deal [with these psychological issues]. It is only after we deal with these problems that the man can go out and look for a job.

Providing psychological support to seafarers and fishers included a raft of challenges, not least because many Ukrainian men felt seeking psychological support was weak and potentially debilitating. Even where the value of this assistance was recognized, it was not always socially acceptable. Services were also not always available in the communities where seafarers were reintegrating or seafarers returned to sea before they had started or completed psychological treatment.

Barriers to seeking out and accepting assistance

Not all men trafficked as seafarers and fishers sought out or accepted assistance. Some seafarers declined assistance because they felt that they could manage on their own. In other cases, needing to work meant that they could not benefit from assistance offers.

Many men were ashamed about being unable to support their families and felt pressure to compensate for this perceived failure. For them, one service provider explained, their priority was their family's financial situation:

> He's been away for six months, he hasn't brought any money, his wife keeps asking: "What happened? What did you do there?" They would be saying: "Why do you go for free medical assistance? There is no such thing now as free medical assistance. You'd just better go find a job or do some useful things at

home." Victims' families often have financial hardships and men would be the ones to deal with this. This is the most widespread reason for refusal.

Reluctance to seek out assistance may also be linked to past, negative experiences of assistance (or lack of past assistance altogether). Another concern was the perceived risk that this would "out" seafarers as trafficked to family, friends, and community (see also Brunovskis & Surtees, 2007). One seafarer explained that, while his family knew that he had problems abroad, they did not know the nature and extent of his exploitation and his neighbors didn't know anything about what had happened.

At a more personal level, men interviewed for this study were previously successful seafarers and, while they did recognize they had been abused and exploited, they did not necessarily see their experience within a paradigm of "victimhood." They were often uncomfortable talking about the experiences they had been through. One man, at least initially, responded to questions about his experience and situation with ambivalence, asking, "Why do we have to talk about this? Men should not talk about their problems" (see also Surtees, 2008).

Conclusion

Trafficking of seafarers and fishers is a less considered and yet important part of the overall picture of human trafficking. Much can be learned from the experiences of the trafficked seafarers and fishers considered in this chapter, from recruitment and exploitation to identification and assistance. At the same time, trafficking at sea can differ substantially from context to context and lessons from one region or one group may not resonate with others' experiences. Moreover, while the experiences and needs of trafficked seafarers and fishers have much in common with those of other persons trafficked for labor in/from Ukraine, there are some specific distinctions that need to be borne in mind when addressing this particular form of human trafficking:

Physical danger and risk of exploitation are unusually high in seafaring and commercial fishing. The very nature of the work—largely out of sight, at sea, moving between various national and international jurisdictions— lends itself to a high risk of abuse. Trafficking and labor exploitation are made significantly more feasible by the limited regulation of labor practices in the seafaring and fishing sectors.

Trafficked seafarers and fishers are not "traditional" victims. The trafficking of highly skilled, professional seafarers goes some way in challenging notions of who gets trafficked and how. Assumptions of vulnerability and risk (which commonly center around poverty, low education, family problems, and social exclusion) do not apply in the same way in these cases. Who gets trafficked and how is highly specific, linked to a localized context and the victim's individual circumstances and personal narratives.

Trafficking threatens seafarers' and fishers' sense of identity. Being trafficked at sea threatens the identity of these men—on a professional level (as a skilled and capable seafarer) as well as on a personal level (as an educated and successful man, husband, and father). Where one's sense of self and identity is intimately tied up in one's profession, having that profession undermined by a trafficking experience can be disorienting, challenging, even debilitating. Trafficked seafarers may also suffer from their failure to earn money and to support themselves or their families, something that can be exacerbated by the need to seek out and accept assistance.

Experiences of trafficked seafarers and fishers challenge victim paradigm. Victimhood is commonly associated with passivity, yet these seafarers were active decision makers, seeking professional satisfaction and to support themselves and their families. Resistance was sometimes subtle—like supporting one another at sea—and sometimes more active—like fighting back against abuse, devising means of exit, seeking help from authorities, giving statements and testimony, bringing legal action against their exploiters, and relating their story for this research to contribute to anti-trafficking efforts.

Identification of trafficked seafarers and fishers is difficult and infrequent. Identifying trafficked seafarers and fishers poses a number of challenges, not least because they are often quite literally "out of sight." Entry points for identification—whether at sea or in port—are case specific and require increasing the engagement of a wide (and expanded) range of stakeholders in the process of identification.

Trafficked seafarers' and fishers' assistance needs are unique and highly specific. The needs of trafficked seafarers and fishers, while not always dissimilar to victims of other forms of labor trafficking, do have some specific features. The specific services that trafficked seafarers require, such as specialized legal aid or psychological assistance as well as decisions around whether to continue to work in seafaring, require careful tailoring of assistance programs to meet their needs.

Human trafficking is a complex phenomenon. Effectively addressing human trafficking involving vessels at sea adds additional layers of complexity. As long as the problem of trafficked seafarers and fishers is not recognized, acknowledged, or prioritized by countries implicated in these activities, steps will not be taken and there will be little if any identification and assistance of trafficked seafarers and fishers. This chapter is offered as a first step in discussing and developing a credible response to modern-day slavery at sea.

Note

* This chapter draws on findings from a study on trafficked seafarers and fishers from Ukraine, *Trafficked at sea. The exploitation of Ukrainian seafarers and fishers* (Surtees, 2012). The study was authored by NEXUS Institute as part of the NEXUS and IOM *Human Trafficking Research Series*, which is funded by the U.S. Department of State Office to Monitor and Combat Trafficking (J/TIP) under the terms of Grant No. S-SGTIP-09-GR-0070. The research series seeks to advance trafficking research by examining less considered aspects of the phenomenon as well as discussing methods and approaches in data collection and research. Sincere thanks are due particularly to the seafarers/fishers who shared their very difficult experiences as part of this study and also made important recommendations for improvements. Thanks also to key informants who participated in the research from both the anti-trafficking sector and the fishing and seafaring fields. I would also like to acknowledge the support provided by staff at IOM Kiev—namely: Ruth Krcmar (CT Programme Coordinator), Hanna Antonova (Senior CT Programme Officer), Ganna Lienivova (Project Specialist), Anh Nguyen (then Counter-trafficking Coordinator, now Senior Regional CT and AVRR Specialist in Vienna), Roman Ilto (Interpreter) and Kukla Petro (Driver)—and staff from NGOs "Faith, Love and Hope" in Odessa and "Youth Centre for Women's Initiatives" in Sevastopol. I am particularly grateful to Sarah Craggs (then Researcher at IOM, now Regional Migrant Assistance Specialist, IOM Regional Office Cairo) with whom I conducted fieldwork in 2010 for this chapter and Anvar Serojitdinov (Project Officer, IOM Geneva), who conducted follow-up interviews in 2011. Amanda Gould (Research and Data Analysis Specialist, IOM Geneva) and Jonathan Martens (Senior Migrant Assistance Specialist, IOM Geneva) reviewed this chapter. Thanks are also due Laura S. Johnson (Research Associate, NEXUS Institute) and Stephen Warnath (Chair/founder, NEXUS Institute, Washington) for their review of and inputs into the chapter. The opinions expressed herein are those of the author and do not necessarily reflect the views of the United States Department of State or IOM.

References

Brunovskis, A., & Surtees, R. (2007). *Leaving the past behind: Why some trafficking victims decline assistance.* Oslo, Norway: Fafo Institute and Vienna: NEXUS Institute.

de Coning, E. (2011). *Transnational organised crime in the fishing industry. Focus on trafficking in persons, smuggling in migrants and illicit drugs trafficking.* Vienna: UNODC.

ILO (2006). *Maritime Labour Convention (MLC).* Retrieved on August 17, 2014 from http://www.ilo.org/wcmsp5/groups/public/---ed_norm/---normes/documents/normativeinstrument/wcms_090250.pdf

— (2007). *Work in Fishing Convention. Convention No. 188.* Retrieved on August 17, 2014 from http://www.ilo.org/ilolex/cgi-lex/convde.pl?C188

Surtees, R. (2008). Trafficked men as unwilling victims. *St. Antony's International Review (STAIR). Special issue: the politics of human trafficking, 4*(1), 16–36.

— (2012). *Trafficked at sea. The exploitation of Ukrainian seafarers and fishers.* Washington, DC: NEXUS Institute & Geneva: IOM.

— (2013). Trapped at sea. Challenges and opportunities in preventing and combatting the trafficking of seafarers and fishers. *Groningen Journal of International Law. Special issue on human trafficking, 1*(2), 91–153.

United Nations (2000). *Protocol to Prevent, Suppress and Punish Trafficking in Persons.* New York: UN General Assembly.

Discussion questions

1. How do the examples in this chapter compare to dominant anti-trafficking discourse?
2. What are some of the challenges related to identifying and assisting seafarers and fishers who have been trafficked?
3. How does masculinity shape vulnerability to trafficking?
4. How does masculinity affect help-seeking for men who have been trafficked?
5. Based on this chapter, what policies might be useful to address trafficking?

Additional resources

'Enslaved—Myanmar' (MTV EXIT Special includes the story of a Myanmar man trafficked onto a fishing boat in Thailand)
http://vimeo.com/39029758

'Enslaved—Cambodia' (MTV EXIT Special includes the story of a Cambodian man trafficked onto a Thai fishing vessel)
http://vimeo.com/39257164

MTV Exit documentary about trafficking in Ukraine (forthcoming)

A Passport to Decent Work (film on the Maritime Labour Convention)
http://www.ilo.org/global/about-the-ilo/multimedia/video/institutional-videos/WCMS_219972/lang--en/index.htm

Sold to the Sea (film on human trafficking in Thailand's fishing industry)
http://ejfoundation.org/oceans/soldtotheseafilm

Chapter 6

Human trafficking in "fresh" organs for illicit transplants

A protected crime

Nancy Scheper-Hughes

Introduction

In this chapter I want to introduce the Organs Watch project—its scholarly, anthropological, and public engagements—as an example of what Pierre Bourdieu called "scholarship with commitment" (2000, p. 40). Elsewhere (Scheper-Hughes 2000, 2002a, 2002b, 2003, 2009, 2011a), I have grappled with the thorny issue of how to frame the problem of the emergence and spread of robust organs and transplant trafficking schemes. Is organs trafficking a solution based on a rational choice model of needs, desires, scarcities, supply, and demand? Is it a problem concerning the commodification of bodies, persons, and organs (Scheper-Hughes & Wacquant, 2002)? Is the question one of human dignity (precious lives) or indignity (wasted lives, wasted bodies)? Is it a narrative of human desperation and despair or is it best understood as a risky and extreme mobilization of hope and optimism ("Yes, I can, I will live!")? Is it a question of human rights, and if so, whose rights are being protected (Friedlaendar, 2002), and whose rights are being denied or negated (Scheper-Hughes, 2003)? Are we best served by using a value-free term, "commercialized transplants" (Turner, 2009), suggesting that this is a problem that can be solved by the application of medical economics and business administration, (Cherry, 2005), or one that requires new laws and regulations (WHO, 2004)? Alternatively, does our subject fall into the domains of organized crime, human trafficking, medical human rights abuses, and even, in the worst instance, crimes against humanity (Scheper-Hughes, 2011a)?

Organ trafficking defined

Organ trafficking made its debut as a much-contested "add-on" to the United Nations Protocol on Human Trafficking (The Palermo Protocol) which defines human trafficking in article 3 as,

> the recruitment, transportation, transfer, harbouring or receipt of persons, by means of the threat or use of force or other forms of coercion, of abduction, of fraud, of deception, of the abuse of power or of a position of vulnerability

or of the giving or receiving of payments or benefits to achieve the consent of a person having control over another person, for the purpose of exploitation. Exploitation shall include, at a minimum, the exploitation of the prostitution of others or other forms of sexual exploitation, forced labour or services, slavery or practices similar to slavery, servitude or the removal of organs.

(emphasis added, UN, 2000)

The protocol recognizes that even willing participants in underworld, black market illicit kidney schemes can be counted as victims. Indeed, most are not coerced by physical threats or force, but by need, and are offered a proposition that, in their weakened condition, they cannot refuse. Some even pay significant amounts of money to be trafficked. While not every transplant facilitated by paid donors falls into the broad category of human trafficking, robust transnational organ trafficking networks exist and are responsible for the recruitment and transport of kidney buyers and sellers through deceit and coercion. These illicit networks account for roughly 15 percent of all unrelated living donor transplants worldwide, according to Organs Watch, the Organization for Security and Co-operation in Europe (OSCE, 2013), World Health Organization (WHO, 2004), and UN estimates. What I wish to present is a conundrum in legal anthropology and criminology: why trafficking of humans for freshly purchased kidneys is to a great extent a protected crime.

Box 6.1 World Health Organization

The World Health Organization (WHO) is a member of the United Nations system and is responsible for matters pertaining to public health. As of 2013, it had a membership of 194 countries. The WHO is accountable for "providing leadership on global health matters, shaping the health research agenda, setting norms and standards, articulating evidence-based policy options, providing technical support to countries and monitoring and assessing health trends." It is the leading public health organization of its kind, concerned not only with accessible health care worldwide, but also with protection from global threats. It plays a significant role in public health policymaking, research, and implementation of programs in member states. The WHO's activities range from mass immunization, to outbreak containment, to emergency disaster management, to the universalization of drug names. Amid its notable campaigns are the identification and control of SARS in 2003, the adoption of WHO's first global public health treaty designed to reduce tobacco-related deaths and diseases in 2003, the launch of the Global Polio Eradication Initiative in 1988, and the eradication of smallpox in 1979. Following the 2000 United Nations Millennium Summit, the WHO became responsible for realizing three of the Millennium Development Goals, namely cutting child deaths, improving maternal health, and combating HIV/AIDS, malaria, and other diseases. The WHO administers a wide-ranging program of activities, addressing matters that relate to women's and children's health, cholera control, oral health, environmental health impacts, social determinants of health, and disabilities and rehabilitation, to name a few. WHO's 2014–2019 budgeted expenditures are US$12 billion.

For further information:

World Health Organization, homepage: http://www.who.int/en

Today, the illicit networks to facilitate organ transplantation through the recruitment and trafficking of kidney providers are conducted in a competitive global field, involving some 50 nations identified by Organs Watch since 1999. While most descriptions of organs trafficking focus on the supplier nations and the individual victims of trafficking located mostly in the global South and the Third World, Organs Watch has focused on the procurer and receiver nations and the individual kidney buyers in the global North and in wealthy countries of the Middle East. In addition to procurer and receiver nations and buyers, a third component of organ trafficking is the set of facilitating nations in which illicit transplants with trafficked persons are conducted. A single illicit transplant tour can bring together actors from as many as four or five different countries: a mobile buyer from one country, a trafficked seller from another location, brokers from two other countries, and mobile surgeons arriving from yet another country, where the kidney removal and transplant actually takes place. In these instances, and the case of the Medicus clinic in Kosovo is perhaps the best example, the participants appear and disappear very quickly, with the guilty parties, including the surgeons, taking any incriminating data with them. When the police finally arrive at the scene, what they discover is the bloody remains of a black market clinic, with traces of forensic evidence, but the key players safely and for all purposes disappear across many borders. Mobility is the essential key metaphor of transplant trafficking. All the actors are counting on a quick exchange of body parts under the gun, so to speak.

The global commerce to provide fresh kidneys to foreign transplant tourists began in South Asia in the late 1970s and early 1980s. The first report on the topic, published in *The Lancet* in 1990, documented the kidney transplant odysseys of 131 renal patients from three dialysis units in the United Arab Emirates and Oman. They travelled with their private doctors to Bombay, India, where they were transplanted with kidneys purchased with the assistance of local brokers, and harvested from living sellers who were recruited from the slums and shantytowns surrounding Bombay. The sellers were paid between $2,600 and $3,300 for their "spare" organ. On return to their home countries, Arab recipients of Indian kidneys suffered an alarming rate of post-operative mortalities resulting from botched surgeries, mismatched organs, and high rates of fatal infections, including HIV and

Hepatitis C contracted from the seller's organ (Salahudeen et al., 1990).There was no medical data or discussion of the possible adverse effects on the kidney sellers, who were an invisible population of anonymous supplier bodies, similar to deceased donors.

Organs Watch was founded in 1999 by me and my UC Berkeley colleague, Professor Lawrence Cohen, following our initial forays into the global sites of what was euphemistically called *transplant tourism*. Cohen focused on various sites in India (Cohen, 1999), while I looked at Brazil and South Africa (Scheper-Hughes, 2000). We decided to take a preferential option for the invisible organs sellers, that is, to make them central to our research.

Before long, I realized that I was documenting more than medical ethical violations, or commerce in organs, which has a long history, with organs, tissues, and body parts being taken from vulnerable dead bodies in forensic and medical morgues as far back as the seventeenth century. Rather, I had unwittingly uncovered the entrée of international organized crime into the secret world of illicit transplant surgeries. Following fieldwork in Turkey, Moldova, Israel, the Philippines, and the U.S., it was apparent that the so-called organ brokers were in fact human traffickers, and the modus operandi involved mobile surgeons, brokers, patients, and sellers from different nations who met up for clandestine surgeries involving cut-throat deals that were enforced, when needed, with violence.

The organs trade as human trafficking

In some respects, human trafficking for organs (primarily kidneys from living donors) is similar to other forms of trafficking—for drugs, arms, sex, and labor—and in some ways it is quite distinct. Like other forms of human trafficking, the kidney trade is organized into donor, recipient, transit, and facilitating sites across national boundaries or within them. Among the key donor/organ selling sites are: Argentina, Bangladesh, Brazil, China, Colombia, Egypt, India, Iran, Iraq (until the war), Israel, Moldova, Romania, Pakistan, Palestine, Peru, Philippines, Russia, U.S., and Turkey. Prominent recipient/organ buyer sites include: Australia, Canada, France, Gulf States, Iran, Israel, Italy, Hong Kong, U.K., U.S., and Taiwan. Facilitating (operating) sites include: China, India, Iran, Iraq (until the war), Philippines, Romania, Russia, South Africa, U.S., and Turkey. How many people are actually trafficked each year for their kidneys? The World Health Organization estimates that approximately 60,000 kidney transplants take place every year. Depending on the country, it is estimated that between 10 percent and 90 percent of organ transplants involve commercial transactions, human trafficking, or coercion. A conservative estimate, based on pooling information from original research, police reports, and from hospital records in key sites of transplant tourism, is that some 15,000 kidneys are sold each year. This is a relatively small and contained problem that could be dealt with efficiently were there the political will to do so.

How many of these brokered kidneys are removed from sellers who are coercively trafficked? How many purchased kidneys are the result of willingly transacted but illegal sales? How many kidneys are procured legally (e.g. in Iran), or through quasi-legal or illegal sales (Egypt, Philippines, Israel, Iraq, etc.)? Where does trafficking end and consensual behavior that may be seen as distasteful but legally ambiguous begin? What are the essential elements of *trafficking* in organs? Does trafficking imply only cross-border transactions involving passports, visa fraud, etc.? What degree of coercion, deception, violence, or threats of violence are necessary to the definition of trafficking? Or, is the intrinsic exploitation of vulnerable populations sufficient to justify the trafficking label?

There are sites where transplant brokers are abusive toward kidney sellers or use hired thugs to back up the verbal contracts agreed to by kidney seller recruits. We have recorded multiple narratives of dirty tricks, threats, and physical abuse among brokers in Moldova, Turkey, Israel, and the United States. My colleague, Lawrence Cohen, has been told of deception and "kidney theft" in isolated areas of India and among Indian guest workers abroad. Threats are common from money lenders, both in Eastern Europe and in South Asia where debt peons are sometimes forced to use their "spare" kidney as collateral. In recent years, the more crude and coercive schemes have been replaced by better organized and ostensibly better educated schemes that pay more attention to the well-being of the kidney sellers, even of trafficked ones, as the Brazil-to-South Africa kidney selling scheme (described below) illustrates.

In-depth interviews with 38 kidney sellers from the Moldovan capital city, Chisinau, and from several villages in central Moldova included many stories of deception, physical threats, false imprisonment in safe houses, confiscated documents, denial of food, and even beatings of those who were recruited to sell kidneys abroad. Some brokers in Moldova and in Turkey, the destination site, used tactics that had already been honed in recruiting naïve Moldovan women into sex work from these same economically forsaken villages. Brokers offered unemployed youth, or household heads in debt or needing cash to support sick spouses or children with severe medical problems, an opportunity to work abroad—especially in Turkey, but also Estonia, Georgia, and Russia—in jobs ranging from construction, painting and plastering, and hotel work, to jobs in grocery stores, restaurants, and dry cleaning factories. On arrival, the young men were kept in safe houses, their passports confiscated, reducing them to total dependency on the brokers for food and housing. A few days later, the local brokers would break the news that it wasn't painting or pressing pants that was needed from the illegal "guest workers," but their kidneys. Those who refused outright, who were shocked and scandalized at the very possibility, were threatened. If they ever wanted to see their villages again, they had best comply. Valdimir, a young man with whom I spent many hours over several days in Moldova, explained his decision to go through with the surgery in Istanbul at the hands of a Turkish doctor whom he referred to as a "butcher" and as a "dog": "Yes, so I did it, I went ahead with it. But if I hadn't given up my kidney to that dog of a surgeon my body would be floating somewhere in the Bosporus Straight."

Following the production in 2001 of an hour-long documentary with Catherine Berthillier for *Envoyé Spécial*, a French TV news weekly, which focused on the lives and stories of the men trafficked from Moldova, I brought the dire situation to the attention of Moldova's prime minister, to the captain of a special force of anti-trafficking police in Chisenau, to the Minister of Health in Turkey, and finally to the Council of Europe at a special investigatory meeting held in Bucharest in May 2002. While efforts to interrupt the trade were initiated in Moldova, the local brokers disappeared while Moldovan kidney sellers continued to trickle in to Turkey, the U.S., and later to South Africa. Perhaps, the initial shock and disbelief that Moldova was infiltrated by internationally linked criminal networks of organ traffickers was replaced with resignation to the local economic facts of life—the rest of the world rejected Moldova's primary export products (including its wine and brandies) in the post-Soviet state. What the world seemed to want from Moldovans was their cheap labor, their pretty women, and their kidneys.

In Israel, a gang of low status new immigrants from the former Soviet bloc nations (Russians and Ukrainians) were utilized by a leading figure in international organ trafficking, Kobi Daan. Following an organized police sting, three brokers were arrested and charged with deception, fraud, and organized crime. A criminal indictment accused Genadi Mishkis, age 32, Albert Chernov, age 41, and Avraham Atias, age 52, of defrauding vulnerable people of their kidneys. All three were arrested in a police raid on June 17, 2003. The alleged ring leader of the organs gang, Kobi Daan, was brought in for questioning and released for want of evidence by police. According to testimonies from the aggrieved kidney sellers, Mishkis and Chernov were merely the brutal underlings who procured kidney sellers and brought them to Atias, who set up the blood and tissue matching and reported directly to Dyan, who set up the transplants abroad or, when he could get away with it, in Israel. Mishkis and Chernov were given $30,000 for each kidney donor procured, half of which was payment to the kidney hunters, half of which went to the sellers. The prey were newly arrived immigrants, mostly Russians, but also Bulgarians, and some Filipino and other guest workers. The accused were brought to trial in 2004 but the state dropped the indictments when state prosecutors told the court that the trial would be unlikely to lead to a conviction due to the lack of cooperation of various key informants and witnesses.

Breaking from anthropological tradition, I made the decision to name the criminals, including the outlaw surgeons, their transplant units and their crime bosses (some of whom were surgeons themselves) (Jimenez & Scheper-Hughes 2002). What followed were several years of advocacy on behalf of the victims of organ trafficking, which included the buyers as well as the sellers and even some of the *kidney hunters*, many of them former sellers who were recruited by organized crime bosses into the tight web of transplant trafficking schemes. I faced considerable resistance from transplant professionals who saw organ trafficking as being relatively rare and consisting of isolated incidents taking place in Third World settings. They were loath to recognize the involvement of transplant trafficking schemes in the West and North (the U.S., Canada, and Europe) as well as in the

South (Asia, South America, and South Africa), where some of the finest public, academic, and private hospitals opened their operating rooms to trafficked kidney sellers and transplant tourists, facilitated by criminal networks.

Box 6.2 Organized crime

The United Nations *Convention against Transnational Organized Crime*, adopted by the United Nations General Assembly on November 15, 2000 and entered into force on September 29, 2003, defines an organized criminal group as a "structured group of three or more persons, existing for a period of time and acting in concert with the aim of committing one or more serious crimes or offences established in accordance with this Convention, in order to obtain, directly or indirectly, a financial or other material benefit." The *Convention against Transnational Organized Crime* clarifies that a structured group can comprise members who unite to commit an offence but are not necessarily confined to fixed responsibilities or permanent membership within the group. Organized crime can take place on local, regional, national, and international levels. Popular media tend to portray organized crime as the conduct of mafia-like groups with hierarchical structures in which members are aware of each other's activities. More frequently, however, organized crime groups comprise loosely allied individuals or small clusters who come together to pursue criminalized activities that appear profitable to them at the time. The corruption of officials is an important dimension of organized crime. The *Protocol to Prevent, Suppress and Punish Trafficking in Persons, Especially Women and Children,* identifies organized crime as a primary cause of human trafficking.

For further information:

United Nations Convention against Transnational Organized Crime and the Protocols thereto
http://www.unodc.org/documents/treaties/UNTOC/Publications/TOC%20Convention/TOCebook-e.pdf

Finckenauer, J. O. (2005). Problems of definition: What is organized crime? *Trends in Organized Crime, 8*(3), 63–83.

In 2008, the climate of denial began to change when the Transplantation Society (TTS) and the International Society of Nephrology held a major summit in Istanbul, attended by more than 150 transplant representatives from around the world. The summit acknowledged organs trafficking as a reality rather than a myth or urban legend, as well as its extent and the need for a unified position among key transplant professionals worldwide against organs trafficking and commerce in fresh kidneys. The Declaration of Istanbul on Organ Trafficking and Transplant

Tourism (2008), followed by the formation of the Istanbul Declaration Custodial Group (DICG) in 2010, applied pressure on countries actively involved in organized or disorganized crimes involving illicit networks of organs traffickers that recruited poor nationals, new immigrants, global guest workers, or political and economic refugees to serve the needs of transplant tourists in countries that tolerated or actively facilitated the clandestine transplant trade.

Despite the recognition of human trafficking for organs as a heinous crime, recent crackdowns, police stings, arrests, and prosecutions of a small number of organs traffickers, criminal networks of brokers and transplant trafficking schemes are still robust, exceedingly mobile, resilient, and generally one step ahead of the game. "They are smarter than you are," Captain Louis Helberg, the head of the commercial crime branch of the South African police in Durban, told me during a police sting. The operation led to the indictment and prosecution of organs brokers, kidney buyers, a transplant nephrologist, surgeons, and transplant coordinators at just one (Saint Augustine's Hospital) of four private Netcare transplant clinics that were involved in hundreds of illicit transplants in South Africa organized by an Israeli organs and transplant trafficking syndicate led by Ilan Pery. The prosecution resulted in several guilty pleas in the famous Netcare ("kidneygate") case, including a plea bargain by the Netcare Medical Corporation itself (Hassan & Sole, 2011).The human organs traffickers (aka *the brokers*) are today more sophisticated and have changed their modus operandi, realizing that their access to foreign outlets in public and private hospitals is time-limited.

Following police crackdowns in Israel since 2008, brokers there confided to me that they either have to find ways to access deceased donor pools in Russia or Latin America (Colombia, Peru, Russia, and Panama) or to set up very temporary transplant sites in new locations (Kosovo, Cyprus, Azerbaijan, and Costa Rica) for a short duration, anticipating police, government, and/or international interventions. Once they suspect a possible sting operation, the international brokers are prepared to move to any of dozens of other temporary and less than ideal foreign sites and clandestine transplant units, some of them unlicensed walk-in medical clinics or rented wards in private hospitals.

The sites of illicit transplants have expanded within Asia, the Middle East, Central Asia, Eastern Europe, Central and Latin America, Europe, and the United States. They have also become more secret, clandestine, and dangerous. The kidney buyers include virtually anyone with the desire and resources to travel, while the brokers include health insurance agents, travel agents, transplant surgeons, transplant coordinators, kidney patient organizations, and religious organizations, or those posing as such, like United Lifeline (Kav L'Chaim) in Brooklyn and Israel. Kidney patients from Taiwan, Japan, Saudi Arabia, Canada, and the U.S. travel to China. People from the Gulf states travel to Egypt, the Philippines and the U.S.. Israelis travel to all of these sites as well as to outpost locations in Kosovo, Azerbaijan, Medellin, Cyprus, Panama, Ecuador, and, most recently, to Costa Rica, where the local organs trafficking broker, Dimosthenis Katsigiannis Karkasi, was also the owner of a Greek pizza parlor, Acropolis Pizzeria. The syndicate used the pizza parlor, which was next door to the Calderón Guardia Hospital in a working class barrio, to recruit kidney sellers (Dyer, 2013).

As for the recruitment of kidney sellers, one economic or political crisis after another has supplied the market with countless political and economic refugees who fall like ripe, low hanging fruit into the hands of the human traffickers. The desperate, the displaced, and the dispossessed can be found and recruited to sell a spare kidney in almost any nation. The new generation of organs traffickers is also more ruthless. When foreign access to transplants in China with organs harvested from executed prisoners shut down during the Olympics, brokers began to pursue transplants with living donors, some of them trafficked Vietnamese people in China, others naïve villagers in parts of the country where blood-selling programs had softened and groomed people to accept kidney selling as another possibility.

In 2009, and again in 2013, I interviewed Ricky Shay, the daughter of a retired Israeli military man, Yechezkel Nagauker, whose kidneys were failing. Meanwhile, his wife was dying of diabetes and had her legs amputated. Fearing a similar fate, Nagauker contacted a broker who guaranteed a kidney transplant in China within two weeks for the price of $100,000. The broker, Yozzie Tezzeri, sent his partner to accompany Naugauker to an unnamed, unlicensed clinic in a peripheral outpost where he was transplanted with a poorly screened and mismatched kidney from a teenage girl. Following an incoherent phone call asking for help from her mortally ill father, Shay flew to China to rescue him. She found him lying unconscious and dying in a filthy hospital bed. The surgeon told Shay that it was too late for her father, and forbade her from removing him from the clinic. But she chartered a special medical emergency flight for her father to Hong Kong, where he was taken to the Intensive Care Unit of a private hospital until he was sufficiently stabilized to fly back to Israel. He died a year later, never recovering from the botched transplant. His 16-year-old kidney seller, a young village woman, also died following her botched nephrectomy. Ricky Shay was shocked that her father, still strong and healthy, was so gullible as to believe what a ruthless broker told him, that he would be in China for only two days, and come back a new man, a gift to his children and grandchildren. Instead he came home a "train wreck," so weak that his voice was close to a whisper. Shay said in 2013 that she was actually angry at her father, a man in his sixties, who would risk the life of a Chinese teenager in order to enhance his own life. But most of all she was angry at the broker, a man she referred to as "my father's killer."

Despite two undercover stories in Israel and TV media coverage by CNN and *Dan Rather Reports* (2013), the broker and his partner were never arrested. When, accompanied by Ricky Shay and two of her relatives, we attempted to confront the broker (Tezzeri) in 2009, a fist fight ensued between the broker and Shay's male relatives. Ricky and I were thrown to the ground by the broker's partner, a feisty Asian woman adept at martial arts. Ms. Shay reported the incident to the police, but clearly the broker had gotten there first and it was Ricky who was cross-examined by the police for having trespassed and arrived unannounced at the home of the broker in his gated community.

In 2013, however, I was able to hear the explanation given by another Israel-to-Asia transplant broker, who requested anonymity. He admitted to facilitating some 50 illegal transplants abroad, some in China, others in the Philippines. He was arrested in 2010, two years after he entered the transplant tour business, first as a minor player, a courier of documents, blood samples, and false affidavits. As he learned the essential aspects of the trade from an older and established broker, he began to recruit buyers from the kidney patient community and even accompanied them to their transplant sites in Asia. What he saw there was not pleasant and he gradually realized what kind of "dirty dealing" the kidney hunters, but not himself, were involved in. He called the kidney hunters low life people, "scumbags." Anyone who sells a kidney, KG said, had to be mentally imbalanced or completely desperate. He had seen both. Although KG pled guilty to some 30 counts of brokering illegal transplants, and had to pay a large financial penalty, losing every cent he had earned, he was freed from prison and today insists that he was morally innocent. He had nothing to do with the kidney hunters and their prey. "I worked only with the patients, the surgeons, and the hospital staff. I helped save the lives of many kidney patients. I regret that I broke the law in doing so and I would never do it again. But if I wanted to, it is easy." It is the easiest thing in the world to find the one thing that drives the entire business: fresh, purchased kidneys.

The new organs trafficking and kidney brokering laws passed in Israel are ambiguous, and the few individual cases brought to the courts have managed to avoid the laws that prohibit trafficking in humans for the purpose of removing organs by being charged under a lesser, regulatory law that prohibits "brokering in organs transactions," a far less serious offense. To date, while several brokers and one Israeli surgeon, Michael Ziss, have been charged with crimes, only one broker, Sammy Shemtov, has served a short prison term. Others, like KG, entered plea bargains, in some cases in exchange for several weeks of community service. No outlaw surgeon has ever been indicted in Israel, nor have any been extradited following requests by Interpol and by prosecutors in South Africa, Turkey, and Kosovo.

In the famous Netcare case in Durban, South Africa, in which more than 100 illicit transplants were performed at the private Netcare Corp transplant unit at Saint Augustine's Hospital, a police sting resulted in several plea bargains from various brokers and their accomplices. Netcare, the largest medical corporation in South Africa, pled guilty to having facilitated the illegal transplants, a first in transplant history anywhere in the world. The immediate result was that Netcare stocks fell worldwide (Hassan & Sole, 2011). The four surgeons and two transplant coordinators who were indicted held fast to their not guilty plea. Their defense was that they were merely employees of Netcare who were deceived by the Netcare Company and its lawyers who initially claimed and defended these international surgeries as legal. In December 2012, the court finally granted a stay of prosecution for the surgeons and their transplant coordinator surgical nurses on procedural grounds (Barbeau, 2012). They were given a permanent stay of prosecution and the state was ordered to pay their defense costs. It is fair to state that rogue transplant surgeons operate worldwide with considerable immunity.

A victimless crime?

Because human trafficking for organs is seen to benefit some very sick people at the expense of other, more invisible or at least dispensable people, some prosecutors and judges have treated it as a victimless crime. When New Jersey federal agents caught Levy Izhak Rosenbaum, a hyperactive international kidney trafficker, as part of a larger police sting of corrupt politicians, in 2009, the FBI had no idea what a *kidney salesman* was. The prosecutors could not believe that prestigious U.S. hospitals and surgeons had been complicit in the scheme, or that the trafficked sellers had been deceived and at times coerced into selling. The federal case, *U.S. v. Levy Izhak Rosenbaum*, ended in a plea bargain in 2011 in which Rosenbaum admitted guilt to just three incidents of brokering kidneys for payment, although he acknowledged having been in the business for over a decade.

At the sentencing in July 2012, citing official court transcripts, Judge Thompson was impressed by the powerful show of support from the transplant patients who arrived to praise the trafficker and beg that he be shown mercy. The one kidney selling victim, Elhan Quick, presented as a surprise witness by the prosecution, was a young black Israeli man, recruited by traffickers to travel to a university hospital in Minnesota to sell his kidney to a 70-year-old man from Brooklyn. Although Mr. Cohen had 11 adult children, not one was disposed to donate a life-saving organ to their father. They were, however, willing to pay $20,000 to a stranger.

Mr. Quick testified that he agreed to the donation because he was unemployed at the time, alienated from his community, and also hoped to do a meritorious act that would improve his social standing. On arrival at the transplant unit, however, he had misgivings and asked his "minder," Ito, the Israeli enforcer for the trafficking network, if he could get out of the deal as he had changed his mind. These were the last words he uttered before going under anesthesia. The seller's testimony had no impact on the court. The judge concluded that it was a sorry case. She hated to send Rosenbaum to a low security federal prison in New Jersey for two-and-a-half years as she was convinced that deep down he was a "good man." As for the kidney seller, the judge argued that Quick had not been defrauded; he was paid what he was promised. "Everyone," she said, "got something out of this deal."

Conclusion: Transplant trafficking as a predatory crime

Illegal, clandestine kidney transplants depend on criminal networks of human traffickers preying on the bodies of both the desperately sick and the desperately poor. At its most exploitative—as when political refugees, displaced persons, prisoners, and the mentally impaired are used as suppliers of fresh kidneys—organs trafficking is a crime against humanity. Legislation and prosecutions are effective deterrents, but to date they have focused on the lowest common denominator, the organs brokers, handlers, and kidney hunters. While prosecutions of the traffickers and their associates are correct they are ultimately inefficient. Brokers may be the most visible players but they are easily replaceable.

What is lost in translation is the difference between *brokering* an organ and *trafficking in human beings* for the purpose of kidney harvesting. Arresting and prosecuting brokers has been ineffective, and has not deterred others from taking their place. Legislation and prosecution must focus on the transplant professionals, the surgeons, hospitals, and insurance companies that have welcomed the trafficking and claimed immunity because the participants in the brokered and trafficked transplants have deceived them.

Ultimately, interventions cannot come solely from within the transplant profession. Bioethics is a weak factor in combating organized crime. Governments face legal obstacles in prosecuting organs trafficking that involves three or more nations in a single illicit transplant. New laws could be passed in the buyer nations to restrict and penalize patients who have acquired a kidney through illicit organs brokering networks. The EU, the United Network for Organ Sharing, Eurotransplant, the United States Department of Justice, and the United Nations Office on Drugs and Crime should pay more attention to combating the global traffic in humans for illicit and clandestine transplants. What remains to be seen is whether the traffic in human beings for their valuable organs will become routinized as something that can be managed through regulation and legal constraints or whether it will continue to be seen either as a "victimless" crime or as an inherently unjust, exploitative, and unacceptable "solution" to the tragic problem of end stage kidney disease.

Given these research quandaries, I do not expect the Organs Watch project to become a model for engaged anthropology (Bourdieu, 2002; Scheper-Hughes, 1995) and I accept that my refashioning of the ethnographer's role has been greeted with lively debate and criticism and I hope that the dialogue continues. From its origins, transplant surgery has presented itself as a complicated problem in gift relations and gift theory, a domain to which sociologists and anthropologists from Marcel Mauss to Levi-Strauss to Pierre Bourdieu have contributed mightily. The spread of new medical technologies and the artificial needs, scarcities, and the new commodities that they demand have produced new forms of social exchange that breach the conventional dichotomy between gifts and commodities and between kin and strangers. Undoubtedly, deathly ill individuals have benefited enormously from the ability to get the organs they need, but the violence—medical, psychological, social, and ethical—associated with these transactions gives reason to pause. Even dedicated attempts to regulate the kidney market in Iran, and more recently in the Philippines, have not been able to eliminate the primary dilemma—the reliance on the bodies of the young and relatively healthy poor, the marginal, the mentally and economically weak, to fortify and supplement the bodies of the old, the mortally ill, and the relatively affluent. The division of the world into organ buyers and organ sellers is a medical, social, and political tragedy of immense and not yet fully recognized proportions.

References

Barbeau, N. (2012). Kidney doctor case collapses. *IOL News*. Retrieved on August 17, 2014 from http://www.iol.co.za/news/africa/kidney-doctor-case-collapses-1.1441346#. U1ib2VcfzvR

Bourdieu, P. (2000). For a scholarship with commitment. *Profession (Journal of the Modern Language Association)*, pp. 40–45. Retrieved on August 17, 2014 from http://www. jstor.org/discover/10.2307/25595701?uid=3737536&uid=2134&uid=2&uid=70&uid= 4&sid=21104061980291

— (2002). Pour un savoir engagé. *Le Monde Diplomatique*, February, p. 3.

Business Report. (2010). Netcare kicked off SRI Index. December 2, 2010. Retrieved on July 28, 2014 from http://www.iol.co.za/business/news/netcare-kicked-off-sri-index-1.912800

Cherry, M.J. (2005). *Kidney for sale by owner: Human organs, transplantation, and the market.* Washington, DC: Georgetown University Press.

Cohen, L. (1999). Where it hurts: Indian material for an ethics of organ transplantation. *Daedalus, 128*(4), Bioethics and Beyond (Fall, 1999), 135–165. Retrieved on August 17, 2014 from http://www.jstor.org/discover/10.2307/20027591?uid=3737536&uid=2134& uid=2&uid=70&uid=4&sid=21104061980291

Dan Rather Reports. "Kidney Pirate." (2013). Retrieved on August 17, 2014 from http:// www.youtube.com/watch?v=ihnwl6lgKcM&feature=youtube_gdata_player

The Declaration of Istanbul on Organ Trafficking and Transplant Tourism (2008). *Clinical Journal of the American Society of Nephrology, 3*(5), 1227–1231.

Dyer, Z. (2013). OIJ arrests 3 doctors and pizzeria owner in organ trafficking sting in Costa Rican capital. *The Tico Times*. Retrieved on April 24, 2014, from http://www.ticotimes. net/2013/10/10/oij-arrests-3-doctors-and-pizzeria-owner-in-organ-trafficking-sting-in-costa-rican-capital

Friedlaendar, M. (2002). The right to sell or buy a kidney: Are we failing our patients? *The Lancet, 359*(9319), 971–973.

Hassan, F., & and Sole, S. (2011). Kidneygate: What the Netcare bosses really knew. *South African Mail & Guardian.* Retrieved on July 28, 2014 from http://mg.co.za/ article/2011-04-29-kidneygate-what-the-netcare-bosses-really-knew

Jimenez, M., & Scheper-Hughes, N. (2002). Doctor Vulture: The unholy business of the organ trade. *Special report*, *National Post* (Canada), March 30, B1, 4, 5.

Organization for Security and Co-operation in Europe (2013). *Trafficking in human beings for the purpose of organ removal in the OSCE region: Analysis and findings.* Vienna: Office of the Special Representative and Co-ordinator for Combating Trafficking in Human Beings. Retrieved on August 14, 2014 from http://www.osce.org/ cthb/103393?download=true

Salahudeen, A.K., Woods, H.F., Pingle, A., Nur-El-Huda Suleyman, M., Shakuntala, K., Nandakumar, M., Yahya, T.M., & Daar, A.S. (1990). High mortality among recipients of bought living unrelated donor kidneys. *The Lancet, 336*(8717), 725–728.

Scheper-Hughes, N. (1995). The primacy of the ethical: towards a militant anthropology. *Current Anthropology, 36*(3), 409–420.

— (2000). The global traffic in organs. *Current Anthropology, 41*(2), 191–224.

— (2002a). Min(d)ing the body: On the trail of organ stealing rumors, in MacClancy, J. (Ed.), *Exotic No More: Anthropology on the Front Lines*. Chicago: University of Chicago Press, pp. 33–63.

— (2002b). Keeping an eye on the global traffic in human organs. *The Lancet, 359*(9310), 971–973.

— (2003). Rotten trade: Millennial capitalism, human values, and global justice in organs trafficking. *Journal of Human Rights, 2*(2),197–226.

— (2009). The ethics of engaged ethnography: Applying a militant anthropology in organs-trafficking research. *Anthropology News, 50*(6), 13–14.

— (2011a). Mr. Tati's holiday and João's safari—Seeing the world through transplant tourism. *Special Issue, Body & Society, Medical Migrations, 17*(2–3), 55–92.

— (2011b). The Rosenbaum kidney trafficking gang. *CounterPunch*, November 30, 1–12. Retrieved on August 17, 2014 from http://bod.sagepub.com/content/17/2-3/55. abstract

Scheper-Hughes, N. and Wacquant, L. (2002). *Commodifying Bodies.* London: Sage.

Turner, L. (2009). Commercial organ transplantation in the Philippines. *Cambridge Quarterly of Healthcare Ethics, 18*(2), 192–196.

United Nations (2000). Protocol to Prevent, Suppress, and Punish Trafficking in Persons, Especially Women and Children, Supplementing the UN Convention Against Transnational Organized Crime. Retrieved on August 17, 2014 from http://www.osce.org/odihr/19223

World Health Organization (2004). *Resolution on human organ and tissue transplantation.* Geneva. Retrieved on August 17, 2014 from http://www.who.int/transplantation/en/A57_R18-en.pdf

Discussion questions

1. How does organ trafficking differ from other forms of human trafficking described in this book?
2. What factors have impeded the prosecution of organ trafficking crimes?
3. Who are the main parties involved in organ trafficking?
4. What does Scheper-Hughes recommend to address the problem of organ trafficking?
5. What is organized crime? How does it relate to trafficking for organs or labor?

Additional resources

Ambagtsheer, F., & Weimar W. (2012). A criminological perspective: Why prohibition of organ trade is not effective and how the declaration of Istanbul can move forward. *American Journal of Transplantation, 12*(3), 571–575.

Bagheri, A. & Delmonico, F. L. (2013). Global initiatives to tackle organ trafficking and transplant tourism. *Medical Health Care Philosophy, 16*(4), 887–95.

Budiani-Saberi, D., & Mostafa, A. (2011). Care for commercial living donors: the experience of an NGO's outreach in Egypt. *Transplant International, 24*(4), 317–323.

Budiani-Saberi, D., & Delmonico, F. (2008). Organ trafficking and transplant tourism: A commentary on the global realities. *American Journal of Transplantation, 8*(5), 925–929.

Caplan, A., Domínguez-Gil, B., Matesanz, R., & Prior, C. (2009). Trafficking in organs, tissues and cells and trafficking in human beings for the purpose of removal of organs. Council of Europe/United Nations Report. Retrieved on August 17, 2014 from <http://www.refworld.org/docid/4b1ce76f2.html

Codreanu, N. (Renal Foundation). (2010). *Identification of victims and collection of cases of organ trafficking*. Presentation held at the 3rd ELPAT Invitational Working Groups Meeting (Sofia, October 8, 2010).

Danovitch, G., et al. (2013). Organ Trafficking and Transplant Tourism: The Role of Global Professional Ethical Standards—The 2008 Declaration of Istanbul. *Transplantation, 95*(11),1306–12.

Delmonico, F. L. (2008). The Declaration of Istanbul on organ trafficking and transplant tourism. *Nephrology Dialysis Transplantation, 23*(11), 3381–3382.

Interlandi, J. (2009). Organs trafficking—not just an urban legend (a report on the research of Nancy Scheper-Hughes and Organs Watch in the USA). *Newsweek Magazine*, January 19.

Rothman, D., et al. (1997). The Bellagio task force report on transplantation, bodily integrity, and the international traffic in organs. *Transplantation Proceedings, 29*(6), 2739–45.

Radcliffe-Richards, J. (2012). *The Ethics of Transplant: Why Careless Thought Costs Lives*. Oxford: Oxford University Press.

The HOTT Project. Retrieved on August 17, 2014 from http://hottproject.com/home.html

Documentary films on organs trafficking

"Tales from the Organ Trade" (2012). HBO. http://www.abc.net.au/4corners/stories/2014/03/03/3953589.htm

"BloodMatch: Israel/USA" (2013). December. Series 7, "What in the World". RTE, Irish Public Television, Dublin, KMF Productions

"Kidney Pirates" (2010). Dan Rather reports on the cost of transplant trafficking (with Nancy Scheper-Hughes) (follows Organs Watch in Turkey, Moldova and Israel).

"H.O.T—Human Organs Traffic" (2009). Lupin Films, Rome. <http://www.imdb.com/title/tt1527626/>

"The Transplant Trade" (2004). Produced and directed by Brian Woods. True Vision Productions, BBC, Channel 4. Trafficking activities in India, Israel and Turkey. <http://truevisiontv.com/shop/product/details/70/the-transplant-trade>

"Transplant Tourism" (2003). David Papery Films. Canadian Broadcast. Follows Organs Watch in Philippines. <http://www.imdb.com/title/tt0389459/>

"Trafic d'Organes."(2002). On site in Moldova and Turkey with "Envoyé Special" documentary filmmaker, Catherine Berthillier. Galaxie Presse, Paris. <http://www.francesoir.fr/actualite/sante/trafic-d-organes-humains-un-marche-qui-explose-232179.html>

Chapter 7

(Not!) child trafficking in Benin

Neil Howard and Simona Morganti

Introduction

Benin has long been identified as an "epicenter" of the international traffic in children (Aide et Action, 2005). This chapter contends that it is not. Using interviews and participant observation conducted with groups of adolescents identified as trafficked—girls who have been in domestic service or market work and boys currently or formerly engaged in quarry-work—the chapter argues that the discourse of trafficking rests on narrow, received ideas that do not correspond to the empirics of young Beninese lives. The trafficking discourse constructs adolescent departures from the family home as the result of corrupted tradition (particularly in the form of "child placement"), economic crisis, or criminality. It also portrays them as nearly always abusive. Our data, however, suggest that things are much more complex, and often a good deal more benign. Teenagers are often highly agentive in their movement, and whether it is they or their families who decide that they should migrate for work, they do so in the pursuit of personal and familial advancement. As such, what is characterized as trafficking would be better understood (and responded to) as youth labor migration.

Research context

Child trafficking emerged as *the* major child protection issue across the Majority World at the start of the last decade (Castle & Diarra, 2003; Hashim, 2003; Huijsmans & Baker, 2012; O'Connell Davidson, 2011; Thorsen, 2007). This was no more apparent than in Benin, where two high-profile events saw trafficking catapulted to the status of "Number One" social policy challenge. The first was the interception of a Nigerian trawler smuggling Beninese adolescents to work in Gabon. The second was the high-profile "rescue" of Beninese teenage labor migrants working in the artisanal quarries of Abeokuta, Nigeria. Both episodes saw young workers identified as "slaves," and both led to Benin's being tarred as the new "epicenter" of the international traffic in children (Alber, 2011; Feneyrol & TdH, 2005; Howard, 2011, 2012; Morganti, 2007, 2011).

It was in this context that the two authors began separately working in Benin in the mid-2000s. Though previously well-versed in the horror stories characteristic of mainstream trafficking discourse, neither of us was prepared for how inaccurate those stories would appear. Indeed, our work with young labor migrants defined as "trafficked" quickly revealed the disjuncture between institutional representations of child trafficking and the lived realities of those represented as trafficked. It was in order to explore this disjuncture that we each began our parallel doctoral research.

Neil's research involved examining what had been identified as one of the country's "classic" examples of trafficking—that of teenage boys moving from the Zou region of Southern Benin to the artisanal quarries of Abeokuta in Nigeria. Neil selected four case study villages from the Zou region, and in these villages he purposively sampled former migrants to the quarries, those involved in the migrant labor network linking the region to the quarries, and village authorities. He also conducted a short period of targeted fieldwork during which he spent time in and around the quarries of Abeokuta themselves, observing the living and working conditions and interviewing representatives of the key actors engaged in the quarry economy.

Simona's research concerned the widespread tradition of child fostering ("*vidomègon*" in the local Fon language), which is considered one of the major elements of trafficking in Southern Benin. After an initial period of fieldwork designed to develop a better understanding of Beninese family structure, traditional education, and child socialization, she examined the "new" forms of child placement and child labor migration from a gender perspective. She focused on the living and working conditions of girls of rural origin, aged between 10 and 15, who had been employed in domestic service or were currently working as domestics and ambulant sellers in Cotonou (Benin's *de facto* capital). Simona collected girls' life stories in various shelters for underage people in difficult situations and in Cotonou's Dantokpa market.

Discourse

The child trafficking discourse in Benin rests on a kind of "pathological paradigm." This paradigm constructs youth work and youth migration for work as inherently problematic. This is because work and migration are seen by child protection actors to belong to an "adult sphere" from which children should be protected and sheltered (see Huijsmans & Baker, 2012; De Lange, 2007; Hashim, 2003; Hashim & Thorsen 2011; Howard, 2011; Morganti, 2008, 2011; O'Connell Davidson & Farrow, 2007; Whitehead, Hashim, & Iversen, 2007). As a result, all labor-related departures from the family home—whether involving young children relocated to work on domestic tasks within the extended family or adolescents migrating to earn some money—are understood as somehow pathological, and the result of unwilled, extraneous cause-factors such as poverty, corrupted tradition, criminal trickery, or parental naivety (Howard, 2011, 2012).

Box 7.1 Child labor

Child labor does not just refer to work done by children. While many forms of work completed by children are harmless and considered to be positive, other forms of work are harmful or exploitative. The International Labour Organization (ILO) defines child labor as "work that deprives children of their childhood, their potential and their dignity, and that is harmful to physical and mental development." Laws regulating children's work vary from country to country. The age at which children can legally be employed, the types of work they may perform, and number of work hours are some of the factors that determine whether children's work is considered to be child labor. Child labor has implications for children's health, education, safety, and social development. Child labor is present in all countries, but varies from region to region. It takes place in formal sectors such as manufacturing and agriculture, and informal economies such as begging and scavenging.

For further information:

ILO Fact Sheet: What is Child Labor?
http://www.ilo.org/ipec/facts/lang--en/index.htm

Child Labor: A Textbook for University Students
http://www.ilo.org/ipecinfo/product/download.do;jsessionid=b12fe9c9a
4efea26855c31e6f39b75b952e16c78089077e00cb0b536edf17859.
e3aTbhuLbNmSe34MchaRah8Tbx10?type=document&id=174

A crucial sub-element in Benin's trafficking discourse revolves around the Fon term *vidomègon* ("child who is with someone"). The socio-cultural phenomenon of *vidomègon* is predicated on the idea of collective education designed to foster social solidarity within the extended family. It involves rural children temporarily being entrusted to a relation in town, who is supposed to offer opportunities to the child that are absent in more remote areas (Morganti, 2006, 2008). Those who take in *vidomègon* children are considered responsible for those children's informal education. Biological parents are often not seen as good educators because they are seen as too soft and, therefore, unable to prepare the young for the tough realities of life. *Vidomègon* children are thus sent to town to "toughen them up" and prepare them for the future. In return for the care, lodging, and protection they receive in the city (Stella, 1996), they are expected to demonstrate obedience and respect for the adults who host them, as well as to help with domestic chores and to help the family business (Morganti, 2007, pp. 90–91).

The engagement of children in this kind of productive economic activity is not considered problematic by most Southern Beninese. Across the region encompassing Benin and Togo, the practice of socializing children through economic activity is well established, possessing in Fon the name "*djoko*," which refers to forms of child work that are both remunerative and convey social responsibility. This is indeed common in much of West Africa, as children are quickly incorporated into the productive collective, according to their capacity.

Box 7.2 Convention 182 Concerning the Prohibition and Immediate Action for the Elimination of the Worst Forms of Child Labour

The Worst Forms of Child Labor Convention was adopted by the International Labour Organization on June 17, 1999 and entered into force on November 19, 2000. The Convention identifies poverty as the cause of child labor and seeks to eradicate the worst forms of child labor, assist in the recovery and integration of child workers, and provide support for families. The Convention defines a child as any person under the age of 18. Worst forms of child labor include:

"(a) all forms of slavery or practices similar to slavery, such as the sale and trafficking of children, debt bondage and serfdom and forced or compulsory labour, including forced or compulsory recruitment of children for use in armed conflict;

 (b) the use, procuring or offering of a child for prostitution, for the production of pornography or for pornographic performances;

 (c) the use, procuring or offering of a child for illicit activities, in particular for the production and trafficking of drugs as defined in the relevant international treaties;

 (d) work which, by its nature or the circumstances in which it is carried out, is likely to harm the health, safety or morals of children."

For further information:

Convention Concerning the Prohibition and Immediate Action for the Elimination of the Worst Forms of Child Labour
http://www.ilo.org/dyn/normlex/en/f?p=1000:12100:0::NO::P12100_ILO_CODE:C182

Increasingly, however, *djoko* and *vidomègon* are demonized and criminalized—seen by child protection actors as *equivalent to child trafficking*, with the words *djoko* and *vidomègon* themselves often used as direct translations for the term "trafficking." The best illustration of this widespread discursive construction can be found in Benin's nationwide anti-trafficking "sensitization campaign" centering on the film and cartoon strip "Ana, Bazil et le Trafiquant." We will discuss it at some length below as it represents an archetype of formal discourse.

Created as part of UNICEF's anti-trafficking work in the early 2000s, "Ana, Bazil and the Trafficker" is the story of a bright young girl, Ana, from a poor village in Southern Benin. The story opens with scenes depicting Ana's home life, her love of school, her housework, and the struggles her family faces to get by. Shortly thereafter, the arrival of a mysterious stranger heralds the shattering of Ana's world. The smooth-talking outsider approaches Ana's loving, yet misguided, parents and begins to persuade them that Ana does not need to remain in school, that she could migrate for work and help the family, and that if she came with him he would be able to place her in a wealthy household that should set her up for life. The man thus implicitly invokes the notions of *djoko* and *vidomègon* and, though at first reluctant, Ana's parents are ultimately persuaded to acquiesce to his suggestion.

At this point in the narrative, "The Trafficker" secretly reveals his plan to take Ana and sell her into servitude. The audience are thereby led to see how the combination of his deviance, Ana's parents' well-intentioned ignorance, and their acceptance of "corrupted" and problematic tradition mean that she is lost. Fortunately for both Ana and the audience, however, Ana's young classmate, Bazil, gets wind of The Trafficker's plan and is able to alert the authorities just after Ana leaves. In the penultimate segment of the story, before the police arrive to rescue her, we see Ana in bondage, an abused *vidomègon* working and being mistreated as a domestic servant. The contrast between her state at this point and her delight at being rescued could not be more stark. The message offered by the cartoon, then, is clear: it is the safe, caring, and protective parental nest, twinned with the school, that represents the appropriate place for children to develop. These differ absolutely from The Trafficker, who embodies at once a real, material threat and also the metaphorical nefariousness that awaits innocence upon its pre-emptive entrance into the world of the "economy," including through *vidomègon* or *djoko*. Though the tale features a young, female protagonist, it is intended to represent the reality of all young labor migrants, including boys heading off to work in sectors other than domestic service.

Youth labor mobility

It is not our contention that child and young workers, youth labor migrants, or those involved in *djoko* and *vidomègon* are always free from exploitation. Nor do we wish to suggest that *djoko* and *vidomègon* have remained unchanged by the entrenchment of capitalism or the concomitant evolution in Southern Beninese social relations. Far from it. Tradition is never static and child or youth work are not always positive. What our data demonstrate, however, is that the trafficking discourse is fundamentally reductive, since it simplistically equates all *djoko, vidomègon,* and youth labor migration with trafficking. Yet the empirics of youth work and youth labor mobility involve a great deal more nuance than this. In the following section, we will seek to highlight that nuance, drawing on our examination of the conditions and context of youth work in and around Southern Benin to do so.

Decision makers

Before we begin to address the conditions and context of youth work, we must first offer a word about *who decides* for children to engage in that work. Where the trafficking discourse implies that decisions are pathological, resulting from trickery, ignorance, or something similar, our research disagrees, showing the labor departure almost always to be highly considered and agentive. As is consistent with social and developmental norms across the African continent, the decision for younger children to leave is almost always taken by the child's parent or guardian (Morganti, 2011). By contrast, when children enter their mid- to late-teens, and as they are both afforded and expected to take on a greater degree of independence, it is more frequently *they* who decide on their own behalf that they are going to migrate for work.

As such, in Simona's research with younger girls who had been sent to the city to a relative or acquaintance in order to work as a domestic servant or market girl, girls frequently reported that they "agreed with" or "were happy with" the decision that their parents had made on their behalf. Neil found similar things with boys, with those who were sent to Nigeria's quarries and those who were sent to undertake non-rural "apprenticeships" in order to acquire practical experience and relieve some of the economic burden felt by the family in the village.

Things were different, however, with older teenage girls and boys. Some of the girls Simona interviewed had decided autonomously to move in order to gain freedom or to find the money necessary to marry. For the boys Neil worked with, money was another central motivator, as will be discussed below, and parents rarely if ever stood in the way of the decision made—since it was understood and considered normal for adolescent boys to begin to articulate their independence through their *djoko* migratory departure.

Content and context of work

The story presented in "Ana, Bazil et le Trafiquant" is said to be "typical" of the trafficking/work experienced by young people in Benin. Our research suggests that this is not the case. In this section, we will discuss the nature and context of the work that our interviewees experienced. We will begin with the teenage girls Simona worked with in Benin's rescue shelters.

These girls were mostly teenagers who had been through more than one "placement" as a domestic servant and had decided to leave their last employer's house. They had generally dropped out of the village school after one or two years in order to follow an "auntie"—often a woman from the extended family—who came to the village looking for a young helper to take back with her to the city. Though often this relationship was described in traditional *vidomègon* terms, it was clear that the girls and their parents expected some form of remuneration from the contract. Often parents received a symbolic amount of money (5,000 CFA, equivalent to US$10) or some gifts (alcohol, fabric), but in general they had to wait for wages to flow as work progressed.

After a few months of domestic and commercial training with the "auntie" and her foster family, the "auntie," legally considered a trafficker, placed her *vidomègon* with another employer who had agreed to pay for the domestic work the girl would perform. Generally, the employer paid the auntie for this service, and the auntie sent money to the girl's parents every two or three months, promising that she would eventually give the girl a dowry (money, clothes, household tools) when the girl finished her contract and returned to the village to get married.

Inevitably, given the sample, the girls in the shelters had all had abusive experiences in this kind of labor arrangement, with most affirming that their host families had no consideration for their well-being. Many said that they were exposed to discrimination, facing various privations, having to do excessive work (12–16 hours a day, six days a week) and at times being subject to physical violence. In this, their experiences clearly recalled those of "Ana," and it would be fair to say that they had, in a legal sense, been "trafficked." However, in contrast to "Ana," none of these girls wanted to go home, none was ready to give up their urban experience, despite its hardships, as all instead wanted to stay in the city but with a "better employer," who would pay them well, help them to start a small business or arrange an apprenticeship (hairdressing, dressmaking) for them alongside their job.

Unlike the girls in care, the teenagers Simona interviewed working in Dantokpa market still lived with their host families or with their employers. They too were considered victims of trafficking simply because they were working children away from their parents' homes, even if the work they did often involved performing the same tasks as girls working alongside their own mothers. The lives of these market girls revolve around trade and they spend about 12–14 hours a day in the streets. Some of them already have their own business and the women they live with act as "economic godmothers" who support and train them. The teenagers divide their time between working for these "godmothers" and working on their own account.

From their point of view, being an itinerant saleswoman is better than being a domestic servant as it has the dual advantage of breaking their isolation and giving them some important economic training. When Simona interviewed them, many took pride in showing the various "tricks of the trade" that they had picked up, and all claimed to want to dedicate themselves to trade. In their opinion, the skills they had learned were crucial, setting them up for life. Although sometimes their work involved unpleasant customer exchanges and occasional exploitation by their "godmothers," none lamented being away from home or school and none wished to stop what they were doing.

Many parallels exist between these experiences and those documented by Neil among teenage boys working in Abeokuta's shallow, gravel-pit quarries. These quarries are operated by the Beninese expatriate community, which provides the labor necessary to extract the gravel. Each small pit is run by a Beninese "boss" who oversees the work of a small gang of Beninese teenage workers. Though they are formally viewed as victims of "child trafficking," in reality these teenage boys are all contracted teenage labor migrants engaged in a period of *djoko*, to which all have offered their consent. Each teenager works six days a week for his boss, and his boss is responsible for sheltering and feeding him. At the end of the two-year contract, each worker receives 140,000 FCFA (about US$260, or an equivalent sum in material terms, e.g. a motorbike). All boys are free to work for themselves on their day off, or when they have completed their day's work for their boss. Though their work is physically demanding, they work in groups of three, with the biggest and strongest pick-axing the ground, the second strongest shoveling the gravel, and the smallest sifting it through a filter. There is a good feeling in the quarries and a lot of jovial banter amongst the workers. All take breaks and they share the workload between them. So while no one ever denies that the work is hard, rarely does anyone claim that it is any worse than the farm work that would occupy them "at home."

We move for the money

When analyzing the reasons given by these teenage boys and girls for their migration to work, the chance to make some money was almost universally identified as the single most significant motivating factor. This is not to say that money was the only factor—indeed, as will be seen below, acquiring social status, experiencing something beyond the village, or becoming socialized into responsible, economically active adulthood were all also important. Nonetheless, and in almost all our interviews, money was the most prominent explanation. This can be illustrated first with Jack's migration experience, as documented by Neil at the site of Abeokuta's quarries.

Jack

Jack was a 15-year-old boy from a village on the border between Za-Kpota *commune* and the *commune* of Bohicon in Benin. Neil interviewed him in Abeokuta at the site of his place of work. He was open, friendly, and confident. The encounter was very cheerful.

Jack came to Abeokuta in 2011 and needed to work in the quarries for another year, in order to complete the standard two-year contract. In return for his labor, he was to receive a motorbike at the end of his two years, which was the price agreed between him, his parents, and his *patron* (boss). On top of this, Jack also worked in his free time and "on his own account." He said that he was able to earn around 2,000 Naira (about US$12) every week by working overtime. His relationship with his boss was also very good and he claimed that he was not mistreated, never shouted at, and was well fed.

Jack was saving his money week-by-week and aiming to return to Benin in order to set himself up in a trade. When Neil asked him why he came to Nigeria, *he was very clear that his goal was to earn money.* Work here was much better than it was at home, he believed, because here he could earn a lot and also got to keep what he earned. *Though the work was hard, earning money made it all worthwhile.* Jack was also very clear that working on the family farm was much more physically demanding than in the gravel pits, even though the former was legal while the latter was not. He was strongly opposed to any laws forbidding young people such as him to migrate to Nigeria to work.

Though Jack is male and his experience as well as his motivations are influenced by the different gender norms that pertain to young males and females in Benin, Simona's research revealed strong parallels among the teenage girls she worked with. This was perhaps most clearly demonstrated by the money-centered narrative frequently recounted by the shelter girls she interviewed who had worked in domestic service. According to them, though they had been unlucky in their domestic placements, if you were a *formally salaried* young housemaid—a *bonne*—you were "made" and your conditions were to be envied, since your job would be "quantified" and that means that every month you can "touch" your own money (10,000–15,000 FCFA, equivalent to US$ 20–25).

Dantokpa's market girls were also highly attuned to the importance of pecuniary gain. All admitted loving the freedom that money offers in Cotonou and all were convinced that in town, even with a few coins, you can always get by—"If you can keep 25 francs, you've already found something to eat!" one would often hear them say. Moreover, when Simona quizzed them on their main reasons for being in the city and working in the market, all explicitly cited the desire to earn money as key. Often they would relate their dream of being able to buy a house for their mothers or for their parents, and to set themselves and their loved ones up in a better future.

What these data all point to, of course, is that money matters to these girls and boys, as it does to people everywhere where economic and social relations are mediated by cash, and in particular where that cash is hard to come by. For these young people, in contrast to the trafficking narrative, migrating is a means to access that which they need in order to advance their life projects.

Relationships and transitions

It is important to note, however, that though earning money underpins all labor migration, we should not see that labor migration simplistically in terms of one-dimensional, personal financial gain. Other factors are important—especially the desire to fulfill one's social responsibility by providing for one's family, or the desire to attain autonomy and social status.

In the anthropology of Southern Beninese societies, the importance of kinship relationships and social ties is understood as paramount. According to traditional educational practice, children belong to their lineage (Rabain, 1979) and they are therefore not socialized as individuals but as members of a larger group of relatives to whom they have collective responsibilities (Morganti, 2006). It is for this reason that child mobility and child participation in the family economy form natural parts of the socialization process. As such, it should come as no surprise that for many of the young labor migrants we interviewed, being able to send money home or "saving to put a roof on [your] father's house" were crucial motivations in their individual experience.

So too was the development of social capital. A high level of labor-related mobility is an integral part of young Beninese lives precisely because that mobility is a strategy that will allow the young both to maintain pre-existing social bonds (with families and with the village of origin) *and* to create new ones (with foster families, employers, patrons, clients, companions, etc.). As is the case in many poor societies, expanding personal networks in this fashion represents a way to overcome the risks and problems of economic isolation. Dantokpa's market girls are perfectly aware of this. In Simona's research, many stated that their staying in Cotonou and working with expert vendors would link their family and the agricultural products they produce with a much wider market.

Personal socio-cultural transitions not linked directly to economic factors are also important in the youth experience of labor migration in Benin (Imorou, 2008). Many of Simona's female interviewees cited the social freedom and emancipation that came from being in the city as of real importance to them. Consequently, though often they would lament the excessive instability related to their employment, few wished to give it up in order to return home before they had had their fill of city life. In cases of difficulty, most attempted to mobilize their urban social networks in order to find alternative employment instead (Jacquemin, 2012).

Neil's research with migrant boys in Abeokuta provided similar data. Central to young male calculations was the desire to attain respect and status. Indeed, one of the major motifs Neil heard when discussing with interviewees the value of labor migration was that, if the migrant were successful, this would allow him to become "considered." Being "considered" (or "known") in Southern Benin means being well thought of or respected as an important or successful person. It is an essential goal for many young males, and successful migration is a principal means of achieving it. Numerous interviewees thus explained that returning from Abeokuta with material goods such as a motorbike, clothes, or a generator represented visible evidence of an individual's success and thus constituted a material path to their being "considered" by those around them on their return.

Major implications

What are the major implications of the discussion outlined above? The first and most simple is of course that anti-trafficking discourse falls well short of accuracy.

As our data attest, the labor-related mobility of children and adolescents in Benin, even where it is abusive, remains a good deal more complex, nuanced, and socio-economically grounded than is suggested by the narrative captured in "Ana, Bazil et le Trafiquant." Instead of child trafficking, we would do better to focus on and discuss child and youth labor migration.

Second, if the disjuncture between discourse and reality is as severe as we suggest, it would imply that the policies designed to "protect" young Beninese people from trafficking are likely to be largely ineffective, if not at times outright counter-productive. Of course, this conclusion is somewhat intuitive—a policy that aims to fix a problem which does not exist is unlikely to achieve its intended results. This is a conclusion that is also supported by our empirical data.

The fundamental actions aimed at combating child trafficking in Benin are: prevention of any child mobility by the adoption of strict laws on child displacement; awareness-raising activities about the risks of migration and child work; detection, care and support of presumed victims; repatriation of presumed victims to their home villages (Howard, 2013). Nearly all anti-trafficking actions in Benin have followed this protocol for almost a decade. Our research suggests that this is futile.

To give only two examples, first, in Neil's case, work in Zou villages targeted with the anti-trafficking message that "migration is dangerous" or that "migration is trafficking" shows how little such messages are heeded. While most have heard them, very few take any notice whatsoever. This is precisely because people understand these messages to be based on false premises. Most often, therefore, migrants or those involved in their migration simply ignore attempts to dissuade or prevent their movement. As one teenager explained in a focus group discussion—"what they say goes in one ear and comes out the other."

At other times, people pretend to take on board the messages they hear, but only because doing so will see them avoid further reprimand (for example, if the message comes from a schoolteacher), or because it is believed that by pretending to play the game, they might be able to entice outsiders to bring rewards for their compliance. In this, the words of one interviewee were particularly telling:

Neil: Do you guys just pretend then [to the organizations trying to stop you moving]?

Artur: Yes, of course. We say "ok" in the hope that they'll bring something, but they bring nothing.

Neil: Wouldn't it be better to be honest and just tell them the truth that their message is useless?

Artur: Sometimes we do. But if we say that or tell them to go away and they don't come back, they will just speak far away on the radio and we will have no chance of getting anything from them.

Our second example is from Simona's research. From this, and in particular from the life stories recounted by girls in care shelters, we see how counterproductive and ultimately naive attempts to repatriate "trafficking victims" to their "home" villages are. After a few weeks in care, "rescued" girls are accompanied back to their villages and their parents are encouraged to put them in an apprenticeship or send them to school. Since most of the girls do not want to return to their village, however, do not consider themselves victims, and would prefer to continue their life in the city, these attempts are likely doomed to failure. The following extracts make this especially clear:

Sabine is about 13. She left her employer's house but she knows that there is no job for her in Abomey and her scars show that her biological mother can be violent too. She wants to remain in Cotonou where she hopes to find "someone better" to work for. She is adamant she will return.

Mama is about 14. She comes from Parakou and she is in Cotonou for her own business and for her mother's one. She had to work for free to receive some merchandise for her mother. She left her mother's creditor because she was a "bad woman" who always accused her, but she doesn't want to go back to the village "before finishing" in the city.

Francine is about 12. She has experienced more than three domestic placements. Her situation is very complicated but she is clear that she doesn't want to go back and stay with her father. She wants to stay with her grandmother in Porto Novo, to work as a housemaid and to start an apprenticeship.

For any migrant in Southern Benin, returning home before having successfully accomplished what he or she has set out to achieve means failure. Migrants, including these young ones, are unwilling to position themselves as victims who have failed, but rather see themselves as workers, in need of good or better work (Morganti, forthcoming). Are policies that seek to repatriate them really in their best interests? And will they manage to prevent the determined from migrating once again?

Conclusion

It is clear that anti-child trafficking discourse is overly simplistic. What is depicted as trafficking in Benin is, according to our research, very often nothing of the sort. Though some of those we have worked with can be considered victims of exploitation, very few would class themselves as anything other than young labor migrants, all working hard, some excessively so, but all moving and working in a social and economic context that values both their labor and their mobility. Until the official narrative is able to reflect this nuance, the policies to which it is related will fail to respond appropriately. It is high time for that to change.

Acknowledgments

Neil Howard thanks Bridget Anderson and Jo Boyden for their supervision and the Economic and Social Research Council for its financial assistance.

Simona Morganti thanks Fabio Viti for his supervision and the Ethnological Mission in Benin and West Africa (MEBAO) for its financial support.

References

Aide et Action (2005). *La problématique des "vidomègons" et du trafic des enfants au Bénin: Regard sur une pratique sociale pervertie*. Cotonou: Aide et Action.

Alber, E. (2011). Child trafficking in West Africa, in Gonzalez, A. M. et al. (Eds.), *Frontiers of globalization: Kinship and family structure in Africa*. London: Africa World Press, pp. 71–93.

Castle, S., and Diarra. A. (2003). The international migration of young Malians: Tradition, necessity, or rite of passage? *Research Report*. London: School of Hygiene and Tropical Medicine.

De Lange, A. (2007). Child labour migration and trafficking in rural Burkina Faso. *International Migration*, 45(2), 147–167.

Feneyrol and Fondation Terre des Hommes (TdH) (2005). *Les petites mains des carrières: Enquête sur un trafic d'enfant entre le Bénin et le Nigéria*. Lausanne: Terre des Hommes.

Hashim, I. M. (2003). Child migration: Pathological or positive? Paper presented at the International Workshop on Migration and Poverty in West Africa. Brighton: University of Sussex.

Hashim, I., and Thorsen, D. (2011). *Child migration in Africa*. Uppsala: The Nordic Africa Institute and London: Zed Books.

Howard, N. P. (2011). Is "child placement" trafficking? Questioning the validity of an accepted discourse. *Anthropology Today, 27*(6), 3–8.

Howard, N. P. (2012). An overview of anti-child trafficking discourse and policy in Southern Benin. *Childhood, 20*(2), 554–558.

Howard, N. P. (2013). Promoting "healthy childhoods" and keeping children "at home": Beninese anti-trafficking policy in times of neoliberalism. *International Migration, 51*(4), 87–102.

Huijsmans, R., and Baker, S. (2012). Child trafficking: "Worst form" of child labor, or worst approach to young migrants? *Development & Change, 43*(4), 919–946.

Imorou, A.-B. (2008). *Le coton et la mobilité: Les implications d'une culture de rente sur les trajectoires sociales des jeunes et enfants au Nord-Bénin*. Cotonou: Plan, TdH, Lasdel-Benin.

Jacquemin, M. (2012). *Petites bonnes' d'Abidjan. Sociologie des filles en service domestique*. Paris: L'Harmattan.

Morganti, S. (2006). Il bambino comunitario. Pratiche di socializzazione infantile nel Sud Bénin, in Viti, F. (Ed.), *Antropologia dei rapporti di dipendenza personale*. Modena: Il Fiorino, pp. 105–139.

Morganti, S. (2007). Il lavoro dei bambini in Bénin, in Solinas, P. G. (Ed.), *La vita in prestito: debito, lavoro, dipendenza*. Lecce: Argo, pp. 75–104.

Morganti, S. (2008). *Bambini dell'altro mondo. Rituali, mobilità e lavoro nell'infanzia del Bēnin meridionale*. Tesi per il conseguimento del titolo di Dottore di Ricerca in Scienze del Linguaggio e della Cultura, ind. Antropologia e Storia del Mondo Moderno e Con-temporaneo, Università di Modena e Reggio Emilia.

Morganti, S. (2011). La mobilità dei minori in Benin. Migrazione o tratta? in Bellagamba, A. (Ed.), *Migrazioni. Dal lato dell'Africa*. Padova: Edizioni Altravista, pp. 127–156.

Morganti S. (Forthcoming). Victims of what? The misunderstandings of anti-trafficking child protection policies in Benin, in Hopkins, L., & Sriprakash, A. (Eds.), *The "poor child": The cultural politics of education, development and childhood*. London: Routledge.

O'Connell Davidson, J. (2011). Moving children? Child trafficking, child migration, and child rights. *Critical Social Policy*, *31*(3), 454–477.

O'Connell Davidson, J., and Farrow, C. (2007). *Child migration and the construction of vulnerability*. Gothenburg: Save the Children Sweden.

Rabain, J. (1979). *L'enfant du lignage. Du sevrage à la classe d'âge chez les Wolof du Sénégal*. Paris: Payot.

Stella, A. (1996). Pour une histoire de l'enfant exploité, in Schlemmer, B. (Ed.), *L'enfant exploité. Oppression, mise au travail, prolétarisation*. Paris: Karthala, pp. 31–48.

Thorsen, D. (2007). "If only I get enough money for a bicycle!" A study of child migration against a backdrop of exploitation and trafficking in Burkina Faso. *Occasional Paper*. Centre for African Studies, University of Copenhagen.

Whitehead, A., Hashim, I. M., and Iversen, V. (2007). Child migration, child agency and inter-generational relations in Africa and South Asia. *Working Paper T24, Working Paper Series*, Migration DRC, University of Sussex.

Discussion questions

1. According to Howard and Morganti, how do their findings contradict dominant dis-courses about trafficking?
2. Based on the chapter, what are some of the unintended outcomes of laws and policies intended to protect vulnerable groups?
3. According to the chapter, what are the misunderstandings of the ways in which young people migrate for work in Benin? How are these important to debates about traffick-ing policy?
4. What factors should policymakers take into account when devising anti-trafficking policies in Benin and elsewhere?
5. Why might anti-trafficking measures not serve the interests of those they are intended to protect?

Additional resources

See *Ana, Bazil et le Trafiquant* here: http://www.dailymotion.com/video/xeekps_anna-bazil-et-le-trafiquant_shortfilms

United Nations Office on Drugs and Crime (UNODC) report Measures to Combat Traffick-ing in Human Beings in Benin, Nigeria and Togo
http://www.unodc.org/documents/human-trafficking/ht_research_report_nigeria.pdf

Chapter 8

Bride traffic

Trafficking for marriage to Australia*

Kelly Richards and Samantha Lyneham

Introduction

Little empirical research has been undertaken on victim/survivors of human trafficking: "the vast majority of academic scholarship addresses trafficking at the legal, policy, or theoretical level" (Bosworth et al., 2011, p. 771). This is largely unsurprising, given that:

- human trafficking is a clandestine crime (Busch-Armendariz et al., 2009; Schloenhardt et al., 2009; United Nations Office on Drugs and Crime [UNODC], 2012);
- people meeting the legal definition of trafficking survivor or victim may not see themselves as having been trafficked (Surtees, 2008b, 2007);
- people who are trafficked to foreign countries may not be able to communicate in the local language well enough to report offenses against them (Richards & Lyneham, 2014);
- people who have been trafficked may mistrust police or other authorities, impeding reporting (Lyneham & Richards, 2014; Richards & Lyneham, 2014);
- people who have been trafficked may fear retaliation against themselves and their families, may fear deportation, may not understand the legal system of the country they were trafficked to, and/or may lack knowledge of available services (Clawson et al., 2003; Lyneham & Richards, 2014; Richards & Lyneham, 2014);
- people who have been trafficked may be misrecognized (for example, as victims of labor law breaches [David, 2010] or as victims of domestic violence [Richards & Lyneham, 2014]); and
- people who are trafficked may be repatriated (Schloenhardt et al., 2009) before being formally identified as victim/survivors of human trafficking.

Other research difficulties stem from deep political divisions in the field and a lack of existing collaborative relationships between academics and practitioners in this area. Bosworth et al.'s (2011) attempts to recruit people who had been trafficked for a study of sex trafficking in the United Kingdom were thwarted by what they perceived as a lack of "buy in" from the relevant gatekeepers, gatekeepers' concerns about the victim/survivors being retraumatized, and a lack of faith on the part of both gatekeepers and potential participants in the capacity of academic research to make a positive difference.

This chapter reports on what is, to our knowledge, the first empirical study of people who have been trafficked in Australia.

The Australian legal and policy context

In Australia, human trafficking, slavery, and slavery-like offenses are prohibited under Divisions 270 and 271 of the Commonwealth *Criminal Code 1995*. This legislation fulfills Australia's obligations under the United Nations Trafficking Protocol by criminalizing:

> recruiting, harbouring, receiving, concealing or transporting a victim using coercion (including psychological oppression, the abuse of power or a person's vulnerability), threat or deception, or by being reckless as to the exploitation of the victim, for the purpose of slavery, slavery-like conditions, servitude (domestic and sexual), forced labor, forced marriage, organ removal and debt bondage.

This definition is applied by the Australian Federal Police to identify victim/survivors of human trafficking who may then be referred to the Australian Government's Support for Trafficked People Program.

The study

The study discussed in this chapter was conducted by the Australian Institute of Criminology (see Lyneham & Richards, 2014; Richards & Lyneham, 2014). It explored the role of partner migration in human trafficking into Australia. A number of factors prompted the research. First, concerns were raised in both the Australian and international research literature that identified partner migration as an area requiring investigation (Attorney-General's Department, 2010; International Centre for Criminal Law Reform and Criminal Justice Policy [ICCLR], 2011; Schloenhardt & Jolly, 2010). Second, stakeholders working with people who had been trafficked presented anecdotal evidence that partner migration had been used to move women into Australia. For example, Australian Catholic Religious Against Trafficking in Humans (ACRATH, 2011) raised concerns in a submission to the Australian government about women coming to Australia and finding themselves "trapped in slave-like sham marriages" (p. 1). Third, research undertaken outside of Australia demonstrated that partner migration had been used to facilitate human trafficking into other "destination" countries, including the U.S.A (Hughes et al., 2007), Europe (Surtees, 2008a, 2007), and Asia (Dinan, 2002). Finally, a small number of media articles (e.g. Hand, 2010) and legal proceedings demonstrated that partner migration had been used to bring women into Australia for exploitative purposes. For example, in the case of *R v Kovacs* [2008] QCA 417, Queensland couple Zoltan and Melita Kovacs were found guilty of "slavery offences" under s. 270.3(1) of the Commonwealth *Criminal Code 1995* after they arranged for an Australian citizen to marry a woman in the Philippines with the intention of bringing her to Australia to work in their takeaway shop and in their home (Anti-People Trafficking Interdepartmental Committee, 2011; David, 2010; Schloenhardt & Jolly, 2010). As Schloenhardt and Jolly (2010) argue, the case of *R v Kovacs* highlights "how the institution of marriage can be used to facilitate [human trafficking]" (pp. 671–672). In order to explore the role of partner migration in human trafficking into Australia, the study included:

- a review of documentary material on identified cases of human trafficking involving partner migration contained in the United Nations Office on Drugs and Crime's (UNODC) international human trafficking case law database and the University of Queensland's case reports on human trafficking in Australia;
- qualitative interviews with key stakeholders from relevant government, non-government, law enforcement and victim support agencies (n = 17);
- analysis of the case files of women identified as victim/survivors of human trafficking involving partner migration or of similar exploitative scenarios related to partner migration (n = 8); and
- in-depth qualitative interviews with these victim/survivors (n = 8).

In summary, the study found that, in line with stakeholders' concerns, the partner migration system had been used to traffic women into Australia to be exploited in slave-like marriages, as domestic servants, and to provide private and commercial sexual services.

While the exploitation associated with human trafficking is commonly dichotomized as "labor" and "sex" exploitation, this study revealed that the experiences of victim/survivors cannot easily be categorized according to these descriptors. Instead, cases of human trafficking involving marriage in this study represented a different category, in which the "exploitation" involved the very personhood of the victim/survivor:

- their labor (domestic servitude, forced commercial labor, or both);
- their body (private and/or commercial sexual servitude, lack of control over childbearing); and
- their self (loss of personal freedom, psychological bondage).

The victim/survivors immigrated and entered their exploitative marriages through diverse circumstances underpinned by the desire to travel, to start a family, and to escape war. Women sought partners through online matchmaking websites, chose to honor an arranged marriage, or met their spouse serendipitously. The women, therefore, consented to marriage and migration. However, the women's consent was negated by the means by which it was obtained, namely through deception about their husband's character, occupation, financial circumstances, living conditions, existing intimate relationships, the nature of their relationship and what would be expected of them once in Australia.

Box 8.1 United Nations Office on Drugs and Crime (UNODC) Human Trafficking Case Law Database

The United Nations Office on Drugs and Crime (UNODC) Human Trafficking Case Law Database contains approximately 1,000 case briefs from 80 countries. Cases included in the Database contain "all the three constituent elements of the internationally agreed upon definition of trafficking in persons," even though the case may not have been prosecuted under trafficking-specific national legislation. The three constituent elements of trafficking in persons are **the act** (what is done), **the means** (how it is done) and the **purpose of exploitation** (why it is done) (http://www.unodc.org/cld/en/about/faq.html). The Database is searchable by keyword and is constantly expanding to include more cases. It is the largest database of trafficking legal cases in the world.

For further information:

http://www.unodc.org/cld/index.jspx

The post-migration experiences of the victim/survivors involved a number of human trafficking indicators (see ILO, 2009), such as assertions of ownership, debt bondage, domestic servitude, restricted movement, threat of deportation, commercial and/or domestic labor exploitation, sexual exploitation, and confiscation of passports. For example, the following extracts taken from victim/survivor testimonies demonstrate the nature and extent of the exploitation:

> [My husband said] "You must iron my clothes and make my food whenever I like and whatever I like . . . You must care for me . . . You are here to do the housework. I brought you to give me money and help me in the house. If you don't do those things I will send you back. Otherwise it's no use keeping you here."

> When I arrived in Australia, my husband and I never shared the same bedroom. There was a room for me to stay in. My husband and his girlfriend left to stay at their own place . . . They only came over when they needed something . . . There were 16 people living in the house . . . My life was like a slave . . . there was always work to do in the house. My mother-in-law was always with me . . . I hardly ever got any rest or break during the day.

If I wanted to go [outside the house and to the city] I had to go with his mother or his sisters or him. They thought that maybe I would get in contact with my parents to tell them what was going on. They didn't want my parents or my family involved because they wanted to keep me under control.

Importantly, the cases examined for the study do not simply reflect instances of domestic violence against migrant women. The exploitation experienced by some of the victim/survivors amounts to servitude (i.e. a slavery-like offence), with the women variously reporting being denied freedom of movement and liberty, being forced to provide sexual and domestic services, and having few genuine opportunities to escape. Further, it appears that the perpetrators of the women's exploitation intended to deceive the women into migrating in order to exploit them.

To exit their exploitative situations, victim/survivors pursued a diverse range of formal and informal avenues, and combinations of these. Most commonly, victim/survivors sought assistance from family members, neighbors and friends, as well as local community centers. None of the victim/survivors was detected by formal authorities, such as police and immigration officials, and few victim/survivors sought assistance from these sources. The majority of victim/survivors were identified as victims of domestic violence, and were therefore offered support and legal remedies appropriate for cases of domestic violence, rather than specialist support and legal provisions related to human trafficking.

Box 8.2 Operational indicators of trafficking in human beings

The European Commission and International Labour Office collaborated to develop a set of operational indicators for trafficking based on consultation with a group of experts "from the 27 EU Member States from police, government, academic and research institutes, NGOs, international organisations, labour inspectorates, trade unions and judiciaries" using an approach called the Delphi method.

The group developed four sets of indicators for adult and child victims of labor and sexual exploitation. The indicators are:

Deceptive recruitment
Coercive recruitment
Recruitment by abuse of vulnerability
Exploitative conditions of work
Coercion at destination
Abuse of vulnerability at destination

and include strong, medium, and weak indicators. This set of indicators is the most robust effort to coordinate data collection and case categorization and investigation to date.

For further information:

http://www.ilo.org/wcmsp5/groups/public/@ed_norm/@declaration/
documents/publication/wcms_105023.pdf

The empirical data collected in our study challenges a number of prevailing misperceptions about human trafficking and add to the emerging body of literature that critiques these misperceptions. The aim of this chapter is therefore to use the data collected from victim/survivors to further critique and/or destabilize some of these assumptions. Specifically, it critically examines the following misperceptions:

- that human trafficking perpetrators are primarily motivated by economic profit;
- that human trafficking victim/survivors are primarily vulnerable to being trafficked due to socio-economic "desperation"; and
- that human trafficking is a type of organized crime.

This type of exercise is important, because the ways in which we understand, define and construct human trafficking influence the ways in which attempts are made to prevent and/or respond to this type of crime. As Schofield et al. (2011) argue—drawing on the work of Bacchi—"the ways in which policy problems are 'represented to be' shapes the types and adequacy of policy actions, including service and program development, to address them" (p. 393).

Assumption 1: That human trafficking perpetrators are primarily motivated by economic profit.

That trafficking perpetrators are motivated solely or primarily by profit is widely accepted in the international scholarship on this crime. For example, Bales (2012) claims that "if slavery stops being profitable, there is little motivation to enslave" (p. 33). A report by the Organization for Security and Co-operation in Europe (Aronowitz et al., 2009) similarly claims that "the expression 'Trafficking pays!' is an apt statement of the *raison d'être* behind all criminal networks and those facilitating this heinous crime" (p. 7), and that "human trafficking is a particularly lucrative business" (p. 25). Even Europol (2007) baldly states that "trafficking in human beings is driven by profit" (p. 2; see also Simmons et al., 2013).

Our exploratory primary research into human trafficking involving partner migration into Australia suggests that this is a limited and potentially unhelpful view. This is not to suggest that profit was not among the motivations of perpetrators who used the partner migration scheme to traffic women. In some cases, it clearly was. For example, in the case of *R v FAS* (*R v Foad Ali Solaiman* [2008] NSWDC 53), in which an Egyptian-born woman came to Australia via an arranged marriage and was then forced into sex work by her husband, economic profit was clearly a motivating factor. The judge ruled that the victim was procured for the purpose of prostitution by threat, and in making his decision accepted "that the offender insisted that she work in the brothel as a means of earning money" and that "she did not have those funds for her own use but rather they seemed to be for either the offender's use or for onward transmission to his family in Egypt" (*R v Foad Ali Solaiman* [2008] NSWDC 53 [80]). For two of the victim/survivors we interviewed, profit also seemed to be among the motivating factors of the men who sponsored them to enter Australia. One woman said that her husband saw her as a "golden egg" and that it appeared in hindsight that he married her to "improve his economic situation." She said:

> When we went to my brother's factory [in my home country] his eyes became very bright like he saw something golden, he was hunting for gold. But when you have desire you can close your eyes to things like that.

Another victim/survivor we interviewed had saved $6,000 in her local currency after years of hard work and saving, only to lose it to her husband after he repeatedly insisted she "loan" it to him.

Profit is therefore clearly among perpetrators' motivations for trafficking women into Australia; somewhat surprisingly, our research shows that this is even the case when the women are trafficked into the domestic sphere, rather than into the sex industry or other industry. To reduce perpetrators' motivations to profit alone, however, is a limited view, and obscures important information about trafficking involving partner migration that is relevant to preventing and responding to this particular manifestation of human trafficking. This approach marginalizes the far more complex and multi-faceted motivations—such as power and control—and the broader underpinnings of these motivations—such as gender and culture—that these trafficking scenarios suggest.

In other words, factors other than monetary gain must be taken into account in the design of prevention measures for trafficking. However, a number of recent anti-trafficking strategies have been premised on the assumption that human trafficking is primarily driven by greed. The "Be Careful What You Pay For" campaign, recently launched in Australia, is a good example. The authors of this trafficking prevention strategy describe this campaign as follows:

> [The campaign is] based on the premise that trafficking in persons is a crime that is demand driven . . . perpetrators engage in trafficking in persons with

profit as their primary goal. This campaign aims to convey the message that consumer decisions are the principal factor determining the extent of trafficking in persons in Australia.

(Schloenhardt, Astill-Torchia, & Jolly, 2012, pp. 430–431)

Aronowitz et al. (2009) similarly recommend that human trafficking be prevented by viewing the crime as a business model, and "considering the demand, costs, risks, revenues, and profit margins and . . . remov[ing] a powerful incentive and disrupt[ing] the trade" (p. 9).

We argue that while prevention initiatives that construct offenders as profit-driven and therefore target consumer decision-making are undoubtedly an important component of the fight against human trafficking, they should not comprise the whole effort. Reducing the motivations of a perpetrator who has recruited a domestic and sexual servant to profit alone simplifies the complex interplay of factors that appear to drive these offenders, and anti-trafficking strategies premised on this construction of offenders would bypass those perpetrators who traffic women into domestic and sexual servitude in private residences.

Assumption 2: That human trafficking victim/survivors are primarily vulnerable to being trafficked due to socio-economic "desperation."

The notion that people become vulnerable to being trafficked primarily due to economic desperation is often repeated in the trafficking literature. Bosworth et al. (2011), for example, claim that "these women . . . may well have suffered considerable economic privations. They are unlikely to have received much formal education . . . the victims came from desperate circumstances in their countries of origin" (p. 774). Bales (2012) similarly argues that "being poor, homeless, a refugee, or abandoned can all lead to the desperation that opens the door to slavery" (p. 32).

Certainly, it is the case that, as Gallagher (2004) argues, "trafficking, like all other forms of irregular and/or exploitative migration, generally involves movement from poorer countries to relatively wealth[y] ones" (p. 9). Further, what Iredale (1995) refers to as "inter-cultural" marriages—those between Western males and women of different ethnic backgrounds (as opposed to intra-cultural marriages, that is those between Western men and women from the man's "home country" [Iredale 1995])—usually occur between men from economically developed countries and women from economically unstable countries (Lan, 2003; Quek, 2010).

A key finding of our study, however, is that women's decisions and motivations to migrate for marriage are far more complex, multi-faceted and, indeed, often more serendipitous than this stereotype allows. While the women in our study came to Australia from poorer countries, these were by no means the poorest countries in the world; nor were the women in most cases among the poorest in their home countries. Many of the women were educated and employed, and as described above, in two instances, women were seemingly targeted for their wealth or ability to work outside the home and earn an income for their husbands. Other victim/ survivors identified corruption, war, and/or the difficulty of succeeding in their home country as influencing their decisions to migrate. While none of the women reported a desire to come to Australia specifically, Australia was described by the women as a place of opportunity, where effort is rewarded. While the women's motivations to migrate to Australia for marriage often included economic motivations, their decision-making processes were much more nuanced and complex than the construction of foreign brides as "desperate" and "poor" suggests.

Further, few of the other women interviewed for our study had specifically sought to find a spouse. Instead, they entered into partnerships with Australian men following chance meetings. For example, one woman married her Australian husband after he saw her in the funeral video of a mutual friend and pursued a long-distance relationship with her, including traveling to her home country to visit. A chance occurrence also resulted in another woman migrating to Australia for marriage when the woman's brother met a man holidaying in their home country in the course of his work as a taxi driver. The woman's brother introduced her to the man, who was from the same cultural background, and the pair married after a long-distance courtship.

Our findings therefore suggest that the construction of migrant brides as motivated primarily by economic desperation is limited and potentially problematic. The study supports the existing work of Constable (2006, 2003), whose research on international marriages found that non-material factors, such as the desire to be married, love, compatibility, and family expectations, can motivate women to seek foreign marriage partners. It also supports the work of Surtees (2007), whose research found that "while many victims originated from 'poor' and 'very poor' economic backgrounds, a striking number of victims also originated from 'average' or 'well-off' families" (p. 40).

This is not to say that economic disparities between developing and developed countries do not influence women's decisions to migrate, but it demonstrates that their decision-making processes are more complex than this. In contrast with Europol's (2007) claim that "victims will inevitably come from countries and regions which are subjected to economic hardship" (p. 2)—a view that also denies the possibility of domestic human trafficking—our study found that women's motivations are influenced by both structural and individual factors.

As the UNODC (2010) puts it:

> There are many factors that can render a source country vulnerable to human trafficking, the most commonly cited of which is poverty. But there are many poor countries that do not seem to produce large numbers of trafficking victims, so poverty alone is not enough to explain this phenomenon.
>
> (p. 41)

Recognizing this complexity is important because assuming that women's motivations are purely or primarily economic fosters a particular construction of victim/ survivors of human trafficking that legitimizes particular prevention and response strategies, which may be limited in their relevance and efficacy. As Vijeyarasa (2010) argues, "if we accord inadequate attention to the decision-making of the victim, we fall short of an in-depth exploration of the socio-economic vulnerabilities that often push potential migrants to engage in unsafe and risky migration where there are barriers to legal migration abroad" (p. 218). We would add to this that an in-depth exploration of factors other than socio-economic vulnerabilities (including individual factors) is vital also.

Assumption 3: That human trafficking is a type of organized crime.

Until recently, another widely accepted belief about human trafficking was that it was a type of "organized crime" and perpetrated by "organized criminal groups" (Goździak & Bump, 2008). For example, Europol (2007) claim that "[human] traffickers . . . are mainly professional and organised criminals" (p. 2). Internationally, the Trafficking Protocol is underpinned by the *United Nations Convention on Transnational and Organized Crime*. In Australia, the Australian Crime Commission has a mandate to respond to serious and organized crime, including human trafficking (Australian Crime Commission, 2011), and the Australian Institute of Criminology's formerly named "transnational and organized crime" team implements the Australian government-funded human trafficking research program. As Goździak and Bump (2008) state, therefore, "the notion that human trafficking and organized crime are closely related is widespread" (p. 46).

Under the *United Nations Convention on Transnational and Organized Crime*, an "organized criminal group" is defined as:

> A structured group of three or more persons, existing for a period of time and acting in concert with the aim of committing one or more serious crimes or offences established in accordance with this Convention, in order to obtain, directly or indirectly, a financial or other material benefit.

The cases examined in our study—both of the eight women we interviewed and those of which the details have been made publicly available—were not perpetrated by organized criminal groups, according to this definition. Rather, they were perpetrated on an *ad hoc* basis by individuals and families. While the literature clearly demonstrates that human trafficking can be and has been undertaken by organized criminal groups (see Aronowitz et al., 2009), our study indicates that, in line with recent scholarship on this issue, the level of organization of human trafficking varies considerably. David's (2012) review of the global evidence about human trafficking and organized crime found that "[the level of organisation varies, from offences] perpetrated either by solo offenders . . . and/or relatively unsophisticated, apparently opportunistic small-scale offenders . . . [to] . . . more enduring groups or networks much closer in nature to 'organised crime'" (p. 7).

Drawing on the existing literature and prosecuted cases of human trafficking (n = 46), Busch-Armendariz et al. (2009) similarly found that the level of organization of human trafficking cases varies substantially. Busch-Armendariz et al. (2009) identified four perpetrator typologies:

- "Mom and Pop" (domestic servitude);
- "Shattering the American dream" (forced labor);
- "The minor pimp" (domestic sex trafficking); and
- "Johns' demand" (international sex trafficking).

The cases of human trafficking involving partner migration in our study most closely align with the "Mom and Pop" perpetrator typology, in which "operations are generally small, involving only a single victim at a given time, although the duration of the victimization can be lengthy" (Busch-Armendariz et al., 2009, p. 19).

Importantly, however, law enforcement stakeholders interviewed for the study raised concerns that organized crime groups have used sham marriages to keep human trafficking victim/survivors in Australia to continue their exploitation in the sex industry. This further highlights the "incredible diversity in the organisation of [human trafficking] offending, even within single markets or geographic areas" (David, 2012, p. 7).

Recognizing that human trafficking offenses occur along a spectrum from *ad hoc*, small-scale "Mom and Pop" operations to operations that might best be understood as "organized criminal groups" is important if this complex crime, in all its guises, is to be effectively prevented and responded to.

Conclusion

Drawing on an exploratory primary research study of human trafficking involving partner migration in Australia, this chapter has sought to critically examine a number of prevailing misperceptions about human trafficking, and to contribute towards the emerging body of empirical analyses that seek to inform evidence-based initiatives that aim to combat it. We have argued here that the data collected for our study indicates that the assumptions that perpetrators are profit-driven, that victim/survivors are motivated by economic desperation, and that human trafficking is a type of organized crime should be reconsidered.

Two key points emerge from this analysis that are worthy of further consideration. First, it is vital that the diversity of human trafficking crimes is recognized in the international scholarship on this topic. As this chapter has sought to highlight, the motivations of perpetrators are highly varied, as are the vulnerabilities of victim/survivors. Further, human trafficking offences occur along a spectrum from highly organized to small-scale, *ad hoc* operations. Despite this, the international body of human trafficking literature often seeks to reduce the complexities of this crime to pithy generalizations (such as that all perpetrators are motivated by profit). Given the vast body of literature on human trafficking, and the numerous and complex manifestations of this crime, it is easy to see why this approach is appealing to those attempting to make sense of this issue and/or contribute towards anti-trafficking efforts. Nonetheless, this chapter cautions against this approach, and highlights instead the importance of challenging generalizations, as these may inform prevention and response strategies that are irrelevant and/or ineffective.

Second, our study suggests that while human trafficking is usually categorized as either "labor trafficking" or "sex trafficking" (Schofield et al., 2011), this categorization is problematic. While scholars have previously argued that the dichotomy of "sex" versus "labor" is false if we accept that sex work is labor (see e.g. David, 2010), this conceptualization is perhaps most problematic because it marginalizes trafficking that occurs in the domestic sphere. According to this taxonomy, "sex traffickers" profit by exploiting their victims as sex workers, and "labor traffickers" profit by exploiting the cheap (or free) labor of their victims in commercial industries other than the sex industry. Our study highlights, however, the importance of considering including domestic servitude in anti-trafficking efforts, as Goździak and Bump (2008) have done. Categorizing the experiences of our study participants as "labor trafficking" reduces their experiences to one aspect of the exploitation they endured (the exploitation of their labor in the home), and ignores the exploitation that occurred as a corollary of the exploitation of the victim's labor (such as sexual violence and a lack of freedom of movement). Categorizing domestic servitude within an intimate relationship as labor trafficking is therefore problematic as it silences aspects of the victim/survivors' experiences that are likely to have been far more traumatic than the exploitation of their labor in the home.

It is important to recognize the many different motivations for human trafficking and other forms of exploitation. While commercial labor enterprises exist specifically and explicitly to make profit, the same cannot be said for private residences. The motivations of those who exploit women in the domestic sphere and those who traffic victims into the commercial sphere are likely to be discrete (although they may overlap, as the case of *R v Kovacs* [*R v Kovacs* (2008) QCA 417] demonstrates). Further, avenues of escape and/or redress available to victims of human trafficking outside of the domestic sphere are vastly different from those available to victims trafficked into domestic servitude. Victims of labor trafficking often work alongside others, sometimes on large-scale projects or for large companies, which are in some circumstances subject to regulatory oversight (e.g. unions; see e.g. David, 2010). In contrast, people exploited in domestic servitude are often isolated, forbidden contact with others, and not subject to any mode of external regulation such as industrial relations oversight. It is important that these differences are taken into account if anti-trafficking initiatives are to be successful.

Note

* This chapter contains revised sections from the report previously published as Lyneham, S., & Richards, K. (2014). Human trafficking involving marriage and partner migration to Australia. *Research and Public Policy Series no. 142*. Canberra, ACT: Australian Institute of Criminology.

References

Anti-People Trafficking Interdepartmental Committee (2011). *Human trafficking: The Australian Government response, 1 July 2010–30 June 2011*. Retrieved on July 29, 2014 from http://www.ag.gov.au/Peopletrafficking/Documents/Trafficking+in+Persons.pdf

Aronowitz, A., Theuermann, G., & Tyurykanova, E. (2009). *Analysing the business model of trafficking in human beings to better prevent the crime*. Vienna: Office of the Special Representative and Co-ordinator for Combating Trafficking in Human Beings.

Attorney-General's Department (2010). *Discussion paper: Forced and servile marriage*. Canberra, ACT: Attorney-General's Department. Retrieved on July 29, 2014 from http://www.ag.gov.au/Documents/Discussion%20Paper%20for%20Public%20Release%20-%20forced%20and%20servile%20marriage.pdf

Australian Catholic Religious Against Trafficking in Humans (2011). *Submission: Sham, forced and servile marriages*. Melbourne, Vic: ACRATH. Retrieved on July 29, 2014 from http://acrath.org.au/wp-content/uploads/2011/04/Sham-Forced-Servile-marriages-1-24-Feb-2011-2.pdf

Australian Crime Commission (2011). *Organised crime in Australia*. Canberra, ACT: ACC.

Bales, K. (2012). *Disposable people: New slavery in the global economy*. Berkeley, CA: University of California Press.

Bosworth, M., Hoyle, C., & Dempsey, M. (2011). Researching trafficked women: On institutional resistance and the limits to feminist reflexivity. *Qualitative Inquiry, 17*(9), 769–779.

Busch-Armendariz, N.B., Nsonwu, M.B., Heffron, L.C., Garza, J., & Hernandez, M. (2009). *Understanding human trafficking: Development of typologies of traffickers*. Austin, TX: University of Texas. Retrieved on July 29, 2014 from http://www.utexas.edu/ssw/dl/files/cswr/institutes/idvsa/publications/humantrafficking.pdf

Clawson, H.J., Small, K.M., Go, E.S., & Myles, B.W. (2003). *Needs assessment for service providers and trafficking victims*. National Criminal Justice Reference Service. Retrieved on July 29, 2014 from https://www.ncjrs.gov/pdffiles1/nij/grants/202469.pdf

Constable, N. (2003). *Romance on a global stage: Pen pals, virtual ethnography, and "mail-order" marriages*. Berkeley, CA: University of California Press.

— (2006). Brides, maids, and prostitutes: reflections on the study of "trafficked" women. *Portal Journal of Multidisciplinary International Studies, 3*(2). Retrieved on July 29, 2014 from http://epress.lib.uts.edu.au/journals/index.php/portal/article/view/164/274

David, F. (2010). Labour trafficking. *Research and public policy series no. 108*. Canberra, ACT: Australian Institute of Criminology. Retrieved on July 29, 2014 from http://www.aic.gov.au/publications/current%20series/rpp/100–120/rpp108.aspx

— (2012). Organised crime and trafficking in persons. *Trends & issues in crime and criminal justice no. 436*. Canberra, ACT: Australian Institute of Criminology. Retrieved on July 29, 2014 from http://www.aic.gov.au/publications/current%20series/tandi/421-440/tandi436.html

Dinan, K. (2002). Migrant Thai women subjected to slavery-like abuses in Japan. *Violence Against Women, 8*(9), 1113–1139.

Europol (2007). *Trafficking human beings in the European Union: A Europol perspective.* Hague: Europol.

Gallagher, A. (2004). Strengthening national responses to the crime of trafficking: Obstacles, responsibilities and opportunities. *Development Bulletin, 66*(December), 8–12.

Goździak, E., & Bump, M. (2008). *Data and research on human trafficking: Bibliography of research-based literature.* Washington, DC: Institute for the study of international migration, Georgetown University.

Hand, J. (2010). I feel like I was used as a slave, woman says. *The Canberra Times,* April 3, 13.

Hughes, D., Chon, K., & Ellerman, D. (2007). Modern-day comfort women: The U.S. military, transnational crime, and the trafficking of women. *Violence Against Women, 13*(9), 901–922.

International Centre for Criminal Law Reform and Criminal Justice Policy (ICCLR) (2011). *Towards human trafficking prevention: National and international expert group meetings.* Report to International Expert Group Meeting on Human Trafficking Prevention, Montreal, March 21–22.

International Labour Organization (2009). *Operational indicators of trafficking in human beings. Results from a Delphi survey implemented by the ILO and the European Commission.* Geneva: ILO. Retrieved on July 29, 2014 from http://www.ilo.org/wcmsp5/groups/public---ed_norm---declaration/documents/publication/wcms_105023.pdf

Iredale, R. (1995). Serial sponsorship: Immigration policy and human rights. *Just Policy, 3,* 37–43.

Lan, P. (2003). Maid or madam? Filipina migrant workers and the continuity of domestic work. *Gender & Society, 17*(2), 187–208.

Lyneham, S., & Richards, K. (2014). *Human trafficking involving marriage and partner migration to Australia.* Canberra, ACT: Australian Institute of Criminology.

Quek, K. (2010). *Empowering the consumer and buying a wife online: Mail-order bride websites and the commodification of women.* Paper presented to the Australian Political Studies Association Conference, University of Melbourne, September 27–29. Retrieved on July 29, 2014 from http://apsa2010.com.au/full-papers/pdf/APSA2010_0099.pdf

Richards, K., & Lyneham, S. (2014). Help-seeking strategies of victim/survivors of human trafficking involving partner migration. *Trends & Issues in Crime and Criminal Justice.* Canberra, ACT: Australian Institute of Criminology.

Schloenhardt, A., & Jolly, J. (2010). Honeymoon from hell: Human trafficking and domestic servitude in Australia. *Sydney Law Review, 32*(4), 671–692.

Schloenhardt, A., Bierne, G., & Corsbie, T. (2009). Human trafficking and sexual servitude in Australia. *University of New South Wales Law Journal, 32*(1), 27–49.

Schloenhardt, A., Astill-Torchia, P., & Jolly, J. (2012). Be careful what you pay for: Awareness raising on trafficking in persons. *Washington University Global Studies Law Review, 11*(2), 415–435. Retrieved on July 29, 2014 from http://digitalcommons.law.wustl.edu/globalstudies/vol11/iss2/4

Schofield, T., Hepworth, J., Jones, M., & Schofield, E. (2011). Health and community services for trafficked women: An exploratory study of policy and practice. *Australian Journal of Social Issues, 46*(4), 391–410.

Simmons, F., O'Brien, B., David, F., & Beacroft, L. (2013). Human trafficking and slavery offenders in Australia. *Trends & Issues in Crime and Criminal Justice* no. 464. Canberra, ACT: Australian Institute of Criminology.

Surtees, R. (2007). Listening to victims: Experiences of identification, return and assistance in South-Eastern Europe. ICMPD. Retrieved on July 29, 2014 from http://www.childtrafficking.com/Docs/listening_to_victims_1007.pdf

— (2008a). Traffickers and trafficking in Southern and Eastern Europe: Considering the other side of human trafficking. *European Journal of Criminology*, *5*(1), 39–68.

— (2008b). Trafficking of men—A trend less considered: The Case of Belarus and Ukraine. *IOM Migration Research Series*. Geneva: IOM. Retrieved on July 29, 2014 from http://publications.iom.int/bookstore/free/MRS_36.pdf

United Nations Office on Drugs and Crime (2010). *The globalisation of crime: A transnational organised crime threat assessment.* Vienna: UNODC. Retrieved on July 29, 2014 from http://www.unodc.org/documents/data-and-analysis/tocta/TOCTA_Report_2010_low_res.pdf

— (2012). *Global report on trafficking in persons*. Vienna: UNODC. Retrieved on July 29, 2014 from http://www.unodc.org/documents/data-and-analysis/glotip/Trafficking_in_Persons_2012_web.pdf

Vijeyarasa, R. (2010). The impossible victim: Judicial treatment of trafficked migrants and their unmet expectations. *Alternative Law Journal*, *35*(4), 217–222.

Discussion questions

1. How do Richards and Lyneham's findings contradict dominant assumptions about human trafficking?
2. How does human trafficking relate to other forms of exploitation and abuse?
3. Where did the authors identify the cases for their study? What might be some limitations of this sample?
4. What might be some unintended consequences of efforts to curtail trafficking via marriage?

Additional resources

The UNODC Human Trafficking Case Law Database
https://www.youtube.com/watch?v=tpyq97aEJ54

Forced marriage in Australia: Part 1
http://www.sbs.com.au/news/article/2013/05/16/forced-marriage-australia-part-1

Forced marriage in Australia: Part 2
http://www.sbs.com.au/news/article/2013/05/17/forced-marriage-australia-part-2

Forced marriage in Australia: Four Corners
https://www.youtube.com/watch?v=CUktnJ49TaQ

Section III

Trafficking policy: Intent and outcomes

Molly Dragiewicz

Section III takes up analyses of human trafficking policy in the United States and United Kingdom, empirically investigating the intentions and values that bring people and organizations to work on the trafficking issue. This section continues scrutiny of international trafficking policies and their intended and unintended outcomes for those affected. While this section draws upon the extensive literature on human trafficking discourse and policy, it contributes empirically based analyses grounded in multiple research methods.

In Chapter 9, "Clinton, Bush, and Obama: Changing Policy and Rhetoric in the United States Annual *Trafficking in Persons Report*," Erin O'Brien and Michael Wilson compare and contrast representations of trafficking across the Clinton, Bush, and Obama administrations. O'Brien is Senior Lecturer in the School of Justice at Queensland University of Technology in Australia. Her background is in Political Science. Wilson is a research student in the School of Justice. O'Brien and Wilson's analysis shows how key political tensions inherent in contemporary debates about trafficking have shifted across the years by comparing the *Trafficking in Persons Reports* from 2001–2012. They argue that while the law of trafficking has not changed much, shifting emphases are manifested via the evolving representation of the problem in the report.

In Chapter 10, Claire Renzetti investigates "Service Providers and their Perceptions of the Service Needs of Sex Trafficking Victims in the United States." Renzetti is the Judi Conway Patton Endowed Chair for Studies of Violence against Women, and Professor and Chair of the Sociology Department at the University of Kentucky in the United States. Her chapter draws on interviews with 43 service providers in order to understand how service providers who have contact with domestic sex trafficking victims perceive their clients' needs, how well service providers believe these needs are being met, and the ways that service providers characterize their relationships with other providers, agencies, and law enforcement. Renzetti found that many service providers articulated a need for residential and drop-in services. Providers articulated different opinions about how rigid or flexible services should be, and were aware of the influence of political debates about prostitution on funding streams. Service providers also shared concerns about trafficking victims accessing services via law enforcement. Many of the participants stressed the need for survivor-informed programming and staffing of services. Others discussed clients' objections to receiving the services offered. This chapter highlights some commonalities and differences among service providers in the U.S. as well as identifying locations to improve anti-trafficking intervention.

Julia O'Connell Davidson discusses anti-trafficking efforts geared to "ending demand" for prostitution in Chapter 11, "On Broken Chains and Missing Links: Tackling the 'Demand Side of Trafficking'?" O'Connell Davidson is Professor of Sociology at the University of Nottingham in England. Her chapter analyzes trafficking discourses focused on the "demand-side" policies which have been adopted in Nordic countries and are now being promoted elsewhere as the solution to human trafficking. Contrasting approaches to prostitution with those to domestic work, pornography, and civilian contract labor in the military, O'Connell Davidson argues that such policies distract us from considering the role of the state in constructing formal and informal labor markets and producing vulnerability to trafficking and exploitation.

Section III presents three quite different takes on anti-trafficking policy and practice in the U.S. and Europe. What the chapters share is an effort to investigate the specific content and impact of anti-trafficking rhetoric and practice in particular historical and geographic locations. These localized investigations can help shape policies that more effectively prevent labor exploitation and the oppression of migrants.

Learning objectives for Section III

1. Describe the ways in which U.S. political discourse on trafficking has changed over time.
2. Compare and contrast the ways that demand for sex work is talked about compared to demand for other types of labor.
3. Identify key debates that are reflected in the U.S. *Trafficking in Persons Reports*.
4. Critique service provider accounts of what trafficking victims need and the services they provide.

Chapter 9

Clinton, Bush, and Obama

Changing policy and rhetoric in
the United States Annual *Trafficking
in Persons Report*

Erin O'Brien and Michael Wilson

Introduction

The United States of America's stance on human trafficking has been shaped over the course of three presidencies, largely under the direction of the Office to Monitor and Combat Trafficking in Persons. The Office (more commonly known as the Trafficking in Persons, or TIP Office) was established through the passage of anti-trafficking legislation debated and enacted during the Clinton administration. It began to produce annual reports and a "watch list" of poorly performing nation states under George W. Bush, and celebrated its tenth anniversary under the leadership of Barack Obama.

The agenda of the Trafficking in Persons Office is not unchanged by political transitions. Disputes over the causes of and solutions to human trafficking are highly politicized, with ideological differences deeply embedded in trafficking discourse (Chuang, 2010). At the heart of many trafficking debates is a dispute over the relationship between prostitution and trafficking. Some anti-prostitution (or abolitionist) activists argue that trafficking is fueled by legalized or tolerated prostitution (Raymond, 2003), while others argue that migrant sex work is distinct to sex trafficking (Kempadoo, 2005). This is not the only point of disagreement in trafficking discourse, with calls for a human rights–based approach often ignored in favor of increasingly restrictive migration regimes (Jordan, 2002). The continued commitment by policy makers from both the Republican and Democratic parties can lead to the assumption that anti-trafficking policy is largely a bipartisan issue (Bernstein, 2010, p. 46). However, the specific policies enacted to address trafficking are frequently the subject of debate, reflecting strong ideological differences about the best ways to combat this problem. Across the Clinton, Bush, and Obama administrations, differences in approaches on trafficking are clearly evident in the agendas set and pursued by the TIP Office. This chapter charts the changes in the policy approaches of the Trafficking Office, through an examination of the annual *Trafficking in Persons Report* published by the U.S. State Department from 2001 to 2012.

The Office to Monitor and Combat Trafficking in Persons operates under the auspices of the State Department, led by an appointed director, often referred to as the anti-trafficking ambassador of the United States of America. The TIP Office plays a central role in articulating the anti-trafficking agenda of the U.S. government. This role is not merely rhetorical. The TIP Office advances its agenda through monetary grants for service provision and research, through diplomatic efforts to shape other nation states' anti-trafficking mechanisms and approaches, and through its annual *Trafficking in Persons Reports*. Through this work, the TIP Office has taken on the role of world watchdog, collecting and reporting information about other nation states' efforts to combat trafficking. Individual nations are given a "tier ranking," designating their efforts as either compliant with the *Trafficking Victims Protection Act*'s standards (Tier 1), not fully compliant but making efforts to improve (Tier 2, or Tier 2 watch list), or not compliant and failing to make appropriate efforts (Tier 3). On the basis of these rankings, the United States of America threatens to impose sanctions on under-performing nations (Chuang, 2006, p. 439).

The *TIP Reports* include these tier rankings as well as individual country reports, though the focus of this research chapter will be the anti-trafficking agendas of the U.S. government as articulated through the extensive introductory and contextual material contained in the *TIP Reports*. The *TIP Reports* include statements by the Secretary of State and the director of the TIP Office, as well as lengthy background discussions about trafficking victims, the causes of human trafficking, and desirable policy responses to the problem. These sections thus articulate a policy agenda for each administration, as reflected through the rhetoric of the reports. The *TIP Reports* are a hugely valuable resource to researchers as they provide an indication of government policy, and demonstrate changes not only across a period of time, but also across different administrations. Additionally, these declared agendas are worthy of examination as they have implications for international policy. Tier rankings potentially affect disbursement of U.S. funding and carry the threat of sanctions for poor performance on anti-trafficking indicators.

To chart the political transitions in the anti-trafficking agenda across three administrations, this chapter will first outline some of the ideological differences in trafficking approaches between Clinton, Bush, and Obama, before engaging in a close examination of the rhetorical changes across 12 years of TIP Office reports. We argue that while the anti-trafficking stance of the U.S. government may appear, at face value, largely unchanged since the establishment of the first anti-trafficking legislation, the rhetoric expressed through the *TIP Reports* indicates fissures between administrations, reflecting changing policy in response to changing leadership.

Anti-trafficking agendas across three presidential administrations

The United States of America signed the United Nations Protocol to Prevent, Suppress and Punish Trafficking in Persons, Especially Women and Children on December 13, 2000, and ratified it on November 3, 2005. The *Trafficking Victims*

Protection Act of 2000 (hereafter referred to as the TVPA 2000), and subsequent Reauthorization Bills in 2003, 2005, 2008, and 2011 form the bulk of the United States' legal efforts to combat trafficking to date. The TVPA thus spans three presidencies, and is the result of significant congressional debate in both the crafting and amendment of the Acts.

Box 9.1

The **Victims of Trafficking and Violence Protection Act of 2000 (TVPA)** is a United States federal law to combat human trafficking. It comprises Division A: *Trafficking Victims Protection Act of 2000*, Division B: *Violence Against Women Act of 2000*, and Division C: Miscellaneous Provisions. Its primary aims are to "combat trafficking in persons, especially into the sex trade, slavery, and involuntary servitude, [and] to reauthorize certain Federal programs to prevent violence against women." The *Trafficking Victims Protection Act of 2000* defines severe forms of human trafficking as "sex trafficking in which a commercial sex act is induced by force, fraud, or coercion, or in which the person induced to perform such act has not attained 18 years of age; or the recruitment, harboring, transportation, provision, or obtaining of a person for labor or services, through the use of force, fraud, or coercion for the purpose of subjection to involuntary servitude, peonage, debt bondage, or slavery." It stipulates that a victim of such trafficking can obtain a temporary work visa if s/he can prove her/his status as such, is willing to participate in the investigation and prosecution of traffickers, and has not been denied previously. The *Act* also encourages states to assist with reintegration of victims in their home countries. The *Trafficking Victims Protection Reauthorization Acts of 2003, 2005, and 2008* introduced several amendments, including the promotion of research on human trafficking, awards for extraordinary anti-trafficking measures, and the *Child Soldiers Prevention Act of 2008*.

For further information:

U.S. Department of State Victims of Trafficking and Violence Protection Act of 2000 TVPA http://www.state.gov/j/tip/laws/61124.htm

---

The Clinton Administration

Congressional debate leading up to the adoption of the TVPA 2000 took place during Bill Clinton's administration and largely centered on a distinction between "forced" and "voluntary" prostitution. At that time, conservative members of Congress and witnesses to congressional hearings from some radical feminist and faith-based organizations argued that all prostitution should be defined as trafficking, with no differentiation made on the basis of consent to participate in sex work (U.S. House of Representatives, 1999, p. 43). The Clinton administration resisted calls to declare all migrant women working in the sex industry as trafficked, regardless of the presence of force, fraud, and coercion (Weitzer, 2007). Instead, the TVPA 2000 adopted a compromise definition, establishing a two-tier definition of trafficking in which "severe trafficking" occurred where force, fraud, or coercion is used to procure labor, or sexual services, or where a child was prostituted. "Severe trafficking" was punishable under law, while transportation for the purposes of consensual prostitution was defined as "trafficking," with no criminal sanctions attached.

For their refusal to declare all migrant sex work as "severe trafficking," the Clinton administration was labeled "pro-prostitution" by some anti-prostitution activists. In 2000, a letter signed by nine organizations led by the abolitionist group Equality Now was released in response to the U.S. delegation's decision to support a United Nations Protocol that referred to "forced" prostitution rather than all prostitution. The letter demanded to know whether Hillary Clinton, in her role as First Lady and Honorary Chairwoman of the President's Interagency Counsel on Women (PICW), was drawing a distinction between "forced" and "voluntary" prostitution. A *New York Post* article reporting the letter referred to Clinton's advisors on the PICW as the "Hooker Panel," naming government officials Anita Botti, Theresa Loar, and Stephen Warnath as advocates of a "pro-prostitution position" (Blomquist, 2000, p. 6). In a scathing *Wall Street Journal* editorial, neo-conservative commentators Charles Colson and William Bennett continued to paint Clinton and the U.S. delegation as "pro-prostitution" by declaring that they had "lobbied for the United Nations to adopt a trafficking protocol that would lend legitimacy to prostitution and hard core pornography" (Bennett & Colson, 2000, p. 26).

The Bush Administration

Following the election of George W. Bush in November 2000, the influence of abolitionist groups increased significantly, with a distinct shift in political climate regarding both domestic and international policy. Milkis and Rhodes (2007) argue that Bush moved away from the "incremental" and "moderate" approaches to domestic policy favored by Clinton (p. 467), while Conlan and Dinan (2007) argue that Bush acted to centralize many policy decisions, often encroaching on issues normally decided at the state level (p. 190). The changes to trafficking policy during the Bush administration are a good example of this, with the *Trafficking Victims Protection Reauthorization Act 2005* directing state authorities to engage in increasing crackdowns on domestic prostitution (TVPRA 2005). Bush also pursued a socially conservative, and often religiously motivated foreign policy agenda, which was clearly evident in several decisions on international aid policy, most notably his decision to reinstate the Mexico City Policy restricting funding for abortion services in developing countries (also known as the Global Gag Rule), which Clinton had rescinded (Crossette, 2004).

This shift towards neo-conservatism created an environment in which anti-prostitution advocates were able to gain support for their agenda of treating all migrant sex work as human trafficking. In particular, advocates renewed their efforts to remove "force, fraud, and coercion" from the TVPA definition of sex trafficking in order to cast all migrant sex work as trafficking punishable under the law. These efforts were led by Congresswoman Carolyn Maloney, who built support in the House of Representatives for the revised Trafficking Victims Protection Reauthorization Bill 2008 in the final year of the Bush administration. However, the Senate refused to accept the removal of the force, fraud, and coercion clause from the legislation, effectively blocking passage of the revised Reauthorization Bill. John Miller, a former Congressman and Director of the TIP Office appointed during the Bush years, wrote a *New York Times* opinion piece in which he attacked the Justice Department and then-Senator Joe Biden (later U.S. Vice-President under Barack Obama) for their resistance to the House version of the Bill, which removed the force, fraud, and coercion elements from the definition of trafficking. Miller accuses them of being "blind to slavery," arguing that they oppose changes to the law that would "make it easier to prosecute pimps, the chief slaveholders in the United States" (Miller, 2008).

Despite ongoing resistance within Congress, particularly from Democratic senators, the Trafficking in Persons Office articulated a strong anti-prostitution agenda throughout the Bush years, clearly reflected in this statement from the 2008 *TIP Report*:

> The United States government opposes prostitution and any related activities, including pimping, pandering, or maintaining brothels as contributing to the phenomenon of trafficking in persons, and maintains that these activities should not be regulated as a legitimate form of work for any human being.
>
> (U.S. *TIP Report*, 2008, p. 24).

This anti-prostitution agenda was also reflected in the release of the *National Security Presidential Directive 22*, which established a funding rule whereby organizations receiving TIP Office funds, foreign aid, and AIDS Outreach funding were required to pledge that they would in no way support or promote the legalization of prostitution (U.S. State Department, 2002, *NSPD 22*). More commonly known as the "Anti-Prostitution Pledge," this policy cemented the anti-prostitution agenda of the TIP Office under the Bush administration.

The Obama Administration

The election of Barack Obama as President of the United States of America in November 2008 gave hope to many in the anti-trafficking field that there would be changes in the State Department's approach to the issue. In particular, it was expected that the influence of conservative and faith-based groups would decline with the departure of George W. Bush (Bernstein, 2010, p. 66; Skinner, 2009).

Senior appointments made in the early days of Obama's presidency seemed to indicate that there would be some shift in approaches to trafficking. Hillary Clinton was appointed as Secretary of State, and in this role would have oversight of the Office to Monitor and Combat Trafficking, and Hillary Clinton's former Chief of Staff, Melanne Verveer, was appointed as Ambassador-at-Large for Global Women's Issues. Verveer not only co-founded and directed Vital Voices, a non-governmental organization working to combat trafficking through the provision of education and opportunities for women in developing nations, she was also integral to the creation of anti-trafficking policy during the Bill Clinton administration as an advisor to the President's Interagency Council on Women. In addition to Clinton and Verveer, Michael Posner was appointed as Assistant Secretary for Democracy, Human Rights and Labor, bringing to the role a reputation for advocating for labor rights and refugee protection (Dietrich & Witkowski, 2012, p. 45). These appointments would seem to indicate that the Obama administration intended to position women's rights and migrants' rights, rather than the sex industry specifically, at the center of their anti-trafficking agenda.

Aside from the role that these appointees could play in guiding policy, the appointment most likely to give an indication of the Obama administration's agenda was Lou De Baca as Director of the Office to Monitor and Combat Trafficking in Persons. When this appointment was announced, De Baca was praised by many activists in the anti-trafficking field for recognizing that human trafficking is not synonymous with sex work, and demonstrating a commitment to addressing labor exploitation beyond the sex industry (Mahdavi, 2011). The hope that De Baca and others would focus anti-trafficking efforts on a wider range of labor exploitation was also shared by some critics of the Bush administration's trafficking efforts. In particular, the Bush administration was criticized not just for an obsessive focus on trafficking for sexual exploitation, but also for the failures of U.S. Immigration and Customs Enforcement (ICE) to adequately identify victims of trafficking due to a tendency to prioritize the rights of employers over workers. Hepburn and Simon (2010) report that many service providers in the field were "hopeful that the relationship between ICE and legal and social service providers may improve with the Obama administration" (p. 16).

At the policy level, the Obama administration has not made significant changes to anti-trafficking legislation, continuing to condemn prostitution as a factor contributing to human trafficking. Many advocates for sex workers' rights were disappointed that the Anti-Prostitution Pledge was not abolished, particularly as Obama quickly repealed the Global Gag Rule. However, the domination of faith-based and conservative agencies in the provision of research and services has begun to decline. For example, the United States Conference of Catholic Bishops, which received significant anti-trafficking grant monies from the Bush administration to distribute amongst subcontractors, is no longer funded under the Obama administration (U.S. House of Representatives, 2011).

Despite the lack of significant legislative change on trafficking during the Obama years so far, there are some clear differences in the anti-trafficking agendas of the Bush and Obama administrations. These are most clearly evident in the annual *Trafficking in Persons Reports* released in June each year. This chapter now moves to an examination of the similarities and differences in anti-trafficking agendas that can be observed across different presidential administrations, as reflected in the *TIP Reports*.

Anti-trafficking rhetoric in *TIP Reports* from Bush to Obama

The *Trafficking in Persons Report* was first published in 2001, following the inauguration of George W. Bush as President of the United States of America. While the groundwork for the establishment of the TIP Office was largely completed during the Clinton presidency, the reports published between 2001 and 2012 primarily reflect the discourses of the Bush and Obama administrations. From Bush to Obama there are some similarities and key differences in anti-trafficking agendas. First, we explore the reports' discussion of the causes of trafficking, with both administrations placing the blame on socio-economic factors and individual criminal responsibility, though to differing degrees. We then consider the ways in which each administration has addressed victim identification and protection. Finally we consider the differences in how the TIP Office under each president has addressed the relationship between prostitution and sex trafficking, demonstrating some of the most significant changes in *TIP Report* rhetoric.

Causes of trafficking

The *Trafficking in Persons Report* across both the Bush and Obama administrations reflects a belief that human trafficking is caused, in part, by socio-economic factors. However, the reports pose these factors as contributing to the vulnerability of populations, rather than directly causative of individual cases of human trafficking. For example, broad socio-economic factors such as the "disruption of societal values" and "political and economic instability" are identified within a framework of social pathologies that render individuals vulnerable to exploitation by criminals (U.S. Department of State, 2003, p. 8). Reports published during the Bush administration repeatedly cite a "lack of employment opportunities, organized crime, violence against women, government corruption, political instability, and armed conflict" as factors contributing to vulnerability to trafficking (U.S. Department of State, 2005, p. 17). This language is closely replicated by the Obama administration (e.g. U.S. Department of State, 2009, p. 32), with the *TIP Report* of 2012 noting that victims "may be poverty-stricken and forced to migrate for work, or they may be marginalized by their society" (U.S. Department of State, 2012, p. 11). Although both the Bush and Obama administrations clearly acknowledge the role of socio-economic inequality as relevant to a population's vulnerability to human trafficking, these social pathologies are largely constructed as the primary contributory factors.

The Obama administration does, however, attribute greater importance to socio-economic factors as a cause of human trafficking, embedded within a more gendered understanding of the trafficking phenomenon. Whereas the Bush administration's *TIP Reports* made reference to the impact of the "low status of women and girls" (U.S. Department of State, 2002, p. 2) on human trafficking as a peripheral factor, the Obama administration's reports have focused in more detail on gender as a factor in human trafficking. *TIP Reports* published from 2009 onwards emphasize the centrality of gender inequality to understanding global trends of human trafficking. The 2010 report declares that women are often victimized when they seek to "escape economic, familial and societal pressures" (U.S. Department of State, 2010, p. 34; 2009, p. 8). The Obama administration's reports further warn against the imposition of restrictive migration practices on women as a potential solution to trafficking, arguing that instead of addressing the problem, this "inevitably pushes migrants . . . to migrate through illegal channels" (U.S. Department of State, 2010, p. 32). The movement of explicit gendered discourses from the margin to the center reflects a more developed understanding of the function of culture and gender in trafficking, which is perhaps an unsurprising result of the leadership of Secretary of State Hillary Clinton, who has advocated for women's rights around the globe for many decades.

Despite the recognition by both administrations that socio-economic factors contribute to the problem of human trafficking, the *Trafficking in Persons Reports* have consistently constructed the locus of human trafficking as originating within the pathology of criminal individuals. The reports during the administrations of both President Bush and President Obama employ language to reinforce the central message that "poverty alone does not explain [human trafficking]" (U.S. Department of State, 2008, p. 8; see also 2011, p. 19). This dominant and recurring discourse minimizes the causative importance of addressing socio-economic global injustices, shifting the responsibility for trafficking from global systems of wealth and resource distribution to individual pathology.

Early *TIP Reports* published by the Bush administration locate trafficking as a consequence of materialistic greed, whereby criminals use means-end reasoning to justify the acquisition of capital through human exploitation (U.S. Department of State, 2003, p. 8). The *TIP Report* released in the final year of the Bush administration expands on this characterization, ascribing responsibility to "fraudulent recruiters, employers, and corrupt officials who seek to reap unlawful profits from others' desperation" (U.S. Department of State, 2008, p. 8). This trend towards constructing the problem of trafficking as centered on the perpetrators of the crime continues throughout the Obama administration.

The *TIP Reports* released so far during the Obama years have used forceful discourse to stress the role of individual criminals exploiting vulnerable victims; where socio-economic circumstances allow, "[t]hat's where the traffickers come in" (U.S. Department of State, 2011, p. 24). The role of the trafficker is described as follows:

> [t]hey prey on their victims' innate hope . . . [t]hey exploit their victims' trust . . . [t]hey find people who have nothing and coerce them into using their lives and freedom as collateral to guarantee a better future.
>
> (U.S. Department of State, 2011, p. 24).

Explicit references to a criminalized "other" by both the Bush and Obama administrations shifts the understanding of the causes of trafficking away from factors influenced by the actions of developed nations, and onto individual criminal entities. Responsibility for perpetuating the gap between rich and poor nations, or failing to improve migration systems, rests with governments in the developed world, but by representing the problem of trafficking as primarily centered on the criminality of greedy individuals, both the Bush and Obama administrations engage in blame shifting.

This construction of the criminalized other also portrays human trafficking as primarily a criminal justice issue, rather than a human rights issue. The reports during the Bush administration in particular relied on this construction, declaring trafficking to be a crime (U.S. Department of State, 2003, p. 10), though also stressing how this crime resulted in a rights violation, denying the "universal human right to life, liberty, and freedom from slavery in all its forms" (U.S. Department of State, 2004, p. 13). The 2012 report, released during the Obama administration, describes trafficking as a "crime, first and foremost" (U.S. Department of State, 2012, p. 7; see also 2003, p. 10), comparable with domestic crimes such as assault and murder (U.S. Department of State, 2012, p. 9).

Constructing trafficking within the framework of traditional interpersonal crime—as the simple violation of another's rights—not only obscures a portion of the U.S. government's responsibility for trafficking, but also acts as a justification for the use of severe punitive measures to "vigorously prosecute traffickers and those who aid and abet them" (U.S. Department of State, 2005, p. 20). Indeed, the state is constructed as the benevolent protector of the victim, as it is the sole responsibility of the state, who "alone has the power to punish criminals and provide legal recourse to survivors," to bring traffickers to justice (U.S. Department of State, 2012, pp. 8–9).

Victim identification and protection

This construction of the state as protector is also evident in both the Bush and Obama administrations' discussion of pre-emptive victim identification. During the Bush administration, *TIP Reports* repeatedly referred to the importance of victim protection, declaring that "victims of human trafficking and slave-like practices must be protected from further trauma" (U.S. Department of State, 2004, p. 5). Protection in this sense is deemed to include the provision of legal, social, economic, and health services, as well as repatriation (U.S. Department of State, 2007, p. 37; also see 2011, pp. 41, 44), an approach consistent with reports released during the Obama administration, which contain a further recognition that different victims require different types of assistance (U.S. Department of State, 2012, p. 30).

Across both administrations, however, the discussion of victim identification serves to implicitly reaffirm state sovereignty and associated forms of border control rather than emphasizing a rights-based approach to the issue. Both administrations call for pre-emptive victim identification systems (U.S. Department of State, 2007, p. 36; 2009, p. 28), with policy language implying the need to strengthen migration controls. For example, the *TIP Report* released in 2007, towards the end of the Bush era, argued for increased policing of "at-risk populations such as persons apprehended for violations of immigration laws, prostitution laws, and begging and labor laws" (U.S. Department of State, 2007, p. 36)—language that would seem to imply a criminalization of vulnerable individuals, rather than a protection of victims.

The reports during the Obama administration use softer language, yet ultimately imply a similar outcome, declaring that nation states should "pro-actively identify victims and potential victims of trafficking" (U.S. Department of State, 2012, p. 21) through the collection of intelligence, which facilitates "smart" rescue raids (U.S. Department of State, 2010, p. 40). While this does not necessarily criminalize certain populations to the extent of the language used in the Bush reports, this stance could still justify an increase in policing of external and internal borders, and directly calls for the use of raid-style techniques, which have been heavily criticized for failing to adequately consider victim circumstances (Busza, 2004).

One key point of difference between the *TIP Report* rhetoric from the Bush to Obama administrations is in a consideration of the role of migration systems in facilitating trafficking. Existing international practices of migration law have become a central concern of the *TIP Reports* in the Obama years, with the 2010 and 2012 reports both specifically considering the use of "sponsorship systems" as a method through which people may be trafficked (U.S. Department of State, 2010, p. 26; 2012, p. 34). Potential victims are recognized as both male and female migrant workers, employed under sponsorship systems that:

> provide excessive power to sponsors in granting and sustaining the immigration or legal status of a migrant worker and . . . do not provide real options for migrants to seek legal remedy for abuses or conditions of forced labor.
> (U.S. Department of State, 2010, p. 26)

The Obama reports shift the focus from a criminalizing of vulnerable populations, towards a consideration of the role of "unscrupulous employers" in perpetuating trafficking systems (U.S. Department of State, 2009, p. 14; 2010, p. 8; 2011, p. 7). This rhetorical shift implies a different policy response to that pursued during the Bush administration through increased "traceability, transparency, and worker protections throughout the supply chain" (U.S. Department of State, 2010, p. 14). While this discourse still places the blame for trafficking either on the vulnerability of victims, or on the greed of individual employers, it reflects a greater recognition of migrant rights and appreciation for the vulnerabilities of migrant workers as a result of existing governmental processes.

Prostitution and sex trafficking

As discussed earlier in this chapter, a major change in the anti-trafficking agenda from the Clinton to the Bush administrations was the greater acceptance of anti-prostitution arguments that all migrant sex work should be viewed as trafficking. Throughout the Bush years, the *TIP Reports* frequently point to the sex industry as a major contributing factor to the problem of trafficking. Prostitution is consistently identified as "inherently harmful and dehumanising" (U.S. Department of State, 2005, p. 19; 2006, p. 21; 2007, p. 27; 2008, p. 23), independent of whether it is voluntary or coerced. The denial of a sex worker's consent implies that consumers and facilitators of the commercial sex industry are inherently deviant and directly engaged in the trafficking chain. At best, consumers are labeled as complicit, "[t]urning people into dehumanised commodities" creating "an enabling environment for human trafficking" (U.S. Department of State, 2008, p. 23). Ultimately, through the reports' rhetoric, the entire commercial sex industry is constructed as being directly causative of sex trafficking, based on the assumption that it invariably fuels the demand for commercial sex (U.S. Department of State, 2007, p. 27; 2008, p. 23), an argument consistent with an anti-prostitution position.

The Bush administration also extends this discursive construction of trafficking and commercial sex to other governments' policies concerning the abolition of prostitution. Indeed, strong language is used to criticize governments who decriminalize or legalize sex work, by implying that they are complicit in the victimization of trafficked persons. This is achieved first through the assertion that "[c]onsiderable academic, NGO, and scientific research confirms a direct link between prostitution and trafficking" (U.S. Department of State, 2004, p. 19). This discourse is furthered by language that explicitly asserts that policies recognizing a difference between migrant sex work and sex trafficking fuel the trafficking of human beings. For example, non-abolitionist policies are described as "a trafficker's best shield" (U.S. Department of State, 2004, p. 22) and providing a "façade behind which traffickers for sexual exploitation operate" (U.S. Department of State, 2005, p. 19), positioning proponents as legitimizing the trade in sex slaves. Where alternative policies are discussed, it is noted that governments have simply "experimented" with decriminalization or legalization, and that as a result "sex trafficking continues to flourish" (U.S. Department of State, 2008, p. 29). It is notable, however, that despite this strong condemnation and rhetorical posturing, the presence of legalized systems of prostitution in countries such as Australia and the Netherlands did not prevent them from consistently achieving a top tier ranking for their efforts to combat human trafficking.

The administration of Barack Obama, despite maintaining some Bush-era abolitionist policies such as the Anti-Prostitution Pledge, has not simply replicated the anti-sex industry rhetoric of the *TIP Reports* up to 2008. The 2009 *TIP Report* (U.S. Department of State), the first released by the Obama administration, reflects a notable absence of much of the abolitionist rhetoric found during the presidency of George W. Bush. In contrast, the narrative shifts the discussion of victims away from a preoccupation with victims of sex trafficking, towards a greater consideration of victims of other forms of labor trafficking (U.S. Department of State, 2009, pp. 14–19). Furthermore, the act of prostitution is no longer as explicitly associated with human trafficking. Instead, the discourse emphasizes that for sex work to constitute trafficking, the worker must be coerced, forced, or deceived (U.S. Department of State, 2010, p. 9; 2011, p. 7; 2012, p. 33). Finally, in stark contrast to the discourse employed during the Bush administration, the criminalization of prostitution is directly linked to heightened levels of sex trafficking, where "[a]s commercial sex is illegal in most countries, traffickers use the resulting status of migrant women that have been trafficked into commercial sex to threaten or coerce them against leaving" (U.S. Department of State, 2009, p. 36). The use of this language affords migrant sex workers some personal agency and legitimacy, while also declaring that the illegal status of prostitution, rather than the legalization of it, may be a more significant contributing factor to the differential power of traffickers over victims.

Conclusion

The ideological differences across the Clinton, Bush, and Obama administrations in relation to human trafficking could be assumed to result in key differences in anti-trafficking policy and agendas. Some of these differences are clearly evident in the rhetoric contained within the annual *Trafficking in Persons Reports*, with transitions in language and focus reflecting key tensions that have dominated congressional debate and trafficking discourse in the United States of America. The conflict between a law enforcement versus a rights-based approach to trafficking, competing approaches on victim protection and identification, and ongoing disputes about the relationship between the sex industry and sex trafficking have permeated the *TIP Report* rhetoric, highlighting both similarities and key points of difference between the presidencies. However, while the rhetoric of the administrations may differ, 12 years of *TIP Reports* also demonstrate clear consistencies in the representation of the trafficking phenomenon.

The *TIP Reports* released during the Bush and Obama presidencies show a consistency in approach in designating socio-economic factors as contributory to, however not necessarily causative of, human trafficking. It is the greed of individual criminals, or unscrupulous employers, which is positioned as the primary cause of trafficking, assisting in the construction of the state as protector and enforcer. The main points of difference between the administrations relate to the discussion of the role of the sex industry in causing human trafficking, with the reports during the

Bush years focusing significant attention on this issue, while the post-Bush reports are largely devoid of abolitionist rhetoric. Instead, the reports during the Obama administration deliver a focus on a wider variety of trafficking for labor exploitation, and a greater understanding of the gendered complexities of trafficking.

While the rhetoric concerning the causes of trafficking across both administrations' *TIP Reports* clearly reflects some points of difference, a consistent agenda of externalizing the causes of human trafficking is maintained. While the Obama administration reports acknowledge the role of migration systems in contributing to trafficking, the declared causes of trafficking within *TIP Reports* from both administrations are still fundamentally rooted in the individual criminal pathology of traffickers and employers, or the failings of developing nations to provide educational and employment opportunities for citizens, and to adequately protect the rights of women, children, and those living in poverty.

This construction continues to justify a law enforcement response to human trafficking, shifting the responsibility for this crime away from the governments and economies of developed countries. The changes in focus of the anti-trafficking agenda from the Bush to Obama administrations are promising, demonstrating a greater awareness of a wider range of factors that contribute to trafficking both as a crime, and a human rights abuse. However, it is hoped that policy in the U.S. will continue to evolve with increased understanding of the causes of, and most effective solutions to, this global phenomenon, including an appreciation of the role that world leaders like the U.S. play not only in combating, but also contributing to human trafficking. Throughout this evolution, the annual *Trafficking in Persons Report* will continue to offer a snapshot insight into the influence changing leadership has on policy agendas.

References

Bennett, W., & Colson, C. (2000). The Clintons shrug at sex trafficking. *The Wall Street Journal*, January 10, A26.

Bernstein, E. (2010). Militarized humanitarianism meets carceral feminism: The politics of sex, rights, and freedom in contemporary antitrafficking campaigns. *Signs*, *36*(1), 45–71.

Blomquist, B. (2000). Hooker panel puts first lady on the spot. *New York Post*, January 8, 6.

Busza, J. (2004). Sex work and migration: The dangers of oversimplification–A case study of Vietnamese women in Cambodia. *Health and Human Rights*, *7*(2), 231–249.

Chuang, J. (2006). The United States as global sheriff: Using unilateral sanctions to combat human trafficking. *Michigan Journal of International Law*, *27*(2), 437–494.

— (2010). Rescuing trafficking from ideological capture: Prostitution reform and anti-trafficking law and policy. *University of Pennsylvania Law Review*, *158*, 1655–1728.

Conlan, T., & Dinan, J. (2007). Federalism, the Bush administration, and the transformation of American conservatism. *Publius: The Journal of Federalism*, *37*(3), 279–303.

Crossette, B. 2004. Hurting the poor in morality's name. *World Policy Journal*, *4*(Winter), 57–62.

Dietrich, J., & Witkowski, C. (2012). Obama's human rights policy: Deja vu with a twist. *Human Rights Review*, *13*(1), 39–64.

Hepburn, S., & Simon, R. J. (2010). Hidden in plain sight: Human trafficking in the United States. *Gender Issues*, *27*(1–2), 1–26.

Jordan, A. (2002). Human rights or wrongs? The struggle for a rights-based response to trafficking in human beings. *Gender and Development*, *10*(1), 28–37.

Kempadoo, K. (Ed.) (2005). *Trafficking and prostitution reconsidered: New perspectives on migration, sex work and human rights*. London: Paradigm Publishers.

Mahdavi, P. (2011). Just the "TIP" of the iceberg: The 2011 Trafficking in Persons Report (TIP) falls short of expectations. *Huffington Post*, September 6. Retrieved on January 20, 2012 from http://www.huffingtonpost.com/pardis-mahdavi/just-the-tip-of-the-icebe_1_b_888618.html

Milkis, S. M., and Rhodes, J. H. (2007). George W. Bush, the Republican Party, and the "new" American party system. *Perspectives on Politics*, *5*(3), 461–488.

Miller, J. (2008). The Justice Department, blind to slavery. *The New York Times*, July 11. Retrieved on February 26, 2009 from http://www.nytimes.com/2008/07/11/opinion/11miller.html

Raymond, J. (2003). Ten reasons for not legalizing prostitution, in Farley, M. (Ed.), *Prostitution, trafficking and traumatic stress*. Binghamton: Haworth Press, pp. 315–332.

Skinner, E. B. (2009). Obama's abolitionist. *Huffington Post*, March 25. Retrieved on November 25, 2010 from http://www.huffingtonpost.com/ben-skinner/obamas-abolitionist_b_178781.html

Weitzer, R. (2007). The social construction of sex trafficking: Ideology and institutionalization of a moral crusade. *Politics & Society*, *35*(3), 447–475.

U.S. House of Representatives (1999). *Trafficking of women and children in the international sex trade: Hearing before the Subcommittee on International Operations and Human Rights, Committee on International Relations*. 106th Congress, 1st Session, September 14.

— (2011). *HHS and the Catholic Church: Examining the politicization of grants, Committee on Oversight and Government Reform*. 112th Congress, 2nd Session, December 1.

U.S. State Department (2002). *National Security Presidential Directive 22 Combating Trafficking in Persons*, December 16.

U.S. Department of State (2002). *Trafficking in Persons Report 2002*. Retrieved on December 20, 2012 from http://www.state.gov/j/tip/rls/tiprpt/2002/index.htm

— (2003). *Trafficking in Persons Report 2003*. Retrieved on December 20, 2012 from http://www.state.gov/j/tip/rls/tiprpt/2003/index.htm

— (2004). *Trafficking in Persons Report 2004*. Retrieved on December 20, 2012 from http://www.state.gov/j/tip/rls/tiprpt/2004/index.htm

— (2005). *Trafficking in Persons Report 2005*. Retrieved on December 20, 2012 from http://www.state.gov/j/tip/rls/tiprpt/2005/index.htm

— (2006). *Trafficking in Persons Report 2006*. Retrieved on December 20, 2012 from http://www.state.gov/j/tip/rls/tiprpt/2006/index.htm

— (2007). *Trafficking in Persons Report 2007*. Retrieved on December 20, 2012 from http://www.state.gov/j/tip/rls/tiprpt/2007/index.htm

— (2008). *Trafficking in Persons Report 2008*. Retrieved on December 20, 2012 from http://www.state.gov/j/tip/rls/tiprpt/2008/index.htm

— (2009). *Trafficking in Persons Report 2009*. Retrieved on December 20, 2012 from http://www.state.gov/j/tip/rls/tiprpt/2009/index.htm

— (2010). *Trafficking in Persons Report 2010*. Retrieved on December 20, 2012 from http://www.state.gov/j/tip/rls/tiprpt/2010/index.htm

— (2011). *Trafficking in Persons Report 2011*. Retrieved on December 20, 2012 from
    http://www.state.gov/j/tip/rls/tiprpt/2011/index.htm
— (2012). *Trafficking in Persons Report 2012*. Retrieved on December 20, 2012 from
    http://www.state.gov/j/tip/rls/tiprpt/2012/index.htm

Discussion questions

1. How has the U.S. conceptualization of human trafficking evolved over time?
2. In what ways has U.S. trafficking policy remained consistent?
3. What is the *TIP Report*?
4. What is the tier system?
5. What factors other than trafficking laws might affect tier rankings by the U.S.?

Additional resources

The U.S. State Department's Office to Monitor and Combat Trafficking in Persons, includ-
    ing links to all previous reports
http://www.state.gov/j/tip/index.htm

Tier placements per country from the 2013 *Trafficking in Persons Report*
http://www.state.gov/j/tip/rls/tiprpt/2013/210548.htm

Newspaper report from the *Guardian* on how non-government organizations use the annual
    Trafficking in Persons Report to campaign for change
http://www.theguardian.com/global-development-professionals-network/2013/jun/21/
    ngos-using-trafficking-persons-report

Chapter 10

Service providers and their perceptions of the service needs of sex trafficking victims in the United States

Claire M. Renzetti

Introduction

In email exchanges with the editor of this volume regarding my chapter, she at one point commented, "I have never seen a topic where the activists have been more studied than the victims or criminals" (M. Dragiewicz, personal communication, August 3, 2012). Indeed, among the more vociferous ongoing debates among feminist scholars is the one concerning sex trafficking, including questions about definitions, frequency and severity, the characteristics of perpetrators and victims and, as the email comment indicates, the characteristics and, especially, the motivations of anti-trafficking activists (compare, for example, O'Brien, Hayes, & Carpenter, 2013 with Raymond, 2013). It's not that scholars involved in this debate disagree over whether sex trafficking is "bad" or problematic. Rather, there is disagreement over such issues as what "counts" as sex trafficking, with concern among some scholars that anti-trafficking activists conflate sex trafficking with all sex work and have embarked on a moral crusade that divests women of agency and the right to control their own bodies (Bernstein, 2010; O'Connell Davidson, 2006; Weitzer, 2010). Other contributors to this volume address various aspects of this debate (see for example Outshoorn, Chapter 2), so I will not explore it in depth in this chapter. Instead, my focus is on how those who provide services to sex trafficking victims in the United States perceive victims' needs and the ability of available services to meet those needs. As Barberet (2014, p. 156) points out, "Scholars—even feminist scholars who resent the imposition of the human trafficking paradigm on all sex work—do not deny that very serious forms of trafficking for sexual exploitation exist," and victims of such exploitation certainly require and deserve effective and helpful responses from service providers. Nevertheless, the data I present in this chapter show that there are important disagreements among service providers regarding such issues as who should provide services to sex trafficking victims and the philosophy of treatment underlying these services.

Before turning to the data, though, let me further make clear what this chapter will and will *not* cover. As noted, I will not delve into the debate about the relationship of sex trafficking to sex work. In my research with service providers, I adopted the U.S. federal government's definition of sex trafficking as specified in the 2008 reauthorization of the Trafficking Victims Protection Act (TVPA, also known as the William Wilberforce Reauthorization Act), largely because this is the definition used by most service providers. The TVPA defines sex trafficking as enticing, harboring, transporting, providing, or obtaining either an adult for commercial sex by force, fraud, or coercion, or a juvenile for the same purpose regardless of the means (U.S. Department of State, 2013).

Moreover, my research focuses on services for *domestic sex trafficking victims*, both adults and children, so I will not discuss services for victims of labor trafficking. I chose this particular emphasis for several reasons. First, although there may be some overlap between labor trafficking and sex trafficking victimization experiences, and some trafficking victims, especially females, may be victims of both types of trafficking, my familiarity with research on sexual trauma led me to conclude that sex trafficking victims are unique in several significant ways and, therefore, likely require responses and interventions different from those that may be effective with labor trafficking victims. The data I gathered for this project, as I will show, reinforce these conclusions.

Second, in preliminary conversations with service providers, several mentioned that they thought domestic victims receive less attention than international victims. Although human trafficking may occur domestically, regionally, and transnationally, it is the latter category that most people think of when they hear the term "human trafficking." Even in the original TVPA and in two subsequent reauthorizations, the United States Congress appropriated funds for the provision of social services for non-citizen victims only. This was not because legislators did not think that U.S. citizens could be trafficking victims, but rather that U.S. citizen victims could ostensibly access services (e.g. legal aid, health care) through the privileges of their citizenship. It was not until passage of the William Wilberforce Trafficking Victims Protection Reauthorization Act in 2008 that Congress officially recognized that U.S. citizen trafficking victims face tremendous difficulties in accessing services for a variety of reasons, some of which I will discuss in this chapter, and so authorized the development of a program to assist U.S. citizens and legal foreign residents who are trafficking victims.

Finally, the official statistics on human trafficking cases (i.e. investigations of suspected trafficking incidents) in the U.S. show that the majority of investigated cases involve sex trafficking. In addition, more than 80 percent of individuals officially identified as sex trafficking victims by law enforcement in the U.S. are U.S. citizens, whereas only about 5 percent of labor trafficking victims are U.S. citizens (Banks & Kychkelhahn, 2011; Farrell, McDevitt, & Fahy, 2008; U.S. Department of State, 2013). Of course, such statistics, especially those on child sex trafficking, must be viewed with a good dose of caution and skepticism given that they derive from "extremely imprecise and speculative methodologies" (Stransky & Finkelhor, 2008, p. 8), and are fraught with political and ideological baggage (Barberet, 2014; Brennan, 2008; Kittling, 2005–2006; Goździak in this volume). But the methodological debates concerning counting and documenting sex trafficking are also beyond the scope of this chapter (see Tyldum & Brunovskis, 2005 for a discussion of the methodological challenges of studying human trafficking).

Service providers' perceptions of the service needs of U.S. sex trafficking victims

I undertook this study because in informal conversations with service providers who had had contact with domestic sex trafficking victims I noted some disagreements in terms of their ideas of how to best serve this client population. In my study, therefore, I sought to get a better understanding of what service providers who have contact with domestic sex trafficking victims perceive to be their clients' most pressing needs, the extent to which the service providers feel that these needs are met with currently available services and resources, and how the service providers characterize their relationships with other service providers and agencies, including law enforcement. Through these discussions, I also sought to understand how the service providers viewed the crime of sex trafficking (for example, versus prostitution and other forms of sex work), and how they viewed victims. For instance, did service providers characterize their clients as "violated innocents" (Chapkis, 2005), or as complicit in some way in the criminal activity? Did their perceptions of their clients vary depending on the clients' characteristics, such as their age? However, no direct questions were asked about these latter issues. Participants were free to lead the conversation in directions they felt were relevant in addition to responding to my direct questions about service needs. The study was exploratory; I came to the project with few preconceived ideas of service providers' perceptions of their work or their clients.

Methodology and data analysis

Between 2008 and 2010 (specifically, a period of 18 months), I conducted semi-structured interviews with 43 service providers who work in the health care sector, in faith-based organizations, in more general service agencies including those that assist the homeless, in domestic violence and sexual assault services, and in legal assistance services. The sample was dispersed across seven states in the South, Midwest, and Northeast and also the District of Columbia. All worked in urban areas. Only two were men, both of whom were white, and only one of the 41 women was non-white (specifically, Latina). All who participated have provided direct services to trafficking victims, although few work at an agency or organization solely dedicated to serving trafficking victims. Nearly all of these service providers focus their efforts and resources on female victims of sex trafficking, although a few also serve both female and male labor trafficking victims.

The sample is obviously by no means random or representative. It is a purposive sample aided by snowballing, whereby participants nominated others whom they thought might contribute to the study by being interviewed. Consequently, the sample reflects the social and professional networks of those who initially agreed to participate. The majority were social workers or counseling or clinical psychologists; four had a background in law, one in theology, and eight were from other disciplinary or work backgrounds. Three were also survivors. Years of experience as a service provider ranged from 3 to 37, but most had had their first known professional contact with a trafficking victim in the 12–36 months prior to the interview.

Although a few of the interviews were conducted in person, the majority were conducted over the phone. None of the interviews was audio-recorded; instead, I took intensive notes during each interview and frequently verified wording with participants to ensure I had recorded their statements verbatim. The interview notes from each interview were compiled into a pseudo-transcript. These were then analyzed using thematic analysis with emergent coding (Miles & Huberman, 1994). More specifically, each "transcript" was reviewed line-by-line to extract salient themes pertaining to study participants' perceptions of sex trafficking victims' needs; available resources and services; and characterizations of victims, perpetrators, and/or the crime of trafficking itself. This process generated a list of thematic codes; the "transcripts" were then analyzed to extract all information relevant to each of the themes and this information was subsequently coded in terms of specific subthemes that emerged as patterns of shared perceptions or experiences across the sample. From this process, three themes (which I pose as questions) and six subthemes were identified. I discuss each of these below, drawing on quotes from the interviews to illustrate key points. No identifying information is provided with the quotes, however, in order to protect the confidentiality of the study participants.

Findings

Theme 1: What services do victims need?

There was remarkable agreement—though not unanimity, as I will discuss shortly—among the service providers I interviewed as to the types of interventions they consider critical for effectively responding to domestic sex trafficking victims, with slight variations depending on whether victims are adults or minors. At the top of most participants' "wish list" of services for both adult and juvenile victims is safe, high quality, residential services or, as one service provider phrased it, "a place where victims can not only be sent, but one where they would want to stay."

The service providers who championed this theme emphasized the need for such facilities to be staffed by professionals trained specifically to understand the causes and effects of trafficking. In the case of minors, who are most likely to come under the authority of Child Protective Services (CPS) and be placed into foster care, the service providers emphasized the need for foster parents to also receive this specialized training or, they predicted, the placement is nearly certain to fail. (Importantly, two service providers mentioned the need to more carefully scrutinize foster care placements, since they may be potential gateways to trafficking of minors.)

All of the service providers who advocated for specialized residential facilities justified this need in terms of the unique trauma that sex trafficking victims experience. As they explained, many sex trafficking victims have a history of neglect and abuse—sexual, physical, and/or psychological—dating from early in their lives; some, they said, had run away to escape their abusive home environments, which made them especially vulnerable to traffickers. While on the street, the service providers explained, they were befriended or taken in by someone who made promises to protect them and led them to believe they could not survive on their own. This individual—the trafficker—may be a woman who initially acts as a mother figure, or a man, who usually acts as a boyfriend. Life with the trafficker may contain coercion and violence at times, but it is also predictable; traffickers convince their victims that if they "behave," they will not have to be "punished."

As the service providers further explained, victims may "traumatically bond" with their traffickers, whom they are with for months, even years, before they are "rescued." (The terms "rescue" and "emancipate" are commonly used by anti-trafficking activists to describe removing someone they identify as a victim from a trafficking situation. For a critique of these and analogous anti-trafficking terminology, see Bernstein, 2010; O'Connell Davidson, 2006.) Consequently, when victims are removed from the trafficking situation, they may behave in ways that would lead one to think they don't want to be rescued. In fact, according to many service providers, they will often actually say they don't want to be rescued. They may behave promiscuously. They may try to use alcohol or drugs. They may try to run away from their rescuers or caregivers. According to service providers, however, such behaviors are symptomatic of the traumatic effects of being trafficked, and if helpers, foster parents, and others don't understand this, they may take to victim-blaming: e.g. "If she acts like that, she's asking for it; she deserves what she gets." Several service providers I interviewed likened these victim-blaming responses to the way people sometimes react to battered women who repeatedly return to their abusers.

While the majority of service providers I interviewed felt that separate residential services with specially trained staff are necessary for sex trafficking victims, a serious disagreement emerged among this group with regard to how such services should be structured, particularly in terms of the level of security required.

Subtheme 1: Security requirements

A major issue of contention among the service providers who advocated for specialized residential services for domestic sex trafficking victims was how secure such facilities should be. Several service providers placed a premium on security, emphasizing the need to make residents feel safe inside the facilities, while simultaneously preventing traffickers and other "bad guys" from finding them and breaking into the facilities. A few also stated that high security is needed to prevent residents from "running away" or "escaping," as they are prone to do. One service provider, who, at the time of the interview, was raising money to fund a residential facility for sex trafficking victims, talked about the possibility of screening potential residents before admitting them to the facility so that only young women who "want to be helped and are ready to be helped" will be admitted. This position regarding security, though, was expressed by a minority of those interviewed.

In contrast, most service providers who favored specialized residential services noted problems with "locking [victims] in." For one thing, such high security measures can be retraumatizing by reproducing the conditions victims experienced when they were trafficked, thereby doing them more harm than good. In addition, the high security approach undermines the trust relationship that these service providers feel is critical to keeping trafficking victims in "treatment", leading to "successful treatment outcomes." One service provider described the appropriate approach to residential security as somewhat "counterintuitive":

> You may think you need to impose more rules, and the more they rebel, or fight with each other, or cause problems, the more you want to lock them up tighter. But you have to give residents some freedom so that they learn to make decisions for themselves . . . they become self-sufficient, because the goal is for them to be able to survive on their own when they do leave. All their decisions have been made for them by their traffickers and now *you're* making decisions for them, they have to follow *your* rules.
>
> (Participant's emphasis)

The level of contention surrounding the issue of security was driven home to me when I witnessed a rather heated disagreement between two service providers, one of whom advocated a "home-like environment" and relatively high freedom in residential facilities for sex trafficking victims, and the other who argued in favor of high security. Said the former, "In this country [the U.S.] we have choices; you can't impose your will on them and not give them any choice." To this the latter replied, "They can have a choice. They can choose to get the service, or they can choose to stay out. Housing comes with conditions." The issue of choice, in fact, emerged as another subtheme in discussions of specialized residential services.

Subtheme 2: Choices come with consequences

In conversations about the pros and cons of specialized residential services, choice emerged as a salient issue, but in different ways. I have already alluded to one of the ways that choice was discussed: in the context of security, freedom, and decision-making. Many service providers expressed considerable ambivalence with regard to providing sex trafficking victims with an array of choices or options. This ambivalence is highlighted in the words of one service provider who said:

> It's important to teach autonomy and independence, and good decision-making. But you also have to ask yourself, how much choice is too much at this point? How much choice actually endangers them? It's very difficult to sort all this out.

Service providers who expressed this view generally felt that sex trafficking victims needed to have choices in order to develop good decision-making skills, but they worried too many choices might overwhelm victims and lead to harmful consequences.

Five service providers discussed choice in a somewhat different way, more explicitly equating it with victims' agency. They raised the issue in the context of their discussion of some victims' resistance to intervention, noting that the choice to refuse services may be a way for sex trafficking victims to exercise some control over their lives. As these service providers explained, victims have been subjected to the control of their traffickers, and once they are removed from that position of extreme subordination, they may try to reassert control over their lives by choosing to strongly resist the rules and authority of their "rescuers." As one service provider expressed it, "Their failure to respond to rescue or treatment in expected ways may be their attempt to exercise personal efficacy in one of the only ways available to them."

Finally, choice was also discussed in terms of the consequences it may have for funding. This particular take on choice was mentioned by only two service providers. Both were advocating the position that "rescued" sex trafficking victims need to have options so that they may influence and participate in their healing and recovery, but both also mentioned that emphasizing "choices" may backfire by making fundraising difficult. One service provider explained, for example, that it is sometimes challenging to raise money for services for adult victims, since many people see them as having made a "lifestyle choice," as having "chosen to be a sex worker," and therefore complicit in the criminal activity. In this service provider's experience, people want to give money to child victims, whom they see as "innocent," not realizing, she said, that "many adolescents aren't willing or wanting services." I will return to the issue of victim agency and choice later in the chapter.

Subtheme 3: Alternatives to specialized residential services

As previously noted, the vast majority of the service providers I interviewed favored specialized residential services for domestic sex trafficking victims, but a sizable minority (n = 9, or about 22 percent) argued against such services primarily because they view them as expensive and a duplication of effort. As one service provider said, "The model of a comprehensive residential system for trafficking victims is not only unnecessary in light of the current array of services that are available . . . it is extremely expensive . . ." These service providers discussed various alternatives to specialized residential facilities.

One popular alternative mentioned is to use existing services for battered women and sexual assault victims. In this view, domestic violence and sexual assault advocates are already prepared to respond to physically and sexually abused women and girls, so they would need only minimal additional training in order to effectively respond to sex trafficking victims. Respondents argued that concentrating services in this way is not simply a cost-saving measure; it ensures, more importantly, that victims receive care from professionals who are likely to be feminists and have a firm understanding of both gender-based violence and the potential for revictimization by various institutional responders, such as the criminal justice system.

Many of the service providers who supported specialized residential services also discussed the use of existing battered women's and sexual assault services, but rejected them as inadequate for meeting the unique needs of sex trafficking victims. One rationale they offered for this rejection is that domestic violence advocates are not likely to see serving sex trafficking victims as within the scope of their mission. Moreover, several service providers mentioned that domestic violence program staff have not been consistent or effective in screening their clients for sexual assault (see Bergen, 2006 for research findings that support this position). Many of these service providers conceded that sexual assault victim advocates would likely be more amenable to serving sex trafficking victims, but they nonetheless argued that extensive training would be required on the causes and unique consequences of sex trafficking in order for the advocates to understand how the trauma resulting from trafficking (e.g. experiencing multiple revictimizations over an extended period of time by multiple offenders) differs from the "typical" sexual assault case they encounter in their practice.

Another service option that was suggested by most of the service providers, not only those who opposed specialized residential facilities, was drop-in centers. Drop-in centers were often discussed in relation to the problem of "rescued" victims rejecting more intensive interventions, such as residential treatment. Drop-in centers open 24/7 and staffed by specially trained professionals were presented as an important point of contact with sex trafficking victims who are not ready or willing to accept comprehensive services. In addition to offering crisis intervention, such centers would provide opportunities to build trust between victims and service providers and to do outreach with victims, raising their awareness of other services available in the community and how to access them, as well as their rights as crime victims.

One common suggestion was to bill drop-in centers as health care centers or clinics. Most of the service providers I interviewed noted that a good way to do outreach to sex trafficking victims is through health clinics and hospital emergency rooms (ERs) because victims often see these services as "neutral" sites and have need for them fairly frequently (e.g. due to their high risk for injury as well as drug overdoses or alcohol poisoning, and treatment for various illnesses, including sexually transmitted infections and hepatitis C). In fact, one service provider mentioned the need to train emergency medical technicians (EMTs) to recognize potential sex trafficking victims and be able to provide victims with information about services "in the form of palm cards, so they have numbers to call and know places they can go when they are ready." However, another service provider argued that one of the reasons sex trafficking victims, especially adolescent victims, do not hold negative views of ERs is because ER staff typically take a "don't ask, don't tell" approach to them:

> ER staff feel they are very limited in what they can do for these patients. For instance, they can't release information about them because of HIPPA regulations [laws protecting patient privacy], they can't keep them in the hospital for long because it's too expensive. They may call CPS or the police, but both tend to give these cases low priority at this stage.

This quote is as important for what it says about ER staff as it is for what it says about the police, another subtheme that emerged from the interview data.

Subtheme 4: Service providers' relationships with law enforcement

All of the service providers in this study noted that most sex trafficking victims access services through the criminal justice system, which, they felt, was problematic more often than not. As they described this process, sex trafficking victims are typically picked up by police on the streets or in raids, and are detained in police stations or jails. Although police were credited for calling service providers after making these arrests, all the service providers emphasized that this point of contact often served to increase mistrust among victims and thereby undermine their ability to provide services. As one service provider explained, "You go interview them in detention and tell them they are trafficking victims and they practically laugh at you. They've been arrested. They're not being treated as *victims*" (participant's emphasis).

Many service providers in this study described their relationships with law enforcement as "tense" at best. They conceded that law enforcement, given the nature of their job, want to question victims and secure their cooperation in investigations and prosecutions, and that often "time is of the essence." But they also pointed out that many victims can hardly be described as "cooperative" with the police, resulting in the police having difficulty seeing them as "victims" and not as "offenders." The service providers, especially those with extensive training or experience with sex trafficking cases, see themselves as the only advocates for victims in these circumstances and expressed that one of their biggest challenges is getting police to "see beyond the law enforcement dimensions of a case."

Consequently, all of the service providers in this study strongly supported more training for law enforcement on sex trafficking (see Farrell et al., 2008 for research that supports the call for more police training). There was disagreement, however, on the need for a coordinated community response (CCR), similar to what has been established in some jurisdictions in recent years for responding to domestic violence and sexual assault victims (see also Caliber Associates, 2007). Although most of the service providers discussed the need for more collaboration across systems, including social services, criminal justice, and health care, many raised questions about the extent to which a CCR is truly collaborative, and whether the divergent foci of the various agencies and responders inevitably engenders conflict among them. Other service providers spoke against establishing a set of cross-agency protocols for responding to sex trafficking victims, arguing that trafficking cases are often highly nuanced and, therefore, victims' needs should be evaluated on a case-by-case basis. As one explained, "A one-size-fits-all approach imposed by the adoption of a protocol will not be beneficial for victims or service providers in trafficking cases."

Despite their concerns with law enforcement, a number of the service providers identified specific programs as examples of good collaboration between social services and the criminal justice system. In most cases, these programs were praised for involving sex trafficking survivors in outreach to and counseling of victims. The role of survivors, in fact, emerged as another subtheme in the data.

Subtheme 5: The role of survivors

Most service providers in this study emphasized the importance of including survivors in programs for sex trafficking victims. Many service providers maintained that survivors are able to establish rapport with victims more easily. Many also pointed out that involving survivor-advocates provides current victims with positive role models, while simultaneously empowering survivors by giving them a significant job, officially recognizing their success, raising their self-esteem and, therefore, helping them maintain the positive behavioral changes they have made.

Nevertheless, while involving survivors in service delivery to victims was praised by most participants, a few suggested this be done with great care. One service provider, for example, who is also a survivor, expressed several serious concerns. First, she said, "it is absolutely necessary to train survivors for this type of work and not simply assume they'll know what to do because they've been there themselves." In addition, she maintained, it is necessary to assess survivors in advance of contact with victims to determine if they have fully healed from the trauma: "If they are not fully recovered, if they still suffer from PTSD, doing this sort of outreach could retraumatize them, which results in harm not only to them, but also to the women and girls they are trying to help."

Theme 2: What works?

In addition to specialized residential facilities and drop-in centers, study participants identified a number of "services within [these] services" that should be offered for domestic sex trafficking victims. Additional services they felt victims need are physical health care; dental care; counseling and mental health care; drug and alcohol treatment programs; education, job training, job placement, and mentoring; basic life skills (e.g. money management); and self-care (e.g. learning meditation or yoga). Significantly, however, nearly all the study participants raised concerns about the lack of evidence regarding the effectiveness of services, programs, and treatment approaches for this specific client population. For example, in a discussion about the debate over specialized residential facilities versus the use of existing facilities such as battered women's shelters, one service provider stated, "We have no proof that one approach works any better, that it's more effective, than any other approach. What we need is evaluation."

The majority of study participants (n = 31) stressed the need for evaluation of services; many explicitly stated that they welcome systematic, long-term evaluation of their services. Some also mentioned the need to "hold service providers accountable" for their treatment of trafficking victims. They expressed concern about what they see as the proliferation of services for sex trafficking victims by agencies and organizations with "good intentions," but without staff trained specifically about sex trafficking victimization and trauma, whose experience is largely with mixed or general client populations. One service provider in the study summed up this worry:

> Just about anybody can hang out a shingle and say they help sex trafficking victims. Yet, even if they have the best of intentions, if they don't understand the causes and consequences of trafficking they could end up doing a lot of harm.

Along similar lines, several participants stated the need for long-term follow-up with clients, although most recognized the practical difficulties in doing this.

At the same time, many of the service providers noted that identifying trafficking victims is often challenging, and they stressed the need for reliable assessment tools that can be used in a variety of settings in which service providers might encounter potential victims, including health clinics, child welfare agencies, and homeless and domestic violence shelters.

Theme 3: Who are domestic sex trafficking victims?

Although the focus of the interviews was explicitly on perceptions of service needs, other topics surfaced during the course of the conversations. One of these was the service providers' perceptions of domestic sex trafficking victims themselves. As I noted earlier, service providers whom I interviewed spoke of sex trafficking victims as in need of being "rescued," which is common among certain groups of anti-trafficking activists. Although some of the service providers talked about victims as having agency or self-efficacy, the majority described victims as "powerless," "docile," and "subordinated and extremely oppressed" by their traffickers. As we saw in the discussion of security, some service providers clearly felt that victims were "brainwashed" by their traffickers, and many stated that victims "traumatically bond" with their traffickers, which is why they do not wish—at least at first—to be "rescued." This characterization is not unlike the depiction of battered women as experiencing "learned helplessness" (Walker, 1984).

Study participants also made distinctions between domestic sex trafficking victims in terms of their age, comparing adult victims with minors. On one hand, several participants mentioned that minors—specifically, adolescents—are often "more rebellious and defiant" than adult victims. They described adolescent victims as more resistant to intervention. One service provider, for example, explained that adult victims are "more tired": "They're tired of turning tricks and they're past the point of seeing the trafficker as their boyfriend or someone who will take care of them. This makes them more open to accepting help." On the other hand, some service providers appeared to be more sympathetic toward minor victims, consistently referring to them as "children" or "kids," implying more innocence with regard to their victimization. As one participant said, "These kids are going through all the normal stuff that kids go through, the typical growing up stuff, but then have all this trauma and abuse on top of it."

Finally, nearly all the service providers expressed concerns about sex differences in victimization, which is the final subtheme to be discussed.

Subtheme 6: Boys are victimized, too

As noted earlier, the study participants provided services to female sex trafficking victims. But while official statistics show that virtually all cases identified as domestic sex trafficking in the U.S. involve female victims, these service providers estimated that 10–20 percent of domestic sex trafficking victims are males, and the vast majority of these are under 18 years old. Many of the service providers with whom I spoke described male sex trafficking victims as even more stigmatized and more likely to be subjected to victim-blaming than are female sex trafficking victims. They attributed these reactions to the fact that most of these boys are gay or transgender, and many are runaways or "throwaways," having been kicked out of their homes by their parents when they came out or their sexual orientation was discovered, or after experiencing abuse and neglect. The service providers described the boys' vulnerability to being trafficked as similar to that of girls: Once they are on the street, they are befriended by or they fall in love with a man who promises to take care of them—and does so for a while—before forcing them to engage in sex work. They are manipulated into believing that prostitution is part of the "gay lifestyle," such that these boys have difficulty seeing themselves as victimized or even exploited.

Despite such sweeping claims, none of the study participants provided services to male sex trafficking victims. At best, some agencies and organizations have street outreach programs, but no one I interviewed knew of specialized services or group homes for young men who had been trafficked. One service provider summed up the views of the majority of advocates when she said that male sex trafficking victims are "probably the most overlooked or ignored and viewed least sympathetically." Yet, these service providers seemed to distance themselves from male sex trafficking, stating that the problem needs to be addressed by the gay community itself. Most characterized the problem as "too political" and some noted resistance to addressing it within the gay community by those who fear that it will be used to discredit gay relationships and reinforce negative stereotypes.

Consequently, while many service providers were concerned that male sex trafficking victims are neglected or overlooked, they also expressed the belief that until leaders in the gay community are "ready to own this issue" and address it themselves, there isn't much service providers can do.

Conclusion

Although the data presented in this chapter are based on interviews with a relatively small, non-representative sample of U.S. service providers, they nonetheless provide us with insights into service providers' perceptions of the service needs of domestic sex trafficking victims, as well as what they see as gaps or problems in meeting victims' needs and how they perceive domestic sex trafficking victims themselves—elements that are interrelated, rather than discrete. For example, one of the significant controversies that became apparent during the interviews involved service providers' differing beliefs about the level of security required at residential facilities for "rescued" victims. But these beliefs, in turn, reflect differences in service providers' notions of victims' vulnerability as well as the effects of trafficking on victims, with some service providers depicting trafficking victims as "brainwashed" and therefore unable to make decisions in their own best interests. This characterization has been criticized by some observers who see it as infantilizing victims and denying their agency (Barberet, 2014). But many service providers struggled to balance their desire to empower victims and their worry about the traumatic effects of trafficking on victims. There was widespread recognition that domestic sex trafficking victims would benefit from a menu of services, selected to meet individual needs, but there was less consensus regarding how these services should be delivered and the treatment philosophy that informs them.

In conclusion, I must note that the service providers with whom I spoke were sincerely and profoundly concerned with effectively meeting the needs of their clients and improving clients' long-term outcomes. Although some observers refer to these victim advocates pejoratively as members of the new "rescue industry" (Agustín, 2007), I found no evidence that any had "refashioned themselves . . . to heighten their attractiveness vis-à-vis funding" (Feingold, 2010, p. 50). Nor did I find evidence, even among those associated with faith-based organizations, of soldiers on a moral crusade. Despite the many criticisms leveled against services for trafficking victims—some of which are undoubtedly justified—the individuals with whom I spoke struck me as genuinely concerned about social justice, and their openness to—indeed, for some, their embrace of—rigorous empirical evaluation of their services reflects their commitment to victim *advocacy*, which, despite their differences, unites them.

References

Agustín, L. (2007). *Sex at the margins: Migration, labour markets and the rescue industry.* London: Zed.

Banks, D., & Kychkelhahn, T. (2011). *Characteristics of suspected human trafficking incidents, 2008–2010*. Washington, DC: U.S. Department of Justice, Bureau of Justice Statistics.

Barberet, R. (2014). *Women, crime and criminal justice: A global enquiry*. London: Routledge.

Bergen, R. (2006, February). *Marital rape: New research and directions*. Harrisburg, PA: VAWnet. Retrieved on December 7, 2013 from http://vawnet.org

Bernstein, E. (2010). Militarized humanitarianism meets carceral feminism: The politics of sex, rights and freedom in contemporary antitrafficking campaigns. *Signs*, *36*(1), 45–71.

Brennan, D. (2008). Competing claims of victimhood? Foreign and domestic victims of trafficking in the United States. *Sexuality Research & Social Policy*, *5*(4), 45–61.

Caliber Associates (2007). *Evaluation of comprehensive services for victims of human trafficking: Key findings and lessons learned*. Washington, DC: U.S. Department of Justice.

Chapkis, W. (2005). Soft glove, punishing fist: The Trafficking Victims Protection Act of 2000, in Bernstein, E., & Schaffner, L. (Eds.), *Regulating sex: The politics of intimacy and identity*. New York, NY: Routledge, pp. 51–65.

Farrell, A., McDevitt, J., & Fahy, S. (2008). *Understanding and improving law enforcement responses to human trafficking: Final report*. Washington, DC: U.S. Department of Justice.

Feingold, D. A. (2010). Trafficking in numbers: The social construction of human trafficking data, in Andreas, P. & Greenhill, K. M. (Eds.), *Sex, drugs and body counts: The politics of numbers in global crime and conflict*. Ithaca, NY: Cornell University Press, pp. 46–74.

Kittling, N. (2005–2006). God bless the child: The United States' response to domestic juvenile prostitution. *Nevada Law Journal*, *6*, 913–926.

Miles, M. B., & Huberman, A. M. (1994). *Qualitative data analysis* (second ed.). Thousand Oaks, CA: Sage.

O'Brien, E., Hayes, S., & Carpenter, B. (2013). *The politics of sex trafficking: A moral geography*. London: Palgrave Macmillan.

O'Connell Davidson, J. (2006). Will the real sex slaves please stand up? *Feminist Review*, *83*, 4–22.

Raymond, J. G. (2013). *Not a choice, not a job: Exposing the myths about prostitution and the global sex trade*. Washington, DC: Potomac Books.

Stransky, M., & Finkelhor, D. (2008). *How many juveniles are involved in prostitution in the U.S.?* Retrieved on December 7, 2013 from http://www.unh.edu/ccrc/prostitution

Tyldum, G., & Brunovskis, A. (2005). Describing the unobserved: Methodological challenges in empirical studies on human trafficking. *International Migration*, *43*(1/2), 17–34.

U.S. Department of State (2013). *Trafficking in persons report 2013*. Retrieved on December 7, 2013 from http://www.state.gov/documents/organizations/210742.pdf

Walker, L. (1984). *The battered woman syndrome*. New York, NY: Springer.

Weitzer, R. (2010). The movement to criminalize sex work in the United States. *Journal of Law and Society*, *37*(1), 61–84.

Discussion questions

1. According to the service providers, what types of resources are needed to best support victims of trafficking?

2.   How might the focus on serving victims of trafficking for sexual exploitation shape service provision in the U.S.?
3.   How do the views of the service providers articulated in this chapter relate to the political debates described by Outshoorn in Chapter 2?
4.   What questions about service provision for trafficking victims does this chapter raise for you?
5.   What do you think should be done to address the lack of services for men described in this study?

Additional resources

Tricked, a documentary directed by John Keith Wasson and Jane Wells, examines sex trafficking in the United States. Wasson and Wells were embedded with the Denver Vice Squad, traveled to Las Vegas, and interviewed not only law enforcement officials, but also trafficked individuals, parents, service providers, and traffickers. The film was released in 2013 and is distributed by Kino-Lorber, New York.

The Office for Victims of Crime Training and Technical Assistance Center provides a website based on data and resources from the Anti-Human Trafficking Task Forces in the U.S.: http://www.ovcttac.gov

The United Nations Global Initiative to Fight Human Trafficking (UNGIFT) also has a resource-rich website that provides data and additional information on both sex trafficking and labor trafficking: http://www/ungift.org

Chapter 11

On broken chains and missing links

Tackling the "demand side of trafficking"?

Julia O'Connell Davidson

Introduction

Politicians, governmental organizations and anti-trafficking non-governmental organizations (NGOs) claim that "trafficking" is a hugely profitable business in which organized criminals transport millions of human victims around the globe in the modern-day equivalent of the transatlantic slave trade. As U.S. President George W. Bush put it in an address to the UN General Assembly in 2003:

> We must show new energy in fighting back an old evil. Nearly two centuries after the abolition of the transatlantic slave trade, and more than a century after slavery was officially ended in its last strongholds, the trade in human beings for any purpose must not be allowed to thrive in our time.
>
> (cited in Bravo, 2011: 563)

Nobody is in favor of slavery, and if "trafficking" is a modern slave trade then everyone must agree on the need to combat it. Given that by 2012 there were 153 State Parties and nine Signatories to the United Nations *Protocol to Prevent, Suppress and Punish Trafficking in Persons, Especially Women and Children*, supplementing the United Nations Convention against Transnational Organized Crime (2000) (hereafter the Trafficking Protocol), it may appear that there is indeed consensus on the issue (UNODC, 2012). But what exactly is it that all these states have signed up to prevent, suppress, and punish? The Trafficking Protocol identifies "trafficking" as a process (recruitment, transportation, and control) that can be organized in a variety of different ways, involve different types and degrees of compulsion (all of which are undefined—What kind of threats? How much deception? Which types of vulnerability?), and lead to a variety of very different outcomes, linked only by a common purpose, "exploitation," which itself is undefined. This definition does not equip us with a standard, universal yardstick against which an individual's status as "trafficked" or "not trafficked" can be assessed, for both "exploitation" and "force" are slippery and context-dependent notions (Anderson & O'Connell Davidson, 2003). Certainly the forced/voluntary dichotomy that informs the imagined distinction between "trafficking" on the one hand,

and "smuggling" and legally sanctioned systems of labor importation on the other, disregards the well-documented fact that there are "elements of both compulsion and choice . . . in the decision making of most migrants" (Turton, 2003, p. 6).

Though "trafficking" is described as a modern slave trade, people are not today being transported into societies where slavery is legally recognized and regulated as a judicial category, and "Victims of Trafficking" ("VoTs") are not people who have been assigned the legal status of "slave." Exploitation, violence, deception, compulsion, and restraints on people's mobility and capacity to retract from contracts and relationships certainly exist, but they vary along a series of continuums. Rather than describing a fixed constellation of these things, the term "trafficking" expresses a set of moral and normative judgments about which particular constellations of coercion, violence, and exploitation, and in which degree, are beyond the pale. And in theory and in practice, these judgments vary according to a host of factors (including the age, gender, race, and nationality of the exploited person; the context in which s/he is exploited; the beholder's normative, political, and moral values; social and political assumptions about what constitutes inappropriate force and about the types and degree of compulsion that nullify consent, and so on) (Ham, Segrave & Pickering, 2013; O'Connell Davidson, 2010; Testai, 2008).

Since "trafficking" does not exist as a prior, objective category, to state "this is a case of trafficking" is not of the same order as stating, "it is raining," or "the sun is setting," but more like stating, "I believe this to be very wrong." This helps to explain why the issue of "trafficking" can be claimed by different groups of actors campaigning for different (sometimes directly opposing) policy interventions, and why alliances between these different groups ebb and flow depending on which particular perceived "wrong" is the focus of attention. It also helps to explain why the "evils" addressed by "anti-trafficking" policies tend to be those things that state actors—especially those from states that occupy powerful positions on the global stage—regard as very wrong, as opposed to the violation of human rights *per se*. As this chapter sets out to show, this point can be well illustrated through a focus on responses to what is termed "the demand side of trafficking." Since space does not permit an analysis of all aspects of demand-side debates, I will focus on calls to address demand for "sex trafficking" by punishing those who purchase commercial sexual services. In exploring how this measure is justified in the context of prostitution but not in other contexts, the chapter draws attention to the political values and interests that inform and are reproduced in the dominant discourse on "trafficking."

Prostitution and "trafficking"

When "human trafficking" emerged as a major policy preoccupation in the 1990s, attention was very much focused on cases in which women and girls were forced into prostitution against the backcloth of the immense political, economic, and social upheavals taking place in former Eastern bloc countries. For governments of affluent liberal democratic states, such cases were indicative of a much wider problem of "transnational organized crime" and other perceived threats to state sovereignty that arose in the context of more porous borders in the post-Cold War era, especially immigration crime. But the association with prostitution made "trafficking" a politically sensitive and potentially divisive issue, for there is much cross-national variation in terms of the legal frameworks and social norms pertaining to prostitution, and in terms of public and political discourse on commercial sex. Certainly in 2000, when the UN Trafficking Protocol was drawn up, there was no consensus upon whether the international community should be attempting to eradicate all forms of prostitution, or whether a distinction should be made between forced and child prostitution (which should be outlawed) and prostitution that is voluntarily chosen by adults (which should be tolerated or regulated).

To sidestep such disputes, the definition of "trafficking" provided in the Trafficking Protocol avoided offering a definition of the phrase "exploitation of prostitution of others or other forms of sexual exploitation" because "government delegates to the negotiations could not agree on a common meaning" (GAATW, 2011, p. 31). This meant that the Protocol could be adopted "without prejudice to how State Parties address prostitution in their respective domestic laws" (Interpretative note 64 to the Protocol), but it also allowed space for conflicting interpretations of what does and does not constitute "sex trafficking" (Anderson & O'Connell Davidson, 2003). Groups that were already campaigning for the abolition of prostitution—including both radical feminist lobby groups like the Coalition Against Trafficking in Women (CATW) and religious groups—could continue to treat the terms "trafficking" and "prostitution" as synonymous. For them, the new international commitment to fighting "human trafficking" promised a means through which to mainstream their understanding of sex commerce as fundamentally wrong, and the issue of "trafficking" thus became the focal point of what Ron Weitzer (2007) has described as a "moral crusade" against the sex industry. Though this crusade finds no favor with governments of states that take a more liberal and/or regulationist approach to prostitution, and is heavily criticized by sex worker rights activists and others concerned with the human, civil, and labor rights of sex workers, governments of states that take a prohibitionist stance on prostitution, in particular the U.S.A, are important and powerful allies, especially in relation to the struggle against "the demand side."

Demand and the "trafficking" chain

Article 9 of the United Nations Trafficking Protocol emphasized the need for State Parties to take measures to discourage the demand that fosters exploitation and, as a result, questions about the demand for the labor/services of "trafficked" persons have been a focus of attention in international policy circles over the past 13 years. Much of this attention has focused on demand in the context of prostitution, and contemporary abolitionists have lobbied hard for the universal introduction of laws to penalize demand. A law passed by the Swedish Parliament in May 1998 criminalizing the purchase or the attempted purchase of "a temporary sexual relationship" has been very effectively sold as model legislation for tackling "the demand side of trafficking." Norway introduced a law criminalizing the purchase of sex in 2008, Iceland did so in 2009, and the same law is currently being debated in Finland, Ireland, and France. The Swedish law was not actually formulated as a response to the issue of "human trafficking," rather it "was the culmination of nearly a decade of work by feminist groups and center/left politicians to convince lawmakers that they should 'send a message' that 'society' does not accept prostitution" (Kulick, 2004, p. 199). However, in international policy circles, it is now discursively framed as an "anti-trafficking" measure, not merely a message about "society's" view of prostitution. This expresses a very particular understanding of the relationship between prostitution and "trafficking," as well as of the relationship between labor exploitation and consumer demand in the context of prostitution.

Box 11.1 The "Swedish Model" or "Nordic Model"

The Swedish Model or Nordic Model refers to a legal approach to prostitution which criminalizes the customer and anyone who profits from prostitution, such as brothel owners, pimps, drivers, landlords, etc. but decriminalizes the sex worker. This law was introduced in Sweden in 1999. Proponents of the law argued that it would send a message that the state does not condone prostitution and would decrease prostitution while holding customers (referred to as prostitution perpetrators by proponents of the law) accountable for the offense. This approach sees prostitution as a form of structural gendered violence and sees sex workers as victims. Advocates for this type of policy would like to see it implemented in more countries. Opponents point out that the sex workers the law was intended to help were not consulted in its formulation and argue that it has made life harder for sex workers by impairing their ability to earn a living, increasing social stigma, and pushing sex work further underground.

For more information:

Opposing the Swedish Model
http://www.nswp.org/sites/nswp.org/files/NordicBrief-ENG.pdf
http://sexworker.wordpress.com

Advocating the Swedish Model
http://exoduscry.com/wp-content/uploads/2010/07/swedish_model.pdf
http://www.equalitynow.org/press_clip/equality_now_advocates_for_
   nordic_model_against_trafficking_and_gender_inequality_the_nor

Many of those advocating measures to penalize the sex buyer accept that people can be "trafficked" into sectors other than prostitution, and do not call for the criminalization of consumers in these other contexts. Prostitution is a special case because, according to contemporary abolitionists, men's demand for prostitution leads directly to "sex trafficking" (Hughes, 1999). Echoing the thoughts of her nineteenth and early twentieth century predecessors in the social purity movement and anti-"White Slavery" campaigns, Janice Raymond (2001, p. 9) of CATW calls on states to:

> Penalize the buyers. The least discussed part of the prostitution and traffick-
> ing chain has been the men who buy women for sexual exploitation in pros-
> titution, pornography, sex tourism and mail order bride marketing . . . our
> responsibility is to make men change their behaviour by all means available—
> educational, cultural, and through legislation that penalizes men for the crime
> of sexual exploitation.

Sigma Huda, who was UN Special Rapporteur on the human rights aspects of the victims of trafficking in persons in 2006 and also a member of CATW, explained why those who pay for sex are uniquely deserving of control and punishment as follows: "Unlike the purchaser of consumer goods produced through trafficked labour, the prostitute-user is simultaneously both the demand-creator and (by vir-tue of his receipt of the trafficked person) part of the trafficking chain." We do not take receipt of the "trafficked" person and personally compel her to pick or process coffee beans when we buy coffee produced by "trafficked" labor, nor is the coffee we drink always or necessarily produced by "VoTs." Thus, according to this line of reasoning, as unwitting consumers, our demand for coffee is not a necessary link in the chain that leads to people being "trafficked" onto coffee plan-tations. But without the men who provide demand for prostitution, there would be no "sex trafficking" and no "masters" to take receipt of "sex slaves."

This argument has been well received in the U.S., where prostitution law is already strongly prohibitionist. Indeed, the U.S. government has exerted great pres-sure internationally for all countries to adopt the "penalize the buyer" approach. A recent report on "the demand side of trafficking" by USAID (2011, p. iv), the U.S. Federal Government agency responsible for providing urgently needed economic, humanitarian, and development foreign aid, states, "Without buyers' demand for prostitution there would be no trafficking for the purpose of prostitu-tion." It then asserts that it is "meaningless to separate demand for prostitution from demand for prostitution provided by trafficked persons," and proceeds to recommend the adoption of legislation that criminalizes buyers, accompanied by enhanced law enforcement efforts that make the threat of arrest tangible, in order to reduce demand for prostitution (USAID, 2011, pp. iv–vii). In the U.S. Depart-ment of State's extremely influential annual *Trafficking in Persons (TIP) Report*, "countries that have not increased criminal punishments against clients of sex workers (with no distinction between consensual commercial sex and trafficked prostitution) are evaluated as not tackling 'demand' adequately" (GAATW, 2011, p. 14), and penalized for this failure.

In theory, this is not about pressurizing countries in need of development aid to bow to the U.S. government's moral stance on prostitution, rather it is justified on grounds that, in the particular context of prostitution, consumer demand drives "trafficking," a slave trade which all states have a duty to eradicate. But is prostitution really the only sector to which "the trafficking chain" argument could be applied?

Invisible chains: The case of domestic work

It is certainly true there are some differences between the consumption of sexual services and the consumption of consumer goods. When consumers buy cheap vegetables, they buy them because they are cheap and not specifically because they have been picked by, say, Ukrainian or Lithuanian workers. But people who buy sex generally wish to consume what has been termed "embodied labour" (Wolkowitz, 2002), which is to say they normally want to consume the services of persons of a specific sex, age, and also often race, ethnicity, or nationality. Few prostitution customers would be equally happy to buy sex from an elderly man or a young woman, and they may also have specific preferences regarding the racial or national identity of the sex workers they use, their language skills, physical appearance, and so on (Anderson & O'Connell Davidson, 2003). It does not follow that those who buy sex uniformly lack all scruples as consumers, however. Indeed, there is plenty of research to show that people who pay for sex are not a homogeneous group. Some of them go to great lengths to avoid buying sex in settings where they believe workers might be coerced into prostitution, and there is no shortage of cases in which clients have actually alerted the police to the presence of forced labor in brothels, precisely because they think it is wrong (Anderson & O'Connell Davidson, 2003; Sanders, 2008).

Furthermore, clients' interest in embodied labor does not actually distinguish demand for commercial sex from demand for services/labor in *all* other sectors in which "trafficking" is said to occur. Those who wish to consume the labor of wives, adopted children, or *au pairs* within the private household, for example, also provide demand for embodied labor, as do employers of domestic workers. Indeed, research on "the demand side of trafficking" found that some employers of domestic workers specifically sought out workers of a particular gender, race, ethnicity, gender, age, and/or nationality precisely because they regarded these "types" of people as better suited to servile labor, more controllable, and somehow less deserving, and even less desiring, of rights. In some cases, employers also expressed a preference for irregular migrants, who were perceived as even less likely to be able to make demands or claim rights (Anderson & O'Connell Davidson, 2003; Bott, 2005; Stock, 2004).

The idea that the sex buyer "takes receipt" of the "trafficked" person is also questionable. Most clients' encounters with prostitutes are fleeting, and even when the prostitute is subject to forced labor, it is normally the brothel owner or pimp, not the client, who dictates the terms on which she works. By contrast, employers of live-in domestic workers do receive the worker into their home for lengthy periods of time. They live with them, they determine their pay and living and working conditions, they know whether the worker remains there of her own free will. Here, the employer is the end consumer and, unlike the coffee buyer mentioned above, s/he does have to personally exact forced labor from the unfree domestic worker. If the logic of the "trafficking chain" case applies in relation to demand for prostitution, it certainly applies equally to demand for live-in domestic workers.

So why are there no calls to penalize *all* buyers of women and girls for exploitation in domestic work? The most obvious reason is that paying someone to live in your home as your servant is not socially stigmatized in the way that paying someone for sexual services is, and that live-in domestic work is regarded as, in some contexts, performing socially valued and necessary functions. In other words, calls to criminalize sex buyers express a set of moral and political values about prostitution, rather than addressing a unique or specific link between demand for prostitution and "trafficking." To this, it is important to add that many of those who make the "penalize the buyer" case in relation to prostitution (including—I would venture to guess—members of radical feminist organizations like CATW as well as state actors) are themselves employers of domestic workers. They have vested interests in domestic work, and so would not accept the argument that because *some* employers of domestic workers are known to imprison, beat, rape, and cheat their employees, *all* employers of domestic workers should be criminalized.

A different set of interests, and a shift of alliances, is revealed if we consider what is perhaps an even more striking absence in talk of the need to "penalize the buyer."

Broken chains: Pornography

Like prostitution, the production of pornography is a segment of the commercial sex market where individuals, including migrants, are sometimes subjected to coercion, exploitation, and violence. What is described as "trafficking" in the context of prostitution can thus also be found in pornography, and if prostitution would cease to exist without buyers' demand, so it might equally be said that without consumer demand for pornography, there would be no economic incentive to coerce or exploit people for purposes of producing it. Radical feminists do say this, and argue for an end to pornography as well as prostitution (e.g. MacKinnon, 2005). But on this issue, the "anti-trafficking" alliance between groups like CATW and governmental actors breaks down. Eliminating demand for pornography is not on the "anti-trafficking" agenda of even the governments that are most enthusiastic about criminalizing the sex buyer in the context of prostitution. The USAID (2011) report mentioned above, for example, identifies pornography as a factor that precipitates male demand for prostitution, and yet banning the production and criminalizing the purchase of pornography is not amongst the list of otherwise draconian measures recommended to eliminate the demand that fosters "sex trafficking" (including the public shaming as well as incarceration of men who buy services from prostitutes).

The disjuncture between how policy makers approach prostitution and how they approach pornography can also be rather nicely illustrated by the views of the former British Home Secretary Jacqui Smith. In November 2008, as Home Secretary, Smith announced proposals for measures designed to tackle demand by shifting the focus onto sex buyers "because they create demand for prostitution and demand for the trafficking of women for sex" (CNN, 2008). A few months later, Smith was caught up in the parliamentary expenses scandal, and it was revealed, among other things, that she had claimed expenses for a telecom bill which included charges for two pornographic films viewed by her husband. After her parliamentary career ended, Smith made a documentary on pornography for BBC Radio 5 Live. Where in relation to prostitution she had stated "There will be no more excuses for those who pay for sex" (CNN, 2008), the documentary demonstrated she was quite able to find excuses for those who provide the demand for pornography:

> I'm pretty sure that there are plenty of people who make an informed decision to work in the porn industry—they make a choice to stay, based on the money they can earn and some even enjoy it. Of course I understand that I was talking to those at the most "legitimate" end of the industry. I know from experience that there are many other women in the broader sex industry who are far from willing participants . . . People use porn because it's enjoyable. Couples sometimes use it together. Men aren't turned into monsters by watching a bit of pay TV!
>
> (Smith, 2011)

In states that already adopt a prohibitionist stance on prostitution, the equation of demand for prostitution with demand for the services of "trafficked" persons legitimates efforts to strengthen and enforce existing laws that construct prostitution as sexual deviance or exploitation, public nuisance, and/or criminality (laws that are widely condemned by groups concerned with the safety, human rights, and civil liberties of those who work in prostitution). That demand for pornography is not similarly equated with demand for the services of "trafficked" persons reflects, I would argue, the fact that the production and distribution of pornography is a multi-billion dollar industry, largely integrated into the formal mainstream taxable economy, and largely controlled and organized by sizeable, sometimes huge, multinational corporations. The politics, not to mention the costs, of attempting to stamp out this industry by penalizing those who consume its products are very different from those of suppressing the relatively far, far smaller market for prostitution by criminalizing and publicly humiliating men caught paying sex workers for services. When it comes to mainstream markets, end consumers and even employers are not automatically regarded as implicated in the demand that fosters exploitation.

From "trafficking chains" to "supply chains"

In dominant discourse on "labor trafficking" into mainstream, state sanctioned markets, talk of "the trafficking chain" is replaced by a preoccupation with "supply chains." In broad brushstroke, the argument goes like this. One of the most striking trends in labor market restructuring over the past 30 odd years has been "the shift from the dominance of a single employer model to complex inter-organizational arrangements including a variety of contracting out arrangements and use of temporary and agency workers in both the private and public sectors" (Thompson, 2013, p. 481). The distance between the workers whose labor-power is consumed in the production of a given product, and the company that sells that end product (and so also between the workers and the consumer of the end product) is often extremely long, and mediated by many third parties along the supply chain. These long chains of subcontractual relations are said to put workers at risk of "trafficking" and exploitation.

Questions about the political context in which these long supply chains have emerged (for instance, about the neoliberal policy measures that have disembedded labor and other markets from regulatory constraints, freeing those higher up the supply chain to squeeze costs by subcontracting risk and responsibility down to smaller, less visible and less accountable units) are not at the heart of dominant discourse on "labor trafficking." However, there are often calls for stronger mechanisms to enforce compliance with applicable labor law, rules and regulations, including harsher legal penalties for those who break laws. Yet the talk here is not all about suppression and punishment. Yes, the end demand for "trafficked" labor may come from unscrupulous and bad individuals or organizations that require control—it can be fueled by companies wanting to cut costs by avoiding "any financial obligation for benefits, taxes, and social insurance," often "fly-by-night companies that are easily dismantled to avoid criminal sanctions" (USAID, 2011, p. 32). But, unlike those who provide demand for prostitution, the individual or organization at the top of the supply chain is not necessarily bad, and may even be keen to work with the authorities to prevent "trafficking." Indeed, "trafficked" persons "may be under subcontract to work for legitimate businesses, government agencies, or individuals who may not be aware of the exploitative conditions of the workers' employment" (USAID, 2011, p. 33).

This is an important proviso in the USAID report given that it includes a case study of "trafficking" allegations made against the United States Defense Department's contractor, Kellogg Brown & Root (KBR), and its subcontractors, involving the recruitment of foreign workers for labor on U.S. bases in Iraq (USAID, 2011, p. 34), and so describes a "trafficking chain" with none other than George W. Bush standing at its very head. One of these allegations involves the case of 13 Nepali men, between the ages of 18 and 27, who in 2004 were recruited in Nepal with promises of a $500 monthly salary to work as kitchen staff in luxury hotels in Jordan. "When they learned that they were actually on their way to Al Asad Air Base in Iraq, the large brokerage fees they owed allegedly kept the men from turning back for home," and as they were driven in cars in the front of an unsecured 17-car caravan along the Amman-to-Baghdad highway in Iraq's Anbar province, they were stopped by insurgents (Barron, 2013). Twelve were kidnapped and later executed. "The thirteenth man survived and worked in a warehouse in Iraq for 15 months before returning to Nepal" (Hedgpeth, 2008). After protracted legal struggles, the families of the murdered men have been allowed to make claims against KBR under the Trafficking Victims Protection Reauthorization, and the trial was scheduled for April 2014 (Business and Human Rights Resource Centre, 2013). If the case had gone to trial, it would have taken ten years for the Defense Department's contractor to be held accountable for its involvement in "trafficking" that led to the violent deaths of 12 young people. Throughout this time, it has been unthinkable that George W. Bush, or even the U.S. Defense Department, would come to feature in dominant discourse as furnishing the demand that fuels "trafficking."

Box 11.2 *Ramchandra Adhikari, et al., v. Daoud & Partners, et al.,* KBR human trafficking case

KBR is the largest U.S. contractor providing civilian labor on U.S. military bases around the world. It was implicated in a human trafficking complaint when a group of 13 Nepali men were kidnapped while driving in an unsecured convoy on the Amman-to-Baghdad highway on their way to work at a military base. Twelve of the men were executed by members of the Ansar al-Sunna Army and the executions were broadcast on television. The men were fraudulently recruited for other work at higher pay, but were told they could not back out of the jobs due to large brokerage fees they had paid to secure the jobs. The one survivor, Buddi Prasad Gurung, was subsequently held on the base for 15 months before being allowed to return to Nepal, whereupon he and family members of the other victims attempted to sue KBR under the U.S. Trafficking Victims Protection Act (2000). However, the case was dismissed on January 15, 2014 when Judge Keith P. Ellison of the U.S. District Court, S.D. Texas, Houston Division, granted the defendants' Supplemental Motion for Summary Judgment on the basis that the Trafficking Victims Protection Act did not apply "extraterritorially" (outside the U.S.). Although extraterritorial jurisdiction for lawsuits against perpetrators for abuses that take place outside the U.S. was written into the Trafficking Victims Protection Reauthorization Act (2005), the law could not be applied retroactively for crimes that took place in 2004.

For more information:

Ramchandra Adhikari, et al., v. Daoud & Partners, et al.
http://iissonline.net/adhikari-v-daoud-partners-dist-court-sd-texas-2014

Conclusion

The concept of "trafficking" presents a panoply of complex and intractable definitional and conceptual problems, which, when unpicked, suggest there is no real consensus on what constitutes, causes, or could prevent "trafficking," or on who counts as a "victim," who as a "trafficker," and who and what "fosters demand for exploitation." But because "trafficking" is popularly imagined as slavery (something universally regarded as wrong), any measure that is described as a means of combating "trafficking" enjoys great moral purchase. Hence, the U.S. government can present the "anti-trafficking" measures it recommends and enacts, from the militarization of borders through to legislation penalizing the purchase of sexual services, as designed to punish "evil" and protect the human rights of the weak and vulnerable. And yet, as Elizabeth Bernstein (2012, p. 6) observes:

> The evidence . . . suggests that contemporary anti-trafficking campaigns have been far more successful at criminalizing economically and racially marginalized populations, enforcing border control, and measuring other countries' compliance with human rights standards based on the curtailment of prostitution than they have been at issuing any concrete benefits to victims.

The intense focus in the "demand-side" policy debate on the idea of fighting "trafficking" by punishing individuals who choose to enter into what are, in the main, consensual sexual acts with adults deflects attention from deeper questions about the role of the state in constructing and shaping *all* markets (informal as well as formal, criminalized as well as sanctioned, stigmatized as well as socially valued) and producing the vulnerability of certain groups to exploitation within them (Anderson, 2013; O'Connell Davidson, 2010; Sharma, 2003).

References

Anderson, B. (2013). *Us and them: The dangerous politics of immigration control*. Oxford: OUP.

Anderson, B., & O'Connell Davidson, J. (2003). Demand for "trafficked" labour? A multi-country study. *IOM Migration Research Series*. Geneva: International Organization for Migration.

Barron, B. (2013). Legal blow for families of slain Nepali laborers. Retrieved October 2013 from http://www.courthousenews.com/2013/08/27/60644.htm

Bernstein, E. (2012). Sex, trafficking, and the politics of freedom, Occasional Paper No. 45, School of Social Science, Columbia University.

Bott, E. (2005). Too close for comfort? "Race" and the management of proximity, guilt and other anxieties in paid domestic labour. *Sociological Research Online, 10*(3). Retrieved October 2013 from http://www.socresonline.org.uk/10/3/bott.html

Bravo, K. (2011). The role of the transatlantic slave trade in contemporary anti-human trafficking discourse. *Seattle Journal for Social Justice, 9*(2), 555–597.

Business and Human Rights Resource Centre (2013). KBR Lawsuit. Retrieved January 2014 from http://www.business-humanrights.org/Categories/Lawlawsuits/Lawsuitsregu latoryaction/LawsuitsSelectedcases/KBRlawsuitrehumantraffickinginIraq

CNN (2008). Retrieved October 2013 from http://edition.cnn.com/2008/WORLD/europe/11/19/uk.prostitution.laws

GAATW (2011). *Moving beyond supply and demand catchphrases*. Bangkok: Global Alliance Against Trafficking in Women. Retrieved October 2013 from http://www.gaatw.org/publications/MovingBeyond_SupplyandDemand_GAATW2011.pdf

Ham, J., Segrave, M., & Pickering, S. (2013). In the eyes of the beholder: Border enforcement, suspect travellers and trafficking victims. *Anti-Trafficking Review*, 2. Retrieved January 2014 from http://www.antitraffickingreview.org/images/documents/Issue2/04_ATR_issue2_ThematicArticle_Ham_Segrave_Pickering.pdf

Hedgpeth, D. (2008). KBR, partner in Iraq contract sued in human trafficking case, *Washington Post*, August 28. Retrieved October 2013 from http://articles.washingtonpost.com/2008-08-28/world/36928422_1_kbr-daoud-partners-nepali

Hughes, D. (1999). Legalizing prostitution will not stop the harm. Coalition Against Trafficking in Women. Retrieved October 2013 from http://www.uri.edu/artsci/wms/hughes/mhvlegal.htm

Kempadoo, K., Sanghera, J., & Pattanaik, B. (Eds.) (2005). *Trafficking and prostitution reconsidered*. London: Paradigm.

Kulick, D. (2004). Sex in the new Europe: The criminalization of clients and Swedish fear of penetration. *Anthropological Theory, 3*(2), 199–218.

MacKinnon, C. (2005). Pornography as trafficking. *Michigan Journal of International Law, 26*(4), 993–1012.

O'Connell Davidson, J. (2010). New slavery, old binaries: human trafficking and the borders of freedom. *Global Networks, 10*(2), 244–261.

— (2013). Troubling freedom: Migration, debt and modern slavery. *Migration Studies, 1*(1), 1–20.

Ramchandra Adhikari, et al., v. Daoud & Partners, et al. (2014). Civil Action No. 4:09-CV-1237. United States District Court, S.D. Texas, Houston Division. January 15, 2014.

Raymond, J. (2001). *Guide to the new UN trafficking protocol*. North Amherst, MA: CATW.

Sanders, T. (2008). Male sexual scripts: Intimacy, sexuality and pleasure in the purchase of commercial sex. *Sociology, 42*(3), 400–417.

Sharma, N. (2003). Travel agency: A critique of anti-trafficking campaigns. *Refuge, 21*(3), 53–65.

Smith, J. (2011). My view of pornography. *The Independent*. Retrieved October 2013 from http://www.independent.co.uk/life-style/love-sex/jacqui-smith-my-view-of-pornography-2229430.html

Stock, I. (2004). Concepts of ethnicity, race and culture in employers' relations with their domestic workers and their implications for citizenship. Paper presented to 4th Congreso sobre la inmigracion en espana: cuidadania y participacion, Girona, Spain, November 10–13.

Testai, P. (2008). Debt as a route to modern slavery in the discourse on "sex trafficking": Myth or reality? *6*. Retrieved June 2012 from http://www.humansecuritygateway.com/showRecord.php?RecordId=21920

Thompson, P. (2013). Financialization of the workplace: extending and applying the disconnected capitalism thesis. *Work, Employment and Society, 27*(3), 472–488.

Turton, D. (2003). Conceptualising forced migration. RSC Working Paper No. 12. Oxford: Refugee Studies Centre.

UNODC (2012). Status of ratification of the United Nations Convention against Transnational Organized Crime and the Protocols thereto as at October 1, 2012. Retrieved

October 2013 from http://www.unodc.org/documents/treaties/organized_crime/COP6/CTOC_COP_2012_CRP/CTOC_COP_2012_CRP1.pdf

USAID (2011). *Tackling the demand side of trafficking*. Retrieved October 2013 from http://socialtransitions.kdid.org/sites/socialtransitions/files/resource/files/Tackling_the_Demand-_Final_8-29-11.pdf

Weitzer, R. (2007). The social construction of sex trafficking: Ideology and institutionalization of a moral crusade. *Politics & Society, 35*, 447–474.

Wolkowitz, C. (2002). The social relations of body work. *Work, Employment & Society, 16*(3), 497–510.

Discussion questions

1. What arguments are made in favor of "ending demand" for prostitution?
2. What are the critiques of the "end demand" approach?
3. What is the "Swedish Model"?
4. What was the *Adhikari v. Daoud & Partners* case?
5. What does O'Connell Davidson say about conflation of trafficking and slavery?

Additional resources

KBR Halliburton Confines 1,000 Workers in Windowless Warehouses. (2011). Retrieved from https://www.youtube.com/watch?v=SScWVfw1JNc

Global Alliance Against Traffic in Women (GAATW) (2011). Moving beyond 'supply and demand' catchphrases: Assessing the uses and limitations of demand-based approaches in anti-trafficking

http://www.gaatw.org/publications/MovingBeyond_SupplyandDemand_GAATW2011.pdf

End Demand ad
https://www.youtube.com/watch?v=E0leBVbZPls

Section IV

Moving forward

Molly Dragiewicz

Section IV showcases two contemporary, critical, human rights–based approaches to human trafficking and exploitative labor conditions. The chapters investigate the impact of international trafficking policies for sex workers in India and Ivory Coast in West Africa. Each of these chapters presents local activism to address trafficking driven by those most involved. This section closes with a conclusion that points the way forward for additional research.

Chapter 12, "'We Have the Right Not To Be "Rescued" . . .'": When Anti-Trafficking Programs Undermine the Health and Well-Being of Sex Workers," was written by Aziza Ahmed and Meena Seshu. Ahmed is Associate Professor of Law at Northeastern University School of Law in the United States. Seshu is co-founder of Sampada Gramin Mahila Sanstha (SANGRAM), a non-governmental organization in India that works with sex workers to stop the spread of HIV/AIDS. This chapter provides a critical perspective on the "raid and rescue" approach used by some anti-trafficking groups. It uses a local case study of Veshya Anyay Mukti Parishad (VAMP), a sex workers' collective in Sangli, India, to explore the impact of raid and rescue efforts on HIV programming. The chapter introduces U.S. anti-trafficking and anti-prostitution campaigns and their impact on law and policy in other countries, especially around HIV prevention programs and sex worker organizing. It also provides an alternative approach to harm reduction, political organizing, and empowerment for sex workers as implemented at the grassroots level.

In Chapter 13, "Nothing Like Chocolate: Sex Trafficking and Child Labor Trafficking," Kum-Kum Bhavnani and Emily Schneider contrast mainstream discourses centered on "sex trafficking" with the realities of child trafficking and exploitation in cocoa production in West Africa. Bhavnani is Professor of Sociology at the University of California Santa Barbara in the United States. She also has formal affiliations with Global and Feminist Studies. Schneider is a Ph.D. candidate in the Department of Sociology at the University of California, Santa Barbara. The authors argue that the focus on sex trafficking has contributed to a distorted view of trafficking which shortchanges international trafficking, other forms of forced and exploitative labor, and leaves out entire regions and groups of people. For example, although dominant trafficking discourses are largely produced by countries with recent histories of colonization and oppression, including legalized slavery regimes, these discourses virtually ignore black workers from

Africa in favor of a focus on white and Asian women. Mainstream discourses also harm the many sex workers who are not trafficked, the authors argue. Their nuanced discussion of the prostitution debates between feminists complements and supplements Outshoorn's overview of the prostitution and trafficking policy debates in Chapter 2. Bhavnani and Schneider recount some of the damaging unintended outcomes of the contemporary focus on prostitution, including further criminalization of sex workers in the name of saving them. Their chapter highlights the main issues that emerge from child trafficking for cocoa production and compares it to sex trafficking.

In Chapter 14, I conclude by pointing to some possible directions for future research on human trafficking. While there is certainly much work to be done to build a research-based foundation for anti-trafficking policy, law, and practice around the globe, the chapters in this section provide a unique contribution by showing what local grassroots activism that is informed by those affected can look like. It is my hope that readers who are interested in doing something about human trafficking will learn from the critical perspectives presented in this book. We should direct our energies to empirical research and interventions informed and indeed guided by those whom we desire to help. There has been plenty of commentary on the trafficking debates, and these chapters provide models for taking the discussion to the next level to effect positive social change. They also provide a caution about the ways in which popular trafficking discourses can backfire despite the best intentions of those reproducing them. We are all opposed to human trafficking, but we need to be critical consumers of trafficking rhetoric and resist the urge to uncritically reproduce narratives that are counterproductive or even damaging to those most affected.

Learning objectives for Section IV

1. Describe the unintended consequences of anti-trafficking policies.
2. Explain how corporations are involved in human trafficking.
3. Discuss who and what is left out of popular discussions about human trafficking.
4. List the authors' suggestions about how to move forward to prevent trafficking and other forms of abuse and exploitation.
5. Propose specific studies that could be undertaken in the future to better understand and prevent human trafficking.

Chapter 12

"We have the right not to be 'rescued' . . ."*

When anti-trafficking programs undermine the health and well-being of sex workers**

Aziza Ahmed and Meena Seshu

Introduction

The United Nations Protocol to Prevent, Suppress and Punish Trafficking in Persons, Especially Women and Children 2000, also known as the UN Trafficking Protocol or Palermo Protocol, defines trafficking in persons as,

> the recruitment, transportation, transfer, harbouring or receipt of persons, by means of the threat or use of force or other forms of coercion, of abduction, of fraud, of deception, of the abuse of power or of a position of vulnerability or the giving or receiving of payments or benefits to achieve the consent of a person having control over another person, for the purpose of exploitation. Exploitation shall include, at a minimum, the exploitation of the prostitution of others or other forms of sexual exploitation, forced labor or services, slavery or practices similar to slavery, servitude or the removal of organs.

While the Palermo Protocol's intention to end trafficking is clear, the meaning of key terms utilized (exploitation, vulnerability, and consent amongst others) is not self-evident, resulting in debate and contestation. Of particular concern to sex work communities is the idea that prostitution is necessarily sexual exploitation and thus qualifies as trafficking. Conflating sex work and trafficking brings sex work under the umbrella of a range of anti-trafficking initiatives that attempt to rescue sex workers through raid, rescue, and rehabilitation schemes with detrimental impacts on HIV programs.

This article uses a case study of Veshya Anyay Mukti Parishad (VAMP), a sex workers' collective in Sangli, India, to explore the impact of anti-trafficking efforts on HIV programming. The paper begins with an overview of the anti-trafficking movement emerging out of the United States. This U.S.-driven anti-trafficking movement supports, through funding and programs, India's state law on trafficking, the Immoral Traffick Prevention Act (ITPA), and works in partnership with domestic Indian anti-trafficking organizations to raid brothels to rescue and rehabilitate sex workers. Contrary to their purported goal of rescuing and rehabilitating women forced into sex work, the anti-trafficking projects that employ a raid, rescue, and rehabilitate model are indiscriminate and often undermine HIV projects at the local level, in turn harming women and girls. We utilize the case of one peer educator in Sangli, India to demonstrate and highlight some of the negative consequences of these anti-trafficking efforts on HIV prevention efforts.

Theoretical framing

This chapter utilizes several theoretical frameworks developed by law and sociology scholars to understand the impact of trafficking programs. In the analysis portion of the paper, we turn to the public health literature to understand and explain the impact of the raid, rescue, and rehabilitation methodology on sex workers caught in the conflation of sex work with trafficking.

Professor Janie Chuang (2010) has documented the rise of "neo-abolitionism," a U.S.-based movement of feminist abolitionists, conservatives, and Evangelical Christians to end trafficking globally. Despite common knowledge that trafficking can occur in many labor sectors, the majority of attention by neo-abolitionists is given to trafficking in the sex sector. The motivations of these various anti-trafficking sub-movements differ considerably. Professor Janet Halley and her co-authors (2006) examine the rise of abolitionist feminism in particular, highlighting the growing influence of abolitionist feminism in the context of international law and inside of international human rights. These feminist abolitionists are often driven by the dominance feminist perspective that all sex work is trafficking and is thereby coerced. This idea is premised on a larger notion of women's lack of agency in sexuality (for a description of the sexual dominance or radical feminist position on sex work see Outshoorn in this volume; Abrams, 1995; Halley et al., 2006). Many radical feminist abolitionists and their allies rely heavily on criminal law as a tool to address trafficking as evidenced by the language of the Palermo Protocol. Sociologist Elizabeth Bernstein (2007) terms the reliance of feminists on criminal law "carceral feminism," reflecting a rightward shift of some feminist organizations that offer increasingly punitive solutions including the use of criminal law as a means to end trafficking. Bernstein's work demonstrates how this rightward shift is part of a growing culture of militarized humanitarianism by the United States (Bernstein, 2007).

The powerful imagery of the modern-day sex slave drives the public discourse on the issue of trafficking in the United States and globally. Fueled by the trope of the captured young sex slave who cannot escape her trafficker and supported by funding from the U.S. government and religious organizations, the neo-abolitionists have become increasingly reliant on "raid, rescue, and rehabilitation" as primary methods of fighting sex trafficking.

While this chapter draws specific attention to the involvement of U.S.-funded organizations and agencies in the raid, rescue, and rehabilitate industry as an international force, it is important to note that many of these projects are implemented by Indian national abolitionist organizations. While there is no comprehensive data available on the abolitionist movement in India, our research demonstrates the active engagement of these organizations in abolitionist work and the receipt of funding and support directly from international funding agencies and religious groups (Consulate General of the United States, 2006).

Drivers of the international anti-trafficking movement: The influence of the U.S. government and civil society

The United States is a key force in the push to end trafficking internationally. The U.S. government has provided a total of 528 million dollars to anti-trafficking projects since 2001 (USAID, 2011). The neo-abolitionists played a key role in demanding the U.S. government address trafficking through funding, programming, and monitoring country progress towards anti-trafficking. Further, the U.S. government through the U.S. State Department Office to Monitor and Combat Trafficking in Persons (TIP Office) instituted a range of disciplinary and regulatory measures for countries that did not meet required standards of laws, policies, and programs and restrictions on U.S. government funding both within and outside the U.S. (Chuang, 2010).

The neo-abolitionist agenda has crept from trafficking and crime control efforts to HIV/AIDS. In 2003, the U.S. enacted the President's Emergency Plan for AIDS Relief (PEPFAR), which states that "no funds made available to carry out this Act, or any amendment made by this Act, may be used to promote or advocate the legalization or practice of prostitution or sex trafficking" (United States Leadership Against HIV/AIDS, Tuberculosis, and Malaria Act of 2003). This language is known as the anti-prostitution loyalty oath (APLO). PEPFAR's 15 billion dollars towards the HIV epidemic made the U.S. government the largest bilateral donor on HIV and AIDS and in turn a heavy hand of influence on the future of the ability of sex workers to respond to the HIV epidemic. The APLO facilitated access to funding for organizations that were willing to sign onto the pledge and resulted in the exclusion of sex work projects from U.S. HIV funding. This resulted in the promotion of the U.S. abolitionist agenda, support for projects seeking to criminalize aspects of the sex industry, and bolstering of organizations seeking to raid, rescue, and rehabilitate. In June 2013 the U.S. Supreme Court found the APLO unconstitutional as a violation of freedom of expression for U.S. organizations.

Box 12.1 The anti-prostitution loyalty oath (APLO) or Anti-Prostitution Pledge in the United States Leadership Against HIV/AIDS, Tuberculosis, and Malaria Act of 2003

The Act was introduced to Congress on March 17, 2003 and enacted on May 27, 2003. Its purpose is to "strengthen and enhance United States leadership and the effectiveness of the United States response to the

HIV/AIDS, tuberculosis, and malaria pandemics and other related and preventable infectious diseases as part of the overall United States health and development agenda." It contained controversial provisions requiring that "No funds made available to carry out this Act, or any amendment made by this Act, may be used to promote or advocate the legalization or practice of prostitution or sex trafficking." A further limitation required that "No funds made available to carry out this Act, or any amendment made by this Act, may be used to provide assistance to any group or organization that does not have a policy explicitly opposing prostitution and sex trafficking." These limitations were found unconstitutional in 2013 by the U.S. Supreme Court as a violation of free expression for U.S. groups in *Agency for International Development, et al. v. Alliance for Open Society International, Inc., et al.*

For further information:

United States Leadership Against HIV/AIDS, Tuberculosis, and Malaria Act of 2003: http://www.state.gov/documents/organization/30368.pdf

Agency for International Development, et al. v. Alliance for Open Society International, Inc., et al. http://www.scotusblog.com/case-files/cases/agency-for-international-development-v-alliance-for-open-society-international-inc/

Supreme Court opinion in *Agency for International Development, et al. v. Alliance for Open Society International, Inc., et al.* http://www.supremecourt.gov/opinions/12pdf/12–10_21p3.pdf

The "raid, rescue, and rehabilitate" industry

So I set off with the I.J.M. [International Justice Mission] investigator (who wants to remain anonymous for his own safety) into the alleys of the Sonagachi red-light district one evening, slipped into the brothel, and climbed to the third floor. And there were Chutki and three other girls in a room, a pimp hovering over them. Perceiving us as potential customers, he offered them to us . . . The Kolkata police agreed to raid the brothel to free the girl. I.J.M. told them the location of the brothel at the last minute to avoid a tip-off from police ranks. The police casually asked us to lead the way in the raid since we knew what Chutki looked like and where she was kept . . . So along with a carload of police, we drove up to the brothel and rushed inside to avoid giving the pimps time to hide Chutki or to escape themselves.

(Kristof, 2011)

Box 12.2 International Justice Mission

According to their 2012 annual report, "International Justice Mission is a human rights agency that brings rescue to victims of slavery, sexual exploitation and other forms of violent oppression." IJM is an Evangelical Christian organization. The website describes IJM as a "non-sectarian community of faith that works with all people to seek justice on behalf of all people regardless of race, religion, or any other status. As a faith community, IJM's core of full-time staff intentionally draw strength and unity from their common commitment to the teachings of Jesus Christ and from their communion of daily prayer and spiritual disciplines. Accordingly, IJM staff seek colleagues who embrace and contribute to the spiritual community through shared Christian conviction and practice." IJM "require[s] that all employees practise a mature orthodox Christian faith, as defined by the Apostles' Creed." IJM claims that it rescued more than 1,000 people from slavery in 2012 and reports US$114.65 million in revenue from 2009–2012. Although IJM has received praise, as illustrated by the quote above, from commentators like Nikolas Kristof and the U.S. Department of State (IJM founder Gary Haugen's former employer), many others have critiqued IJM based on the harm their programs cause to HIV prevention and local campaigns for sex workers' rights. For critiques of IJM see: Bernstein & Jakobsen (2010), Chuang (2010), Thrupkaew (2009).

For additional information:

IJM 2012 Annual Report
https://www.ijm.org/sites/default/files/download/IJM-2012-Annual-
    Report.pdf

Bernstein, E., & Jakobsen, J. R. (2010, August 25). Sex, secularism, and religious influence in U.S. politics. Retrieved from Open Democracy website: http://www.opendemocracy.net/5050/elizabeth-bernstein-janet-r-jakobsen/sex-secularism-and-religious-influence-in-us-politics

Chuang, J. A. (2010). Rescuing trafficking from ideological capture: Prostitution reform and anti-trafficking law and policy. *University of Pennsylvania Law Review, 158*, 1655–1728.

Thrupkaew, N. (2009, October 5). The crusade against sex trafficking. *The Nation*. Retrieved from http://www.thenation.com/article/crusade-against-sex-trafficking

The raid, rescue, and rehabilitate scheme refers to a process by which brothels are raided by police or NGO workers, women are removed from brothels (rescued), and then placed in a rehabilitation facility. Raids are typically conducted by police officers at the behest of local and international organizations seeking to rescue and rehabilitate sex workers. The International Justice Mission, described in the *New York Times* op-ed by Nikolas Kristof above, was the recipient of over US$900,000 from the U.S. government between 2001 and 2005 (*Boston Globe*, 2006). In a recent evaluation, USAID detailed IJM's raid and rescue process in detail:

> IJM employs two methods for rescuing victims, one is brothel raids in coop-eration with the police, and the other is the "buy-bust" operation. In the latter, undercover agencies attempt to purchase the services of an underage girl. Once the perpetrator accepts the money, the police who are watching and waiting, step in and arrest them. These raids and "buy-busts" are targeted at perpetra-tors discovered through information provided by undercover operatives.
>
> (USAID, 2006)

The raid and rescue is the first part of the process. Heavily reliant on local police, raids are often violent not only for those accused of being traffickers but also for the sex workers themselves. This has been documented in numerous contexts including Southern Africa (Arnott & Cargo, 2009), Eastern Europe (Sex Workers Rights' Advocacy Network, 2009), and India (World Health Organization, 2005). The insistence on using police forces in the context of raids and rescues has been pushed by neo-abolitionists despite evidence of police violence against sex work-ers. The level of violence experienced by sex workers in the context of raids (both for the purposes of arrest and rehabilitation) was noted by the World Health Orga-nization and the Global Coalition on Women and AIDS in a 2005 Informational Bulletin on violence against women:

> However, both trafficking and violence against trafficked women need to be understood more broadly in the context of migration, and examined sepa-rately from sex work. At the same time, it is important to note that in several countries, certain activities such as rescue raids of sex establishments have exacerbated violence against sex workers and compromised their safety. For example, research from Indonesia and India has indicated that sex workers who are rounded up during police raids are beaten, coerced into having sex by corrupt police officials in exchange for their release or placed in institutions where they are sexually exploited or physically abused. The raids also drive sex workers onto the streets, where they are more vulnerable to violence.
>
> (World Health Organization, 2005, p. 2)

The final step for anti-trafficking organizations is often rehabilitation of women in the sex industry. Rehabilitation programs are run either by non-governmental organizations including churches or are government programs. The commonly told trope of the rescued woman ends here; she is now in the safe hands of the state or an NGO which will rehabilitate her, find her a new source of employment, and at some point release her from the rehabilitation home. In reality this is not the way the story typically ends. Frequently sex workers are taken to rehabilitation programs where they are kept in jail-like conditions, may experience abuse, and then are eventually released. Rehabilitation programs have come under increased scrutiny by public health bodies and sex worker organizations concerned for the health and safety of women removed from brothels. Documented extensively by sex worker projects and human rights organizations (and often acknowledged by the anti-trafficking programs and police), rehabilitation programs often undermine the very purpose of their existence given the high rates of violence experienced by women in rehabilitation homes, the return of women to sex work (perhaps due to a lack of employment opportunities otherwise, or because they wanted to remain in sex work and/or rejected the rehabilitation plan thought up for them) after being detained for extended periods of time, disrupting their everyday existence (Overs, 2009; Soderlund, 2005). To illustrate the harm of raid, rescue, and rehabilitation schemes in India we turn to the case of VAMP in Sangli, where anti-trafficking efforts driven by abolitionists have severely undermined programming recognized for its success in addressing the HIV epidemic.

The case of VAMP in Sangli, India

About VAMP

Approximately 2.1 million people in India are living with HIV (UNAIDS, 2012). Sex workers are amongst the groups most affected by the HIV epidemic in India. Approximately 17.1 percent of female sex workers in Maharashtra are HIV positive. A four-state survey found that the prevalence of HIV amongst sex workers is approximately 14.5 percent (Ramesh et al., 2008).

In 1992, SANGRAM initiated a 5,000-person sex worker collective called VAMP in Sangli, Maharashtra that mobilizes and empowers sex workers to address the various challenges faced by the sex worker community. The early inspiration for the movement came from the impact of HIV on the sex work community. The program distributes around 470,000 condoms a month (Association for Women's Rights in Development, 2011).

A central component of the work of VAMP revolves around delivering HIV information, care, and support and ensuring that sex workers are able to access treatment services. VAMP staff and leadership have received numerous accolades and awards for a demonstrated impact on the lives of individuals in Sangli living with and at risk of HIV including from the U.S. government (USAID, 2011). Despite the public acknowledgment of their success as an HIV program—including a case study featuring them on a USAID website—SANGRAM and VAMP are subject to the swinging political pendulum of U.S. foreign assistance (USAID, 2011). The rise in influence of the neo-abolitionists, for example, brought VAMP under the scrutiny of the U.S. government for providing sex worker services (Souder, 2005). Despite the simultaneous accolades, SANGRAM was publicly accused of trafficking women and girls in both India and the United States. VAMP has also become the target of a locally operated and internationally funded raid and rescue industry (Pawar, 2011).

This confluence of forces, the targeting of SANGRAM by neo-abolitionists and the increasing focus on SANGRAM by local and international anti-trafficking organizations, exemplifies the negative consequences of how uninterrogated anti-trafficking initiatives under the local umbrella of the ITPA can go very wrong at the expense of successful HIV programming. In particular, peer-educators are arrested and charged with trafficking under the ITPA. Thus the push for anti-trafficking efforts undermines HIV programming.

The impact of the raid, rescue, and rehabilitate model on HIV programming in Sangli

The routine and common occurrence of raids and rescues severely disrupts the lives of sex workers and the work of HIV programs. This section seeks to highlight the primary negative consequences of this and other raids on the health and well-being of sex workers in Sangli. First, the raids themselves may have a negative impact on sex workers' lives, increasing violent and unsafe sex work. The violent and disruptive raids mean that clients do not come to the brothel areas (Field Notes, 2011). This doesn't result in stopping sex work (as perhaps hoped by the abolitionists who push for criminalization of clients). Instead, it displaces sex work as sex workers begin to seek out clients and makes sex work unsafe by driving sex work underground resulting in sex workers taking greater risks with their safety and health in their engagement with clients. In the brothels where VAMP works the sex workers are less prone to client violence because VAMP organizes sex workers to root out violence and oppression, taking care to report violent clients to other sex workers and then working to exclude those clients from brothel areas. This provides a safety mechanism premised on trust and cooperation between sex workers. The ongoing raids disrupt systems of self-governance and safety established by sex worker collectives.

Second, the unrelenting raids on brothels that are structured to facilitate the delivery of HIV programming have a detrimental impact on a well-established public health principle: that the collectivization of sex workers reduces HIV risk (Shannon & Csete, 2010). For example, with the assistance of VAMP, sex workers have developed a means of monitoring condom use and encouraging HIV testing. Initially, peer workers collected used condoms and counted each sex worker's used condoms to compare the number of condoms to the number of clients. Where there is a discrepancy the sex worker is encouraged to go for an HIV test immediately and then again a few months later. If the sex worker tests HIV positive she joins a community of sex workers who care for and monitor the health of sex workers living with HIV. These mechanisms of care and support established by sex workers have resulted in a destigmatization of HIV and a support infrastructure necessary for women living with HIV. The raids and rescues disrupt the support systems which are often reliant on interpersonal relationships and trust.

Third, the arrest and detainment of sex workers in jails, remand homes, and rehabilitation centers often disrupts HIV care and exposes individuals with HIV to tuberculosis and other diseases which are often rampant in closed confined settings. This is of extreme concern given the high number of sex workers living with HIV. The remand homes, rehabilitation centers, and the jails are not equipped to address the treatment and health needs of sex workers living with HIV. Often when VAMP knows that a sex worker living with HIV has been taken to a remand home, rehabilitation site, or arrested they attempt to locate her to ensure she is getting HIV medication. In many cases attempts to locate sex workers to ensure that HIV care is continued fail because women and girls who are rescued flee rescue homes or because VAMP staff are not allowed to meet and inquire about their well-being.

Fourth, violence against sex workers at the hands of the state during raids, rescues, arrests, in remand homes and rehabilitation centers is well-documented (Overs, 2009). Despite this, organizations employing a raid, rescue, and rehabilitate scheme rely heavily on the police. This has two primary impacts. First, it subjects the sex workers to violence at the time of the raid as well as in state custody. Second, where organizations like VAMP, amongst many other sex worker organizations, have effectively altered their relationship with the police to be able to call on the police for support, these anti-trafficking efforts undermine the new and often delicate positive engagement with the police.

Finally, the conflation of sex work and trafficking that drives the assumption that all sex workers must be rescued undermines the innovative and effective anti-trafficking efforts being taken on by sex workers who see the difference between sex work and trafficking. A recent study of over 3,000 female and 1,300 male sex workers in India found that the majority of females entering sex work did so independently (Sahni & Shankar, 2011). VAMP sex workers effectively identify underage girls in brothels because they are the first to encounter them. Upon identification they work to get them into safer living conditions. This has proven to be an effective process because the underage girl's first point of contact may be other sex workers. Working directly with sex workers is an effective alternative to the raid and rescue model.

Conclusion and recommendations

This case study demonstrates how the conflation of sex work with trafficking at the international and local level, encouraged by the neo-abolitionist movement inside the United States, impacts HIV programs at the local level. In the town of Sangli the ongoing presence of internationally supported abolitionist groups impacts the capacity of VAMP to implement HIV programming by destabilizing projects, undermining progress made with local police with regard to building relationships, and disrupting the lives of sex workers. Further, the raid, rescue, and rehabilitation scheme itself is flawed—the reliance on the most oppressive arm of the state, in this case law enforcement, results in greater violence against sex workers during the process of rescuing them and rehabilitating them into government-run facilities that sometimes operate as detention centers.

In order to effectively address the HIV epidemic amongst sex workers and end truly coercive practices in the sex industry it is necessary to learn from the success of effective programming. VAMP provides a model for anti-trafficking efforts as well as HIV prevention for sex workers. The lessons are clear: allow for the participation and leadership of sex workers in projects and programs; learn from the local organizations that remain consistently on the ground and work every day within the nuances of the state–sex worker dynamic; and allow for sex workers to define the terms of their engagement in projects and programs designed to assist sex worker communities.

Acknowledgments

Many thanks to J. Kirby, Adam Cernea Clark, and Sonia Haerizadeh for research assistance, the ClassCrits Conference, the organizers and participants of the Governance Feminism Workshop, members of the Anti-Trafficking Roundtable. Thanks also to Wendy Parmet, Sutapa Majumdar, Caroline Jones, and Jason Jackson for various insights during the research and writing process.

Notes

* From SANGRAM Bill of Rights (2010).
** A version of this paper was previously published in the *Anti-Trafficking Review*. Ahmed, A. & Seshu, M. (2012). "We have the right not to be 'rescued' . . .": When anti-trafficking programs undermine the health and well-being of sex workers. *Anti-Trafficking Review, 1*, 149–168.

References

Abrams, K. (1995). Sex wars redux: Agency and coercion in feminist legal theory. *Columbia Law Review, 95*, 304–376.

Arnott, J., & Cargo A. L. (June, 2009). *Rights not rescue: A report on female, male, and trans sex workers' human rights in Botswana, Namibia, and South Africa*. Retrieved on August 18, 2014 from Open Society Institute website: http://www.opensocietyfoundations.org/sites/default/files/rightsnotrescue_20090706.pdf

Association for Women's Rights in Development (2011). The VAMP/SANGRAM sex workers' movement in India's southwest. *Building feminist movements and organizations initiative*. Retrieved on August 18, 2014 from http://www.google.com/url?sa=t&rct=j&q=& esrc=s&source=web&cd=1&ved=0CCEQFjAA&url=http%3A%2F%2Fwww.awid. org%2Fcontent%2Fdownload%2F117347%2F1335451%2Ffile%2FCTW_VAMP_ Movmnt_ENG.pdf&ei=-kjyU9jtPNH7oASm4IK4BQ&usg=AFQjCNFt7GYlsa8DMr1R qHKHMM9YPvzngg&sig2=7x4yVd76-XNqJjvqVgt1rw&bvm=bv.73231344,d.cGU

Bernstein, E. (2007). The sexual politics of the new abolitionism. *Differences, 18*(3), 128–151.

Bernstein, E., & Jakobsen, J. R. (August 25, 2010). *Sex, secularism, and religious influence in U.S. politics*. Retrieved on August 18, 2014 from Open Democracy website: http://

www.opendemocracy.net/5050/elizabeth-bernstein-janet-r-jakobsen/sex-secularism-and-religious-influence-in-us-politics

Boston Global (2006). USAID contracts with faith based organizations October 8. Retrieved on August 18, 2014 from http://www.boston.com/news/special/faith_based/faith_based_organizations.htm

Chuang, J. A. (2010). Rescuing trafficking from ideological capture: Prostitution reform and anti-trafficking law and policy. *University of Pennsylvania Law Review, 158*, 1655–1728.

Consulate General of the United States, Kolkata (2006). U.S. grants $600,000 to anti-trafficking initiatives in eastern India [Press release]. Retrieved on August 18, 2014 from http://kolkata.usconsulate.gov/wwwhipr040706.html

Halley, J., Kotiswaran, P., Shamir, H., & Thomas, C. (2006). From the international to the local in feminist legal responses to rape, prostitution/sex work, and sex trafficking: Four studies in contemporary governance feminism. *Harvard Journal of Law and Gender, 29*(2), 335–424.

Kristof, N. (May 26, 2011). Raiding a brothel in India. *The New York Times*. Retrieved on August 18, 2014 from http://www.nytimes.com/2011/05/26/opinion/26kristof.html

Overs, C. (2009). Caught between the tiger and the crocodile: The campaign to suppress human trafficking and sexual exploitation in Cambodia. Retrieved on August 18, 2014 from http://www.aidslex.org/site_documents/SX-0046E.pdf

Pawar, Y. (November 20, 2011). "DNA" Special: Rogue NGO separates "sex worker" mother from baby. *DNA India*. Retrieved on August 18, 2014 from http://www.dnaindia.com/mumbai/report-dna-special-rogue-ngo-separates-sex-worker-mother-from-baby-1614950

Ramesh, B. M., Moses, S., Washington, R., Isac, S., Mohapatra, B., Mahagaonkar, S. B., . . . & Blanchard, J. F. (2008). Determinants of HIV prevalence among female sex workers in four south Indian states: Analysis of cross-sectional surveys in twenty-three districts. *Aids, 22*(5), S35–S44.

Sahni, R., & Shankar, V. (2011). *The first pan-India survey of sex workers: A summary of preliminary findings*. Retrieved on August 18, 2014 from SANGRAM website: http://www.sangram.org/resources/Pan_India_Survey_of_Sex_workers.pdf

Sex Workers Rights' Advocacy Network (2009). Arrest the violence: Human rights abuses against sex workers in Central and Eastern Europe and Central Asia. Retrieved on August 18, 2014 from http://swannet.org/files/swannet/File/Documents/Arrest_the_Violence_SWAN_Report_Nov2009_eng.pdf

Shannon, K., & Csete, J. (2010). Violence, condom negotiation, and HIV/STI risk among sex workers. *The Journal of the American Medical Association, 304*(5), 573–574.

Soderlund, G. (2005). Running from the rescuers: New US crusades against sex trafficking and the rhetoric of abolition. *Feminist Formations, 17*(3), 64–87.

Souder, M. (October 6, 2005). [Letter to the Honorable James Kounder].

Thrupkaew, N. (October 5, 2009). The crusade against sex trafficking. *The Nation*. Retrieved on August 18, 2014 from http://www.thenation.com/article/crusade-against-sex-trafficking

UNAIDS (2012). India, HIV/AIDS estimates (2012). Retrieved on August 18, 2014 from http://www.unaids.org/en/regionscountries/countries/india

United States Leadership Against HIV/AIDS, Tuberculosis, and Malaria Act of 2003, Pub. L. No. 108–25, §2, 117 Stat. 711, 716 (2003) (current version at 22 U.S.C.A. §§7601(23) (West 2010)).

USAID (2011). SANGRAM's collectives. *AIDSTAR-One Case Study Series*. Retrieved on August 18, 2014 from http://www.aidstar-one.com/focus_areas/gender/resources/case_study_series/sangrams_collectives

UN Office on Drugs and Crime (2003). *Protocol to Prevent, Suppress and Punish Trafficking in Persons, Especially Women and Children*.

World Health Organization (2005). Violence against women and HIV/AIDS: Critical inter-
sections. *Information Bulletin Series.*

Discussion questions

1.   What are the critiques of the raid and rescue approach?
2.   What new problems do raid and rescue missions cause?
3.   What impact does raid and rescue have on HIV prevention?
4.   How does the raid and rescue approach differ from the approach of SANGRAM?
5.   What is the anti-prostitution loyalty oath?

Additional resources

SANGRAM: Sex Worker Organizing in India
http://blip.tv/sexworkerspresent/sangram-sex-worker-organizing-in-india-2978073

Caught Between the Tiger and the Crocodile
http://blip.tv/sexworkerspresent/caught-between-the-tiger-and-the-crocodile-1165299

Asia Pacific Network of Sex Workers YouTube channel
https://www.youtube.com/user/apnsw

NBC in-depth news report on IJM in Cambodia
https://www.youtube.com/watch?v=6OZjJUpHv6Y

SANGRAM
http://www.sangram.org

Chapter 13

Nothing like chocolate

Sex trafficking and child labor trafficking

Kum-Kum Bhavnani and Emily Schneider

Introduction

Trafficking has become a key buzzword for Third World development in the twenty-first century. As this volume demonstrates, there is no shortage of writing on the topic. The question remains, however: why is it that discussions of trafficking focus almost exclusively on sex and related aspects? It is, of course, true that sex trafficking does damage substantial numbers of people, women and children in particular. Our chapter certainly reminds readers of that. But why is it that sex trafficking is not usually linked to other forms of trafficking of children and adults, such as in the trafficking of labor, sexual or otherwise? Tackling that question in any depth is beyond the purview of our chapter, although we do discuss it briefly at the end of this chapter. However, it is this question that informs our writing, as we illustrate how sex trafficking is a symptom of the current world we inhabit, as indeed are other forms of trafficking in scholarly writings and campaigns. In this chapter, we first critique the overemphasis on sex trafficking. We next discuss the trafficking of children in the Ivory Coast who are used as workers to harvest cocoa beans.

The United Nations defines trafficking as:

> The recruitment, transportation, transfer, harboring or receipt of persons, by means of the threat, or use of force or other forms of coercion, of abduction, or fraud, of deception, of the abuse of power of a position of vulnerability or of the giving or receiving of payments or benefits to achieve the consent of a person having control over another person, for the purpose of exploitation.
>
> (UN, 2000)

It is generally accepted that trafficking arises in situations of acute inequality, where power dynamics are so extreme that some individuals and organizations are able to assume total control over another person's life.

It is commonly claimed that women and girls are the primary targets of international trafficking. Brysk argues that of the 800,000 people trafficked across borders each year (Brysk, 2012), two-thirds are women. Murray (2008) asserts that 65 to 95 percent of these are women trafficked into the sex industry. In response to this perception of the problem, countries identified as destinations for trafficked sex workers such as Sweden and the Netherlands have put legal measures in place to combat trafficking, and residents of these countries who commit acts of sexual exploitation abroad may be prosecuted in their home countries (Brysk, 2012).

However, contrary to the popular focus on international sex trafficking, most trafficking occurs within a person's own country or region, and often for non-sexual forms of labor (Brysk, 2012). It is thought that domestic trafficking usually affects men in the Third World, who may be forced into debt-slavery or hard labor by dictatorial regimes. In addition, many children are trafficked within and from Third World nations to become soldiers (e.g. Uganda), domestic servants (Philippines; Pakistan), or laborers on plantations and in factories. Despite the variety of contexts for trafficking and other exploitative labor conditions, sex trafficking makes up the primary focus of anti-trafficking media campaigns and legislative measures (e.g. Brysk, 2012; Chang & Kim, 2007). While these initiatives have been successful in arousing public concern and spurring more countries to create anti-trafficking legislation, many contend that they do more harm than good (e.g. Peach, 2011).

The nearly exclusive focus on international sex trafficking, as distinct from other forms of forced migration and labor exploitation, can be a problem for several reasons (Chang & Kim, 2007). First, the prioritization of sex trafficking overshadows other forms of forced labor, which affect greater numbers of people, as we discuss later. Second, it steers attention away from domestic trafficking, which is more common than international cases of trafficking. Third, current characterizations of sex trafficking have used tactics similar to the "white slavery" slogan deployed historically, privileging white women and ignoring entire regions and groups of people. For example, despite the frequent use of slogans about "modern-day slavery," the history of legalized slavery regimes and their legacies of inequality are marginalized in these discussions. Further, contemporary representations of trafficking largely omit Black workers from Africa as mainstream conceptions of trafficked women focus on Asian and White women trafficked for sex work. Likewise the plight of trafficked children is highlighted much more than the situation of trafficked women, and women victims receive greater attention than men (Brysk, 2012).

In addition to the dynamics described above, the rhetoric around sex trafficking has proved to be damaging for the many sex workers who are not victims of trafficking. For example, Alison Murray cautions against the overemphasis on sex trafficking, warning against the sensationalism often employed by journalists, activists, and even researchers. She argues that a focus on a minority of trafficked women among sex workers inaccurately dramatizes reality and obscures statistics so as to promote a patriarchal moral crusade against prostitution and women's sexuality (Murray, 2008). This creates an environment where all sex workers are seen as victims in need of rescuing, including those who view themselves as workers. The result is that this approach denies both agency and human rights to all in this category.

Behind Murray's position lies an intense debate over whether prostitution is inherently a form of violence against women. On one end of the spectrum are those who believe that all women who go into prostitution are forced to do so, and no woman voluntarily chooses to become a sex worker. All, including scholars and activists, who hold this view can be categorized as representing the abolitionist stance. Abolitionism characterizes prostitution as a "hierarchically gendered relation that must be understood through the lens of male domination and women's oppression" (Schotten, 2005, p. 212), a position favored by a number of radical feminist scholars such as Kathleen Barry, Sheila Jeffreys, and Catharine MacKinnon. Alongside advocacy organizations, such as the Coalition Against Trafficking in Women, they argue that prostitution is organized gang rape and an inherent violation of women's rights (Alexander 1997). As Kathleen Barry explains:

I am taking prostitution as the model, the most extreme and most crystallized form of all sexual exploitation. Sexual exploitation is a political condition, the foundation of women's subordination and the base from which discrimination against women is constructed and enacted.

(Barry, 1995, p. 11)

Barry goes on to argue that once a person is reduced to a body that is used to sexually satisfy another, with or without consent, a violation of that person has taken place (Barry, 1995). Abolitionist scholars contend that prostitution is not a voluntary decision; women are either overtly coerced into prostitution or they are indirectly forced into it by extreme conditions such as poverty and abuse (Farley, Baral, Kiremire, & Sezgin, 1998). MacKinnon argues that all sexuality is an expression of male power, and that sex, sexuality, and gender are male constructions that are outside the scope of women's choices (MacKinnon, 1989). Barry echoes this view as she states:

Can women choose to do prostitution? As much as they can choose any other context of sexual objectification and dehumanization of the self . . . [W]omen actually do not consent to prostitution or any other condition of sexual exploitation—in rape, in marriage, in the office, in the factory, and so on.

(Barry, 1995, p. 33)

The problem is that issues of consent, as well as issues of sexual and other human desires on the part of those who pay for such labor, as well as on the part of the workers, is not even hinted at in such discussions (for example, is sex within marriage a form of sex work/prostitution, or is it consensual sex?), and this creates a significant gap when discussing the meaning of sex work for the women who perform it.

In contrast, the "sex-as-work" approach maintains that prostitution is "primarily an economic relation, and must be understood as a form of labor under capitalism" (Schotten, 2005, p. 212). Pro-sex worker scholars such as Kamala Kempadoo, Laura María Agustín, and Carol Queen reject the abolitionist stance, and define prostitution as a form of labor (Kempadoo & Doezema, 1998). This frame of thinking is largely supported by sex workers' rights movements and organizations such as COYOTE, the International Prostitutes Collective, and the Sex Workers Outreach Project, as well as prominent sex workers and advocates such as Margo St. James, Norma Jean Almodovar, and Carol Leigh. This sex-as-work view finds its roots in Gayle Rubin's "sex-positive" position, which opposes the idea that sexuality is merely a symptom of gendered oppression (Rubin, 1984). Instead, the sex-as-work approach identifies oppression in terms of social relations and that prostitution is illegal, and implicitly rejects sexuality as an essential representation of the self. It emphasizes that most labor is exploitative, citing poverty, inadequate wages, and abusive conditions to be the sources of sex workers' alienation and exploitation, not the actual act of having sex with strangers (Showden, 2009). For us, the issue of desire is central—desire/need for money, a desire/need to support children and others, and a desire/need to have some autonomy in one's working life.

A second debate that affects efforts to combat trafficking is the question of forced vs. free sex workers, a debate spelled out by Doezema two decades ago. In response to blanket characterizations of prostitution as violence, the prostitutes' rights movement successfully pushed for a distinction to be made between forced and voluntary sex work (Doezema, 1998). Motivating this distinction is a respect for adults' agency in decisions to voluntarily engage in sexual labor.

The debates are not limited to theory and academia, as they have serious repercussions for sex workers' lives around the world. Lucinda Peach (2011) argues that the infusion of American conservative morality into anti-trafficking measures has devastating impacts for both sex workers and victims of trafficking. American Christian conceptions of prostitution represent a distinct perspective on sexuality that employs moralizing notions such as "sin" and "impurity" that are not found in other cultural and religious perspectives. For example, Thai Buddhism does conceive of prostitution as inherently sinful while Indian Hinduism took a much more nuanced approach to prostitution prior to British colonialism. By forcing other cultures to conform to repressive American Christian notions of sexuality and prostitution, we facilitate harsher forms of patriarchy and weaken the possibility of culturally sensitive solutions to exploitation.

This type of religious condemnation of prostitution can be found in the highest levels of legislation and anti-trafficking measures. For example, organizations that provide vital services to sex workers such as HIV/AIDS prevention and treatment are required to sign anti-prostitution pledges that force them to either abandon their clients or lose their funding (Chang & Kim, 2007). This type of codification of moral opposition to prostitution fuels deeper stigmatization and criminalization of sex workers. This in turn leads to the general defunding of social programs for vulnerable communities, especially reproductive healthcare programs for poor women of color.

The problem with the "forced vs. free" dichotomy mentioned earlier is that it often translates into a disregard for the rights and well-being of voluntary sex workers. It allows for the application of moralistic categories such as guilty/innocent and whore/virgin to stigmatize sex workers, deny them services, and criminalize them. This leads advocates to be more concerned with whether a sex worker is pure and innocent, rather than developing strategies to fight systems of debt bondage and slavery (Doezema, 1998). It also relieves advocates of their responsibility to consider the rights of *all* sex workers, glossing over the urgent need for greater protection of sex workers' rights. While there are legitimate distinctions to be made in terms of involuntary and voluntary labor, relying too heavily on this approach enables organizations to ignore the mistreatment or abuse of sex workers, so long as the "innocent" women are protected or "rescued" (Doezema, 1998).

Furthermore, the forced vs. free dichotomy does not always accurately reflect the lived experiences of sex workers. Kaoru Aoyama (2009) reports that, in a sample of Thai sex workers, understandings of their labor as voluntary or forced were dependent on a variety of factors such as working conditions, access to social resources, and networks of human relationships. In this sense, it was the general conditions of unjust exploitation and not the nature of sex work itself that caused them to sometimes define their work as forced. Aoyama explains that these women's relationships to their work were highly contextual, with external factors creating a wide range of perspectives even within the same woman. As she explains,

> The experiences of being a happy sex worker and a suffering victim of sexual slavery were very different things but not mutually exclusive, in the sense that they often existed not only within women who found themselves in different situations but also within the same woman at different points in time.
>
> (Aoyama, 2009, p. 32)

Sex workers who independently decide to migrate in search of better economic opportunities find themselves in a particularly precarious position. Laws prohibiting the rights of sex workers to work abroad create a dependence on traffickers, "middle-men," and "promoters," who take advantage of the illegality of prostitution in order to exert excessive, and often abusive, control over the sex workers' lives and economic resources. Anti-prostitution laws prevent people in the sexualized entertainment industry from independently seeking contracts, which forces them to rely on promoters and managers. This creates a situation where the worker becomes indebted to her "promoters," because the promoter or manager arranges for visas, auditions, required training, or other services that are necessary for legal migration and temporary work. Usually without the funds to pay up front for such services, which are largely symbolic and bureaucratic, workers become indebted to their promoters who gain control of their salaries. This then affords the "promoters" the ability to manage the workers' salaries, which often encourages the entertainment workers to turn to informal sex work in order to supplement their income (Parreñas, 2011). Parreñas describes the mechanisms by which Filipina women who enter Japan on an "entertainer visa" are subject to conditions comparable to indentured servitude as a result of their dependence on middle-man brokers. For these reasons, amongst others, the worker is rarely able to attain actual control of her own labor in the formal labor market.

In addition, as for all undocumented migratory workers, restrictions that result from citizenship status have additional detrimental effects on sex workers. A sex worker can be doubly denied protections from the state, not only because she may be undocumented, but also because she is engaged in an illegal form of labor. In addition, even if she is documented, such workers also lack protections from the state because they are often employed by bodies that are not always subject to the host country's laws, such as with Filipino promotion agencies in Japan. These examples complicate the lines between trafficking, sex work, voluntary and involuntary labor. Accordingly, we can begin to eliminate the mechanisms for the trafficking and exploitation of sex workers only by focusing broadly on the policies and movements that seek to secure greater control for migrant workers over their own labor.

In addition to legal and monetary sanctions for sex workers, trafficked or not, "raid and rescue" (Chang & Kim, 2007) missions may translate into repressive and dangerous situations for sex workers. While these missions claim to be supporting the victims of trafficking, in reality they frequently result in the arrest and deportation of the "rescued" women. This can put sex workers in an even more precarious position than they were before, while simultaneously infringing on their most basic rights such as deciding what job they want, who they wish to live with and how they want to live with children. Furthermore, if sent back to their home communities, many women face ostracism due to stigmas against sex work, or even revenge from criminals as well as punishment from the local government (Murray, 2008). Such missions also assume that all sex workers want to be "rescued," something that is not borne out by research (e.g. Wilson, 2008).

The rescue/abolitionist approach is also problematic in that it shifts the focus towards a need for humanitarian protection rather than a human rights approach that recognizes sex workers as "displaced agents in need of migration rights" (Agustin, 2007 cited in Brysk 2009, p.17). Grace Chang and Kathleen Kim argue that current U.S. policies divert attention away from the actual causes of trafficking (poverty, discrimination, political unrest), and subsequently deprive trafficked persons of their rights (Chang & Kim, 2007). By focusing exclusively on sex trafficking, the U.S. government is able to ignore its own role in the creation and perpetuation of global inequality by framing trafficking as a "moral" rather than structural issue. As Chang & Kim explain:

> Through these policies, the U.S. government and many other nations promote human trafficking and labor exploitation, while simultaneously creating the conditions of poverty through neoliberal economic policies that compel people to migrate. The selective criminalization of "sex trafficking" ensures

that the root causes of all forms of human trafficking, and state responsibility for or complicity in these structural causes, remain unchallenged.

(2007, p. 13)

The rhetoric is such that it becomes possible and reasonable to explain trafficking in isolation from the negative effects of globalization and neoliberalism. The public comes to understand the trafficking of sex workers as the result of a few evil people rather than a structural process rooted in the demand for cheap, foreign labor.

Child trafficking for cocoa production in Ivory Coast

In the next section we examine the issues associated with trafficking in children in West Africa, specifically Ivory Coast. This issue has been known about for some time (Raghavan & Chatterjee, 2001) but has only started to gain international attention in the past few years. The following discussion highlights the main issues that emerge from this form of trafficking.

Child trafficking for cocoa

Chocolate is consumed virtually everywhere in the world. Chocolate production is an extremely profitable business. In the U.S.A., people spent close to $16 billion on chocolate products in 2006, while in Britain—a population less than one-third the size of the USA—close to $7 billion was spent in this way. In 1989, *The Economist* stated that people in Britain spent more money on chocolate than on bread (Satre, 2005). More than 65,000 people are employed in the chocolate industry, which yields profits of nearly $13 billion per year. Chocolate is central to the sweets and candy industries, and is simultaneously touted as offering health benefits such as protection against high blood pressure (e.g. Santa Barbara News-Press, February 2006). Almond (2004) argues that a unique emotional bond with the commodity creates a deep need for chocolate among consumers. Despite the size of the chocolate business, the processes by which this product/commodity arrives into the hands of consumers have been given comparatively little attention.

Research on chocolate has tended to have an historical focus (e.g. Coe & Coe, 1996; Satre, 2005), an horticulturalist/health orientation (Young, 1994), or has been of the coffee-table book genre (e.g. Scharffenberger & Steinberg, 2006). In the past decade, however, empirically based books have become available regarding the growing and harvesting of cocoa and the inhumane conditions for some of the workers (e.g. see Off, 2006; Woods, 2003; van den Anker, 2004).

In 2001, allegations were raised that child enslavement and trafficked child labor were key to the cocoa harvesting labor force, especially in West Africa. July 2005 marked the date by which chocolate producers around the world agreed, through a voluntary protocol, to end the use of child slavery on cocoa farms. This 2001 voluntary protocol followed a measure passed by the U.S. House of

Representatives that a federal system be established which could be used to certify chocolate as "slave-free." The measure, itself a rider to an agricultural bill, was proposed by Senators Tom Harkin and Eliot Engel following an investigative report written in June 2001 (Raghavan & Chatterjee, 2001) published in 32 Knight-Ridder newspapers in the USA (Rosenblum, 2005). These two reporters wrote poignantly about the harvesting of cocoa by enslaved labor and themselves tracked this harvest from the Ivory Coast—where over 40 percent of the world's chocolate is produced—to London and Philadelphia. In fact, Ghana and Ivory Coast produce over 70 percent of the world's cocoa.

On seeing the measure passed by the House of Representatives, the producers of chocolate, represented by the Chocolate Manufacturers Association, prevented the bill from reaching the Senate by adopting a voluntary protocol to end slave labor on cocoa farms. Some have claimed that this voluntary protocol was promised in order to avoid consumer boycotts and circumvent imposition of stringent federal rules (e.g. the Anti-Slavery website; Lutheran World Relief Chocolate Project). Others have suggested that the initial reports about child labor were exaggerated (e.g. Doyle, 2002, cited in Rosenblum, 2005, p. 113; International Institute of Tropical Agriculture, 2002; Berlan, 2004). It is clear that the controversy created by Raghavan and Chatterjee's investigative report necessitated drastic action on the part of the manufacturers, even if there is no agreement on the precise accuracy (are the children actually enslaved? are they trafficked?) of the allegations.

This situation had not changed a few years later. For example, a report from Tulane University (2011) on child labor in the cocoa sector in agriculture argued that over 800,000 children in Ivory Coast, and close to a million in Ghana, work on "cocoa-related activities" (Payson Center, 2011, p. 7) and that this constitutes about 25 to 50 percent of all children who work in agriculture in Côte d'Ivoire and Ghana. They argue that the International Labour Organization's Convention 182 to eliminate the worst forms of child labor is not in place, or even near to being so, in the cocoa industry.

It is this type of research, funded by the U.S. Department of Labor, that led the U.S. Department of Labor Child Labor Cocoa Coordinating Group to issue its report in March 2013, with the following statement:

> By 2020, the worst forms of child labor as defined by ILO Convention 182 in the cocoa sectors of Côte d'Ivoire and Ghana will be reduced by 70 percent in aggregate through joint efforts by key stakeholders to provide and support remediation services for children removed from the worst forms of child labor, including education and vocational training, protective measures to address issues of occupational safety and health related to cocoa production, and livelihood services for the households of children in cocoa growing communities; the establishment and implementation of a credible and transparent sector-wide monitoring system across cocoa growing regions in the two countries; and the promotion of respect for core labor standards.
>
> (CLCCG, 2013, p. 19)

Box 13.1 The Protocol for the Growing and Processing of Cocoa Beans and their Derivative Products or Harkin–Engel Protocol

The Harkin–Engel Protocol was passed in 2001 as a compromise proposed by the Chocolate Manufacturers Association and signed by the World Cocoa Foundation which implemented a voluntary, self-regulatory process to address child slavery in cocoa production. The Protocol circumvented a proposed bill which would establish slavery-free labeling guidelines on chocolate by the U.S. Food and Drug Administration.

In 2010, chocolate and cocoa companies including ADM, Barry Callebaut, Cargill, Ferrero, The Hershey Company, Kraft Foods, Mars Inc., and Nestlé proposed a new voluntary Framework for Action which established a public/private partnership with ILO to address the worst forms of child labor in Ivory Coast and Ghana.

For more information:

Text and signature of the protocol
https://lms.manhattan.edu/pluginfile.php/51668/mod_resource/content/1/
   HarkinEngelProtocol.pdf

Framework of Action to Support Implementation of the Harkin-Engel Protocol
http://responsiblecocoa.com/wp-content/uploads/2010/09/Cocoa-Framework-
   of-Action-9-12-10-Final.pdf

The Cocoa Protocol: Success or Failure?
http://www.laborrights.org/sites/default/files/publications-and-resources/
   Cocoa%20Protocol%20Success%20or%20Failure%20June%202008.pdf

Slavery and trafficking are both terms that can mask the lived experiences of those who are part of these events. Sometimes, as Orla Ryan (2011), amongst others, explains, this work of children is a financial necessity for their households.

> Roughly one-third of farms yield as little as 137.5 kg per hectare. What this means is that the poorest farmers can make just $500 a year, an income which makes it impossible to do little more than survive, let alone hire laborers, buy fertilizer, or invest in new seedlings . . . in this scenario, it is not difficult to understand why smallholders choose to use the cheapest labor they can find, often their own families.
>
> (Ryan, 2011, p. 59)

The large chocolate manufacturers are important components in understanding why this child labor occurs, why it is necessary for small farmers, and why so much of it is trafficked (Off, 2006). Hersheys is one such example.

The story of Milton Hershey and his rise to fame as a very successful chocolate maker has been documented (e.g. D'Antonio, 2006). The familiar story is that Milton Hershey established a very large chocolate factory in 1903 near Derry Church in Pennsylvania, "in the middle of the corn field" (Brenner, 1999, p. 105). He sited it there so that the surrounding land would offer pasture for cows whose milk could be used to make chocolate. Simultaneous to the building of the factory, Hershey established the town of Hershey (known by that name even though it remains unincorporated as Hershey town)—which presently has a 91 percent white population—outside Harrisburg, PA. The story of Hershey's life—including his creating an orphanage in Hershey so that he and his wife, Kitty, could have close relationships with children—because they did not have any biological children of their own—is a story of naïveté, eccentricity, sadness, and greed. The Hershey factory is now acknowledged to be one of the very largest chocolate factories in the world. In fact, the Raise the Bar Campaign to petition Hersheys has estimated that this company has approximately 42 percent of the market share in chocolate in the USA (http://www.GlobalExchange.com).

In this context, in order to undermine this forced labor, often what is discussed is the issue of boycotts and petitions. For example, the International Labor Rights Forum, in Washington, DC, organized a petition against Hersheys, who had always refused to discuss the issue of slave-free beans in their chocolate, with the result that Hersheys has promised to remove such beans from its chocolate by 2020. In addition, Hersheys, along with many of the other major chocolate manufacturers such as Mars, has offered $600,000 between 2011 and 2014 to discourage farmers from using child labor. It is worth noting that Mars has offered $2.7 million for the same issue over a shorter period of time (2011–2013) (Kaitlyn, 2012). In fact, Mars has said that by 2016 it will have 50 percent of its cocoa purchased from certified cocoa producers, who offer "credible assurance" that their cocoa is being produced in line with the ILO Convention 182, and by 2020 that will be 100 percent.

Where does this leave us? Chang and Kim (2007) argue that sex workers' organizations, as well as trafficked workers and other groups who do not usually make alliances with the first two groups, should create coalitions. This is clearly critical and is a suggestion that all activists in the field of trafficking must pay attention to. To clarify, the issue of trafficking in children for cocoa harvesting has a number of facets. Agricultural labor is often dependent on children around the world, including in the Third World. While, again, involuntary forced labor trafficking is not condoned by us, of course, we also want to state that when households or neighbors rely on the labor of children for a harvest, it is often because the family income is so low that they cannot afford to pay adult laborers. That is, the amount that farmers receive for their cocoa beans does not allow them to subsist or have enough income to support their household without using the (forced) labor of children. We do not support this forced labor, but we mention it to complicate the issue of trafficking in children for cocoa harvests. We are not saying we agree with it. What we are saying, however, is that in order to undermine forced trafficking in children for the cocoa harvest, farmers need to be paid a much higher price for their beans. That is, the solution to stop forced trafficking is not necessarily only to institute harsher and harsher penalties for those who organize this trafficking, and who make profits out of this trafficking, but, in addition requires an examination of the reasons parents and guardians, and the receiving farmers, participate in this trafficking.

And this is where the identity between the two forms of trafficking enters, apparent in the United Kingdom's annual Anti-Slavery Day of 18 October (http://www.ecpat.org.uk/content/anti-slavery-day). However, differences between the two must also be taken into account. Is it domestic or international trafficking? What is the reason for the trafficking? Different reasons suggest different solutions. Sex trafficking relies on women, to a large extent, while cocoa harvest trafficking relies on children. How do the initial stages of trafficking differ from each other? Are women and children who are trafficked all infantilized in the same way, and cowed into submission? How do we tackle trafficking in which the person who is trafficked is "tricked" into believing they are going for something other than forced labor, sexual or otherwise? We raise these questions because, in the early stages of trafficking "trickery," there is a seeming degree of voluntarism on the part of the trafficked person. Some say it is a truism to assert that migrant labor is a form of economic refugee-ism. Yet, the main similarity between trafficked children and sex trafficking is just that—economic refugee-ism. And it is this identity of intentions that could help to create an identity of goals for activists who wish to change the situation: goals that might be able to avoid a moralistic stance on either sex work, or the labor of children.

However, we wish to take this point further, and suggest that because political coalitions are works of identity and difference simultaneously, issues of difference within political coalitions also have to be foregrounded in such work. We argue this because, as we suggested earlier, issues of sexual desire enormously complicate how sex work, and therefore how forced sex trafficking, which is often equated with other forms of sex work, operates. We are not saying that all, or indeed the majority of, people who work in sex work do it out of sexual desire. However, it is the case that sexual desire can undermine a straightforward and simplistic understanding of the work that is to be done. In a similar vein, the issue of children working/laboring can also be complicated. Many have argued, including Nadezhda Krupskaya during the Bolshevik revolution of the early twentieth century, that it is important that children learn the difference between work (tasks that are done, without pay, and often of a more domestic nature such as cooking and cleaning and tending to animals to ensure human social reproduction) and labor (which requires a contract, informal or otherwise, between the laborer and their proprietor, and which is done for money), and that they learn to do both at an early stage. All of this complicates our thinking and is why we therefore conclude it is important to ensure that there is a coming together of activists who work on all forms of trafficking. "If you're in a coalition and you're comfortable, you know it's not a broad enough coalition" (Johnson Reagon, 1983).

References

Agustin, Laura Maria (2007). Sexual commotion, in *Sex at the margins: Migration, labour markets and the rescue industry*. London: Zed Books.

Alexander, P. (1997). Feminism, sex workers, and human rights, in Nagle, J., *Whores and other feminists*. New York, NY: Routledge, pp. 83–97.

Almond, S. (2004). *Candyfreak: A journey through the chocolate underbelly of America*. New York: Harcourt.

Aoyama, K. (2009). *Thai migrant sexworkers: From modernisation to globalisation*. Basingstoke, England: Palgrave Macmillan.

Barry, K. (1995). *The prostitution of sexuality*. New York, NY: New York University Press.

Berlan, A. (2004). Child labor, education and child rights among cocoa producers in Ghana, in van den Anker, C. (Ed.), *The political economy of new slavery*. Basingstoke, UK: Palgrave Macmillan, pp. 158–178.

Brenner, J. G. (1999). *The emperors of chocolate: Inside the secret world of Hershey and Mars*. New York, NY: Broadway Books.

Brysk, A. (2012). Beyond framing and shaming: Human trafficking, human security and human rights. *Journal of Human Security, 5*(3), 8–21.

Chang, G., & Kim, K. (2007). Reconceptualizing approaches to human trafficking: new directions from the field(s). *Stanford Journal of Civil Rights and Civil Liberties, 3*(2), 318–344.

Child Labor Cocoa Coordinating Group (March 2013). Child Labor Cocoa Coordinating Group 2012 Annual Report. Prepared by the Offices of Senator Tom Harkin, Representative Eliot Engel, the United States Department of Labor, the Government of Côte d'Ivoire, the Ghana Ministry on Employment and Social Welfare, and the International Chocolate and Cocoa Industry. Retrieved on July 30, 2014 from http://www.dol.gov/ilab/issues/child-labor/cocoa/2012-CLCCG-Report.pdf

Coe, S. D. & Coe, M. D. (1996). *The true history of chocolate*. London: Thames and Hudson.

D'Antonio, Michael (2006). *Hershey: Milton Hershey's extraordinary life of wealth, empire and utopian dreams*. New York: Simon and Schuster.

Doezema, J., 1998. Forced to choose: Beyond the voluntary v. forced prostitution dichotomy, in Kempadoo, K., & Doezema, J. (Eds.), *Global sex workers: Rights, resistance and redefinition*. New York and London: Routledge, pp. 34–50.

Farley, M., Baral, I., Kiremire, M., & Sezgin, U. (1998). Prostitution in five countries: Violence and post-traumatic stress disorder. *Feminism & Psychology, 8*(4), 405–426.

International Institute of Tropical Agriculture (2002). *Child labour in the cocoa sector of West Africa: A synthesis of findings in Côte d'Ivoire, Ghana and Nigeria*. Sustainable Tree Crops Program. Washington, DC: USAID/USDOL/ILO.

International Labor Rights Forum (September 27, 2012). *Chocolate company commitments to ending abuses in cocoa production in West Africa*. Retrieved on July 30, 2014 from http://www.laborrights.org/publications/chocolate-company-commitments-ending-abuses-cocoa-production-west-africa

Johnson Reagon, B. (1983). Coalition politics: Turning the century, in *Home girls: A Black feminist anthology*. New York: Kitchen Table Women of Color Press.

Kaitlyn (2012). The dark side of chocolate blog. Retrieved on July 30, 2014 from http://bizgovsoc6.wordpress.com/2013/04/07/the-dark-side-of-chocolate

Kempadoo, K., & Doezema, J. (1998). *Global sex workers: Rights, resistance, and redefinition.* New York, NY: Routledge.

MacKinnon, C. (1989). *Toward a feminist theory of the state.* Cambridge, MA: Harvard University Press.

Murray, A. F. (2008). *From outrage to courage: Women taking action for health and justice.* Monroe, ME: Common Courage Press.

Off, C. (2006). *Bitter chocolate: Investigating the dark side of the world's most seductive sweet.* Toronto, Canada: Random House.

Parreñas, R. Z. (2011). *Illicit flirtations: Labor, migration, and sex trafficking in Tokyo.* Stanford, CA: Stanford University Press.

Payson Center (May, 2011). *Oversight of public and private initiatives to eliminate the worst forms of child labor in the cocoa sector in Côte d'Ivoire and Ghana.* New Orleans: Tulane University.

Peach, L. (2011). Sin, salvation, or starvation? The problematic role of religious morality in U.S. anti-sex trafficking policy, in Bergoffen, D. B. (Ed.), *Confronting global gender justice: Women's lives, human rights.* London: Routledge, pp. 66–82.

Raghavan, S., & and Chatterjee, S. (June 24, 2001). Sweet, beloved chocolate a product of child slavery. *The Miami Herald.*

Rosenblum, M. (2005). *Chocolate: A bittersweet saga of dark and light.* New York, NY: North Point Press/Farrar Strauss and Giroux.

Rubin, G. (1984). Thinking sex: Notes for a radical theory of the politics of sexuality, in Vance, C. (Ed.), *Pleasure and danger: Exploring female sexuality.* Boston, MA: Routledge, pp. 267–319.

Ryan, O. (2011). *Chocolate nations: Living and dying for cocoa in West Africa.* New York, NY: Zed Press.

Santa Barbara News Press (February 28, 2006). Sweet surprise for chocoholics, p. A-1.

Satre, L. J. (2005). *Chocolate on trial: Slavery, politics and the ethics of business.* Athens, Ohio: Ohio University Press.

Scharffenberger, J., and Steinberg, R. (2006). *The essence of chocolate.* New York, NY: Hyperion.

Schotten, C. H. (2005). Men, masculinity, and male domination: Reframing feminist analyses of sex work. *Politics & Gender, 1*(2), 211–240.

Showden, C. R. (2009). Prostitution and women's agency: A feminist argument for decriminalization. Presented at the American Political Science Association Annual Meeting, Toronto, Ontario.

United Nations (2000). Protocol to prevent, suppress and punish trafficking in persons, especially women and children. Retrieved on July 30, 2014 from www.uncjin.org/Docu ments/Conventions/dcatoc/final_documents_2/convention_%20traff_eng.pdf

van den Anker, C. (Ed.) (2004). *The political economy of new slavery.* Basingstoke, UK: Palgrave Macmillan.

Wilson, A. (2008). Plural economies and the conditions for refusal: Gendered developments in Bangkok, in Bhavnani, K., Foran, J., Kurian, P., & Munshi, D. (Eds.), *On the edges of development.* London and New York: Routledge, pp. 38–51.

Woods, D. (2003). The tragedy of the cocoa pod: Rent-seeking, land and ethnic conflict in Ivory Coast. *Journal of Modern African Studies, 41*(4), 641–655.

Young, A.M. (1994). *The chocolate tree: A natural history of cacao.* Washington, DC and London: Smithsonian Institution Press.

Discussion questions

1. According to Bhavnani and Schneider, what are some of the negative outcomes of the focus on sex trafficking rather than trafficking for other forms of labor?
2. How did chocolate manufacturers undermine Engel's efforts to impose a labeling system to identify slave-free chocolate in the United States?
3. How does child labor for cocoa production challenge traditional understandings of trafficking as organized crime?
4. What do Bhavnani and Schneider recommend to address the conditions for children working in cocoa production?
5. What do you think Bhavnani and Schneider mean when they write that "Slavery and trafficking are both terms that can mask the lived experiences of those who are part of these events?"

Additional resources

Nothing Like Chocolate, a film by Kum-Kum Bhavnani
http://nothinglikechocolate.com

International Labor Rights Forum
http://www.laborrights.org/industries/cocoa

Anti-Slavery Website
http://www.antislavery.org/english/campaigns/cocoa_traders/default.aspx

The Dark Side of Chocolate, a film by Miki Misrati and U. Roberto Romano
https://www.youtube.com/watch?v=JCb06GOjkrg

The Child Labor Cocoa Coordinating Group 2012 Annual Report
http://www.dol.gov/ilab/issues/child-labor/cocoa/2012-CLCCG-Report.pdf

Stop Chocolate Slavery website
http://vision.ucsd.edu/~kbranson/stopchocolateslavery/index.html

Chapter 14

Conclusion

The future of human trafficking research

Molly Dragiewicz

As the chapters in this collection show, empirical research on human trafficking is in its infancy. Plagued by definitional uncertainty, appropriation by competing political interests, and the difficulties involved in studying any clandestine activity, human trafficking research has been substantially outpaced by the proliferation of anti-trafficking funding streams and programs. Nonetheless, a growing number of scholars are conducting empirical research on human trafficking and the impact of the laws and policies intended to address it. As this book illustrates, many of these scholars have come to question the utility of the concept of trafficking altogether. Others point to concerns with labeling people as victims of trafficking who would not describe themselves that way. Some view trafficking law as a badly needed avenue to prosecute crimes that are impossible to otherwise address, but most note that criminalization is at best an inefficient response to the problem. Despite precocious claims by governments and advocates about "best practices" for preventing and responding to human trafficking, it is difficult to imagine a future in which there is scholarly agreement on the best way forward in addressing this issue. Certainly there is no empirical, research-, or evidence-based foundation for sweeping generalizations about best practices at this point.

Scholarly publications to date have overwhelmingly focused on describing general dynamics of trafficking and trafficking routes, based largely on anecdotal information. Another of the largest segments of the research literature so far comprises commentary on the human trafficking policy debates. Although these debates are often described as fairly homogenous across the globe, this collection reveals substantial regional variation in this discussion. Political, epistemological, and resource differences between governments have had a profound effect on legal and social responses to trafficking. Therefore, attention to the theories of trafficking propagated in specific locations will continue to be essential to research in the field. Despite the challenges of studying trafficking, there are several possible directions for future research. The preceding chapters exemplify innovative approaches to radically contextualized research, providing some potential ways forward. I will outline a few of these possibilities here.

Research on human trafficking lawsuits and prosecutions

Although one might assume that each country which has made trafficking a prominent political issue might publicize the details of trafficking cases and especially the prosecutions that trafficking laws have sought to increase, this is not the case. Indeed, in researching possible contributors to this book over a period of several months, I sought out empirically based articles on human trafficking prosecutions across the globe with little success. While there are methodological challenges to reviewing trafficking prosecutions due to regional variations in criminal code offenses related to trafficking, a growing number of countries have established federal trafficking offenses. This is due in part to U.S. pressure to criminalize trafficking related offenses or potentially be shamed in the U.S. *Trafficking in Persons Report*'s tier system. Even though research on federal cases would only represent a small fraction of trafficking cases, this could provide essential, foundational information about government efforts to address trafficking via criminalization. Information about the types of cases that have been brought, the locations and industries in which they occur, the legal arguments made, and the ultimate outcomes of the cases would provide some empirical foundation for understanding the impact of anti-trafficking laws.

Research on service provision

Millions of dollars have been spent to provide services to trafficking victims, yet few people who have been victims of trafficking have been identified relative to the many other crime victims who report victimization and request assistance every day. In the U.S., local efforts to address trafficking have focused on young women in prostitution, and it is unclear if those identified as trafficking victims are victims of sexual exploitation, child sexual abuse, women who entered prostitution as minors, or simply sex workers. Despite limited research with small samples of service providers (such as Renzetti in this volume), it is not clear how many of what kind of organizations are providing what services to whom for what types of trafficking. Basic documentation of service provision would be fairly straightforward to accomplish. It is surprising that no such data exists given the large amount of government spending that has been allocated to service provision and federal imperatives for "evidence-based practice" and program evaluation in other areas of criminal justice practice.

Research with trafficked persons

The few existing databases on human trafficking contain information about identified trafficking cases drawn from victim and case accounts. This is a potential starting point for research. However, to date the databases are not readily available for access by independent scholars. As Goździak pointed out in this volume, restrictions on the U.S. case database have increased rather than decreased over time as data would have accrued. The U.S. has had a National Human Trafficking Hotline since 1998. The hotline is currently housed at the Polaris Project, an NGO founded by Brown University students. The Polaris Project website claims that it gathered information on "9,298 unique cases of human trafficking" over five years from 72,543 interactions via the hotline, email, and an "online tip form." In addition, they say they have provided services requested in 588 cases from 2007 to 2012. Yet their website also says that they assisted 150 survivors during 2012, including "survivors impacted by Hurricane Sandy," and "victims who would have otherwise been homeless." Since the client services page on their website is out of order, it isn't clear what services they actually provide or for victims of what. As the federally funded hosts of the hotline, perhaps Polaris will share data they have gathered on trafficking cases with scholars.

Research on implementation and outcomes of anti-trafficking law and policy

Without the most basic baseline data on even those trafficking cases identified for prosecution, it is impossible to assess the impact of the slew of anti-trafficking laws and policies that have been drafted in the past 20 years. While the U.S. and UN call for criminalization of trafficking, there is no effort to collect evidence on the effectiveness of this approach to the problem. It is not yet clear if, how, and to what effect anti-trafficking programs are being implemented.

Research on trafficking for other forms of labor than prostitution

To date, the majority of scholarly publications on trafficking have been focused on prostitution. Indeed, interest in prostitution is the reason many groups with no previous history of interest or expertise in women, human rights, or violence and abuse became involved in trafficking. Research on trafficking for labor in other sectors is badly needed if we are to understand the issue and craft inclusive policies for preventing and responding to exploitative labor and migration conditions.

Trafficking is in the middle of an extended period of heightened public and political interest. The reasons for state engagement with trafficking differ substantially from place to place. While research on trafficking is important, especially in light of the millions of dollars being poured into anti-trafficking programs, I urge readers to think critically about the ways in which trafficking is discussed and deployed as a political issue. What is gained and lost when we conflate the vocabulary of child sexual abuse, labor exploitation, illegal migration, and violence against women with human trafficking? Where do the varied and conflicting voices of those affected by anti-trafficking policies fit in? Why is there so much effort being expended to locate and identify victims of trafficking when adults and children who report sexual abuse, physical abuse, and exploitation by relatives and employers are routinely discredited and treated poorly by justice and social systems? Like other social problems, human trafficking has been taken up because it resonates with deeply held values and interests. It is essential to reflect on the impact of interventions that have been designed without the input of those who will be most affected. I hope that this book has provided some new information to readers that will inform future research, study, and action against contemporary human rights violations including human trafficking.

Index

Page numbers in **bold** refer to boxes.